W9-BRU-653

OUT OF THIS WORLD

ALSO BY MARY SWANDER

POETRY

Heaven–and–Earth House
Driving the Body Back
Succession

NONFICTION

Parsnips in the Snow
(with Jane Staw)

EDITED COLLECTIONS

Land of the Fragile Giants
(with Cornelia Mutel)

OUT OF THIS WORLD

A Woman's Life Among the Amish

MARY SWANDER

VIKING

VIKING
Published by the Penguin Group
Penguin Books USA Inc., 375 Hudson Street, New York, New York 10014, U.S.A.
Penguin Books Ltd, 27 Wrights Lane, London W8 5TZ, England
Penguin Books Australia Ltd, Ringwood, Victoria, Australia
Penguin Books Canada Ltd, 10 Alcorn Avenue, Toronto, Ontario, Canada M4V 3B2
Penguin Books (N.Z.) Ltd, 182–190 Wairau Road, Auckland 10, New Zealand

Penguin Books Ltd, Registered Offices: Harmondsworth, Middlesex, England

First published in 1995 by Viking Penguin, a division of Penguin Books USA Inc.

1   3   5   7   9   10   8   6   4   2

Copyright © Mary Swander, 1995
All rights reserved

Grateful acknowledgment is made for permission to reprint excerpts from the following copyrighted works: Stringtown Grocery Almanac Calendar. Copyright 1994 by Skinner and Kennedy Co., Inc., St. Louis, MO. All rights reserved. "Ruby, Don't Take Your Love to Town" by Mel Tillis. Copyright © 1966 Cedarwood Publishing. Used by permission. All rights reserved.

The author wishes to thank the editors of the following publications where portions of this book first appeared: *The Christian Science Monitor, Cream City Review, Garden Letter, Green Prints, The North Dakota Quarterly, Natural Health,* and *The New Republic.*

Many of the names of the characters and places in this book have been changed.

Library of Congress Cataloging in Publication Data
Swander, Mary.
Out of this world : a woman's life among the Amish / Mary Swander.
p.   cm.
ISBN 0–670–85808–0
1. Amish—Iowa—Social life and customs.   2. Swander, Mary—Homes and
haunts—Iowa.   3. Iowa—Social life and customs.   I. Title.
F630.M45S93   1995
811'.54—dc20   95–10002
[B]

This book is printed on acid-free paper. ∞

Printed in the United States of America
Set in Adobe Sabon
Designed by Katy Riegel

Without limiting the rights under copyright reserved above, no part of this publication may be reproduced, stored in or introduced into a retrieval system, or transmitted, in any form or by any means (electronic, mechanical, photocopying, recording or otherwise), without the prior written permission of both the copyright owner and the above publisher of this book.

for Thomas and Barbara,
Linus and Mary

The goal of the Amish schools is to prepare children for usefulness by preparing them for eternity.
— The Amish School,
by Sara E. Fisher and Rachel K. Stahl

Acknowledgments

The completion of this book was made possible in part by a grant from the Iowa Arts Council, and by assistance from Iowa State University. I also wish to express my appreciation to my neighbors, who inspired me and generously gave of themselves; my friends, who encouraged me and pulled me through difficult times; and Elizabeth Grossman, Jane von Mehren, and Barbara Grossman, who supported me from the conception of this book to the finished manuscript, and throughout my past writing career.

Contents

1

To Start a Cold Motor

TO START A COLD MOTOR

A 100 watt electric light bulb makes a practical heating unit for your car and if kept lighted through the night will keep motor and radiator warm. This will not only greatly assist in starting on snappy winter mornings but eliminates possibility of a frozen radiator.

By covering hood of car with blanket and allowing same to touch the floor, heat will also reach crank case and keep lubricating oil warm. A 100 watt lamp will cost approximately 5 cents a night to operate.

—Stringtown Grocery Calendar

A BRIGHT RED BOW and harness bells tied on the horse, Donna, Stu, and I set out in their cart to greet our neighbors and bring in the New Year. "Dashing through the snow, in a one-horse open sleigh," we sang, a sleeping bag draped across our laps and tucked around our knees, with Emily's legs prancing, her hooves tapping the rhythm on the ice-covered gravel road. The horse loved the task. With Emily we didn't have to worry about a cold radiator. She had to be held back from a gallop, her mane flopping and fluttering in the wind. Mason jars full of preserves rattled on the cart floor, and brightly wrapped boxes of goose and duck eggs careened into one another as we rounded the corner and headed south toward the Amish General Store and the extended family who minded it.

"If we bring our neighbors gifts every year on New Year's Day," Donna said, "they'll think that's *our* custom." Tall and certain, Donna sat in the front seat of the two-seater cart. Part Native American, her black hair streaked with silvery gray and pulled back from her high, broad forehead and straight nose, she had the presence of one who knew how to invent ritual.

A week before, on Christmas Eve, we hadn't been prepared for the Amish custom of neighborly gift exchange. In their buggies, they drove from house to house and arrived at our door with pickles and relishes from their gardens.

"Merry Christmas," Lydia had said, appearing on my stoop and handing me a pint-size mason jar, a red ribbon looped around its belly, a handwritten label neatly affixed to the lid that read, "Sorghum Molasses." She stood bare-legged in the cold, her feet pushed down in buckle-jangling galoshes, her plain black dress, fastened with straight pins, hitting just below her knees. A purple wool shawl wrapped around her head and shoulders framed her face, skin scrubbed, without makeup and with a pink hue that reflected both years of hard work and a life free from the pressures of normal American culture.

"Merry Christmas, and thank you so much," I said, worrying that I had nothing to offer her.

Donna and Stu worried about the same thing. We are some of the few "English" in the area, immediate neighbors and definite outsiders. As simply as we live, as much as we try to preserve the environmental integrity and blend in with the spirit of the landscape here, we also know that we, with our cars and telephones, are worldly. Yet, because the Amish are freed from competitiveness and striving, because they maintain a real sense of community and live a life I wish I could, I'm drawn to the them and feel honored whenever they include me in their gatherings and customs.

Donna, Stu, and I wanted to reciprocate. We had had our little Christmas among ourselves. I had given them a calendar from the Seed Savers Exchange, complete with full-blown color pictures of heirloom varieties of squash and chili peppers. They had given me an almanac calendar from the Amish grocery three miles up the road. That calendar sported no glossy photos, just plain black and red numbers and grids marking off the days, surrounded by tables, graphs, and inserts explaining everything from how to start a cold motor to the maturation rates for corn. We wanted to share something in return with the Amish from our gardens, something we had made by the work of our own hands, to let our small individual plots become a link to a larger community.

Emily veered into the General Store's parking lot—one of her more usual stops. The store blended into the snow drifts, a small, white, one-story wooden building squatting in the middle of a soybean field. A tiny, hand-scrawled sign hung in the window: CLOSED. When open, the store bustled with customers wedging their way down the crowded aisles to try on a pair of Red Wing work boots, find a sharp paring knife, buy a card of pearl buttons, or a rag rug. Then, Emily liked to stand at the hitching post and whinny to the other horses, each attached to a black buggy and waiting patiently for the return of his or her owner.

"Come on, Em. Not today." Donna snapped the reins and guided her away from the post to the family's drive.

We could only guess where the family might be gathered. The Amish often live three or four generations together, clustered in several houses on one farmstead. It isn't unusual to find a large main farmhouse, a smaller "grandpa's house," and a mobile home all grouped close to shelter parents, grandparents, and married children. We tried the main house, knocking on the door and tapping the glass, getting no response.

Worried that the pickling juices would freeze, we pushed open the door and set down our gifts on the long dining table—massive, oak, and draped with a plain white cloth. Chairs were pushed out and left at odd angles, as if the occupants had been suddenly called away. I felt as if any minute someone would step out of the kitchen and catch me, a voyeur, a violator. The very house seemed alive, driven by the heartbeat of the potbellied stove in the center of the room, waves of hot air wafting toward us from its five-foot-tall cylindrical box.

Black socks, tights, and diapers hung clothespinned and drying from cords that stretched from wall to wall. A quilting frame took up the rest of the space, the traditional strips of purple and black cloth stretched between its clamps, a star pattern just beginning to be embellished by tiny, regular stitches. Above the frame, a hook marked a prominent place in the ceiling where at night a kerosene lantern hung, casting its light on the artistry below.

We tiptoed out, whispering, as if fearful of being found, and climbed back into the cart. Just then Fannie, Lydia's mother, rounded the barn, shawless, her bare arms crossing her chest. "Won't you come in and have a cup of coffee? We're all in the little house," she called.

"We'd love to," I said, "but . . ."

"We have eight more households to visit," Stu tried to explain.

"We'll come back another time," Donna said, pulling back on the reins and maneuvering Emily out of the drive. Inside the little house, the adults waved and a bevy of small faces pressed to the window. Emily snorted and retraced her route past the store. We trotted on through the afternoon, the wind stinging our faces, our double-mittened hands and double-socked feet growing colder and colder, the cart straining to creak up the hilly lanes and turn in the drives, making sharp turns around windmills and pumps. Donna clicked her tongue and flicked the whip above Emily's head to urge her on, and in the backseat Stu worried over every dip and swerve, every mud rut and loose pocket of gravel.

"Watch this dip in the road, easy, easy," he said. From the backseat of the cart, he waved his arms and directed traffic, warning Donna to advance slowly. A police officer and transplanted New Yorker, Stu has seen enough of the world's problems to make him fret over the smallest safety issue, and even in the country he retains an air of alertness. In times of stress, his hand automatically brushes his side in search of his gun or billy club.

"Whew, now we're over that one," Stu said when we passed the small dip.

In the winter, I worry more about my garden than the roads. Most people in Iowa find January the one month that they can wrap themselves in a quilt next to the fire, feast on that jar of last fall's sorghum molasses, and thumb through the garden catalogues, imagining their next year's tomatoes and pumpkins just as shiny and big as the ones in the ads. In their grim way, midwesterners find the dark, cold month of January joyful. Even though they fight the wind and ice, they have a little more time for their own thoughts, for their hobbies, before the spring, with its frenzy of tilling, planting, and weeding.

During the last decade, Iowa winters have been mostly mild. The January thaw has now routinely found us playing tennis in light sweaters for at least one day mid-month, and conversations with snowbird grandparents overwintering in Florida almost always find their way to jokes about coming on back home to warm up. However, we are mistrustful of surprises, no matter how seemingly good, and can view them only as bad omens. These mild rainy winters have been indicators of either summer floods or hot, dry drought years that have had the same relatives reminiscing of the Dust Bowl and the Depression.

"Last summer, we only got one haying," Moses, my neighbor and the local patriarch, had told me. "Never been that bad since back in thirty-six. We planted that year, all right, then nothing."

So on December thirty-first I had been excited to be standing inside at my window, looking out at the drifts circling and swirling, piling higher and higher, the wind howling and billowing the snow into the air. The night before, the evening had been crisp and calm, then about midnight, large dry flakes began falling, covering my front stoop, the cornfields across the road that the pheasants and sheep were still gleaning. I pulled up my comforter and eased into a gentle sleep only to wake at four A.M. to the hammering wind driving the snow against the window, the glass rattling in the frames, the flakes seeping through the storm windows.

The cacophony, the power of the storm, was too much to allow me to return to sleep. I rose and sat in the dark for several hours, watching the blizzard force itself down upon the countryside, and realized how "normal" it was for this time of year, how it provided needed moisture and ground cover, how it would provide the perfect backdrop for our New Year's Day outing. Perhaps it even proved the weather report wrong, for on the radio it had warned every noon of yet another el niño and its possible devastating effect on the crops.

"Whoa, Emmie, it's okay." Stu tried to calm the horse, who edged closer to the ditch, a pickup passing us on the other side of the road. Brome grass brushed the spoke of the cart's wheels. All around us, the snowy fields stretched into the horizon, the stubble of cornstalks sticking up here and there, the crops put up in silos, barns, and corncribs.

I grow my crops in a 20-by-40 plot just outside the door of my home, the Fairview School, an old one-room country schoolhouse. The building, a white square box built in the 1920s, sits on top of a hill in the very center of the United States. From my garden, I watch the corn and bean fields unfold in the valley below, the scraggly beard of trees following Picayune Creek as it cuts across the landscape, the bright red barns and white farmhouses receding into the horizon. I watch the red-tailed hawk swoop and glide on thermals, dipping down for the kill. I see the turkey vultures already down, pecking away at the raccoon hit and left for scavenge on the gravel road. I see the dried stalks of the big bluestem grasses shoot up out of my prairie patch in the ditch and bend with the wind.

From my garden, I hear the coyotes howl at night as they slink out of the creek cover and prowl toward the farmsteads. Their barking carries over the plains in the cold air, piercing and clear. In the dark, the battery-powered reflectors on the Amish buggies blink on and off, their horses clip-clopping up the hill, the wheels churning on the gravel, flinging up mud and muck. Sunday is Amish date night, when buggy after buggy rolls by, the young couples inside driving home from evening services sometimes as late as midnight. Late Sundays, I like to stand out in my garden, trace the constellations in the black sky, and take in the buggy parade, the noise rising to a crescendo, the horses breaking into a gallop as they approach my hill. I watch them disappear down the road, the black carriages like shooting stars, their orange triangular slow-moving-vehicle signs fading from sight.

A buggy passed our cart on the left and Emily turned her head toward the other horse in greeting.

"Watch this now, Donna, take it easy, easy," Stu chanted.

Calmly and steadily, Donna steered the horse through the misty fog that moved in toward late afternoon.

"Whoa, these bridges are slippery. That's it, slow down, Em. Slow, slow."

Sweat trailing down her flanks, Emily kept up her pace throughout the countryside as we surprised the families of the cheese man, the horse trainer, the painter, and the turkey farmer who brings us dressed birds—heart attack victims, scared to death on the days of the roundups. The smaller Amish children, solely German speakers until school age, bashfully clung to their mothers' skirts when we offered them pretty ribboned boxes. They smiled excitedly when they found huge goose eggs inside, and the next day, a ten-year-old boy stopped, pounded on the door, his stocking cap pulled down nearly over his eyes, and asked if our gifts were "fertile."

Some of the older children seemed anxious to volunteer a list of their Christmas spoils. As we left the last house, our fingers and toes just beginning to go numb, a seven-year-old boy stood on the mudroom porch, the door flung wide, and shouted after us, lisping, "I got a manure spreader!"

Home, Emily found her way to her stall, her blanket cinched around her rib cage, the sun setting behind the barn, bringing the day to a close in a hushed gray tone, a few flakes of wet snow beginning to light on the garden fence, on the dried relics of cucumber vines that still twined up the wire. The garden gate cast an eerie last shadow on the drifts inside, now shiny with crusted snow. Our fingers and toes nearly frostbitten, Donna, Stu, and I quickly said good-bye, heading into our houses. Inside, I huddled near the stove, my hands almost touching the cast iron, and I knew that the world had been brought into balance. The snow meant faith in a bountiful garden to come, and a bountiful garden meant a continuation of gifts that would bond neighbor to neighbor. Yes, this would be our custom. My fingers warming and thawing, I felt reassured that nature had settled some of its debts and that I had settled some of my own.

TO WELCOME in the New Year, I stood in my kitchen browning ground bear, the little chunks of red meat dancing and sizzling in my cast iron pan, the aroma wafting through my house. As I cooked, I sang and yodeled to the radio, Emmy Lou Harris creating a steady, cheerful beat for the stirrings of my wooden spoon. On the kitchen counter waited piles of vegetables from my cache pit—carrots, potatoes, turnips, and onions, scrubbed, sliced, and diced, all ready to be added to the pot, then placed atop my wood-burning stove to simmer and steam for several hours, blend and ooze into a delicious winter stew.

Moses and his wife, Miriam, had given me my first package of bear, part of a kill their grandson had brought back from a hunting trip in Colorado. They gave the other neighbors homemade glazed doughnuts done up in Saran Wrap and bright red bows, but were stumped for a while over my gift. They knew I have a medical condition that has not only eliminated sugar from my diet but has made me intolerant of most normal American fare and sent me off on a journey of experimentation with less common, more exotic foods.

"Here, would you like to try this?" Miriam asked one night in late December, pulling the package from her propane-propelled freezer, the light from the kerosene lamp casting a shadow across her face.

The package, white and glistening in its butcher paper, weighed and chilled my hand. I thanked her and walked up the gravel road toward my house with my gift, the solstice stars bright in the clear sky, Ursa Major, the Big Bear constellation, radiant above me. Bear. I'm going home to try to eat bear, I thought. What would it taste like? Greasy and gamy? No, that stereotype had long vanished from my culinary vocabulary. Since the onset of my illness, I have eaten venison, moose, wild duck and goose, pheasant, even possum and squirrel. Greasy and gamy, my friends had predicted before each attempt. After having given each meat an honest try, though, and the meat, in return, providing needed protein for me during a time of crisis, I began my own list of descriptions, ranging from delicate, to nutty, to succulent.

My first bite of bear brought a lift to my eyebrows. Bear was nothing like any of the other critters on my "safe foods" list. Bear was spicy. Plain ground bear, shaped into a patty, broiled in the oven without salt, pepper, herbs, or sauce, was the tastiest meat I'd ever put into my mouth. The bear hummed on my plate, its hearty bouquet filling my nostrils and lungs, resting on my tongue with pure pleasure. With my eyes closed, bear was barbecue. Bear was bratwurst. Bear had a bite, a growl, a scratching, clawing taste that stayed behind to make me feel satisfied, fortified, whole. O Artemis. O Callisto. O Goldilocks, I cried to myself, embrace the great beast of the night. You are in heaven!

FOR YEARS I had been in hell. As a child I was repulsed by certain foods. I hated many fruits and would go without breakfast rather than take a bite of grapefruit. The spray of its juice across the dining-room table, my parents and brothers plunging their spoons into its fleshy fruit, made me want to dart from the room. Raspberries ruined a good dessert, and the very smell of eggs cooking in the kitchen made me gag. I complained that drinking a whole glass of milk made me stop breathing.

My mother thought I was simply a picky eater and swung between ignoring my dislikes and providing me with substitute foods, allowing me to go hungry or, in real irritation and fear of malnutrition, requiring a kind of force-feeding, commanding me to sit at the table until I "cleaned" my plate. I remember sitting in my chair for what seemed like hours with a dish of pineapple in front of me, the sun going down, the rest of the family in the living room gathered around the newly purchased TV, watching "I Love Lucy," my favorite show. I fell asleep there, spoon never touched, the pineapple pieces floating belly up in a pool of melted lime Jell-O.

My older brother had a hostility toward vegetables. Since we sat next to each other at the table, we often made quick trades—his vegetables for my fruit or eggs—gobbling up the evidence before we could even be accused of a crime. But some nights the two of us became bound to our seats, broccoli untouched on his plate, a full glass of milk in front of mine. A double hunger strike. In our imprisonment, we fantasized broccoli stems growing wings and flying out the window, and tiny vacuums magically popping out of the dining-room walls to suck up milk. We imagined small trapdoors in our abdomens that were direct routes to our digestive tracts. We could simply open them, shovel in food, and bypass our mouths and taste buds altogether.

When I matured, I tried to "grow out of" my food dislikes. I found I could tolerate an egg if it was scrambled or cooked into something, but most of my other aversions remained firm.

As I moved through my self-conscious teen years, I found my-self embarrassed by the handful of foods that I couldn't bring to my mouth. I no longer blended invisibly into my peer group and I offended hosts by my refusals. In my more sophisticated twenties, I tried again and again to choke down soufflés and garlic-drenched pastas, only to break out in inexplicable rashes and to become plagued by sinus headaches. Finally, my head booming every afternoon with a pain that no aspirin could control, I visited a doctor, who determined that I was allergic to just those ten or fifteen foods that had kept me constrained to my chair as a child.

For a half dozen years, I did well, strictly avoiding my "bad" foods. I read and reread labels. If I bought bread, I made sure the ingredients didn't include milk. Happily, I never bought another egg, and also gave up ice cream, noodles, pas-try, pies, and dozens of other things that contained eggs. My doctor said I absolutely had to give up booze, as alcohol wildly exacerbated any allergic condition. At the time, I was drinking fairly heavily, and spent several days in bed shaking and sweating from withdrawal, but came out on the other end feeling better. My diet clipped my social life a bit, but I could always pass for normal by ordering club sodas in bars, and picking carefully from restaurant menus.

Then, in my early thirties, my headaches began to return and my skin became even more sensitive, so I visited yet an-other allergist, a skinny grandfatherly physician with bushes of white hair in his ears, who spent a week testing me to hun-dreds of foods, chemicals, and inhalants. Up and down my arms, and over my back, he pricked my skin with dilute prep-arations of various substances, from eighteen different kinds of molds to eighteen kinds of grains and cereals, and watched for reactions—mostly itchiness and swelling. He then prepared a vaccine and sent me home to self-inject what turned out to be a mis-mixed, overdosed vial of nearly fifty antigens.

This second allergist had promised that, through his treatment, I would not only be rid of my headaches but be able to sit down to a whole bowlful of strawberry ice cream. As soon as I had depressed the needle's plunger into my thigh, I felt dizzy and soon found I had violent reactions to all foods. One bite of rice made me black out, one leaf of lettuce made my mouth break out in huge, raw sores. Even brushing my teeth with baking soda made me keel over on the floor. I dropped twenty pounds in ten days and ended up in a hospital trying to find a food—any food—I could tolerate enough to keep myself alive.

MY DIET HAD never been loaded with McDonald's hamburgers and fries. Before I became severely food allergic, I ate an occasional piece of meat, chicken, and fish, beans, grains, granola, and vegetables from my own garden. I was content fixing simple, wholesome recipes and getting together a fancier, large meal once a year for Thanksgiving. When I traveled, I enjoyed eating out in restaurants, but if it came down to a decision about whether to sample French haute cuisine or tour the Country Music Hall of Fame, I'd go for the latter. I ate better, and liked food and cooking more than my mother, who never had much of an appetite and would from time to time "forget to eat." I'd lived in both Europe and hippie artist colonies, and understood the value of both presentation and nutrition, but was too much of a midwesterner to veer away from anything but a practical diet.

M.F.K. Fisher said she had her Irish grandmother to thank for launching her into her lifelong love of fine food. Her grandmother's cooking was so bad that, once Fisher left home, she became enthralled with any morsel with a hint of flavor. I come from a matriarchy of three generations of Irish-Iowa cooks. My great-grandmother, born during the Irish potato famine, immigrated to the United States as soon as she was old enough to get herself on the boat and arrange with relatives in Illinois to barter several years of cooking, cleaning, and child care for her steerage passage. Once in America, my great-grandmother put in a year of service, then got so sick of dirty dishes that she jumped bail. In the middle of the night, she packed a knapsack and set out alone westward toward the Mississippi on foot, free at least for a while of the skillet and saucepan, the cinders and woodstove.

Of course, her dream of a life without cooking turned to ashes once she married and raised her family of ten. As soon as she could, she turned over all the food preparation to my grandmother, the youngest child and the only girl. My grandmother dutifully roasted meat and whipped potatoes, adding milk and butter, plunging the masher down into the ceramic bowl until her arms ached. Then, just when all of her older siblings had left the house and her chores had dwindled, her mother loaned her out to her brothers, to help cook for their families and threshing crews. To escape her servitude, my grandmother began teaching, then to escape teaching, she married, and the cycle began again.

In my genetic code, cooking spiraled down with a whole set of chains that rattled from one generation to the next. Food was something we always reminded ourselves we were most grateful to have. We never sat down to dinner without first saying a prayer. *Bless us, O Lord, and these Thy gifts. . . .* The potato famine remained in our collective consciousness, and the Great Depression only reinforced our thankfulness for our rural bounty. *It was hell being poor in the country,* my grandmother used to say, *but it was worse in the city, where they didn't have enough to eat.* Food meant survival, but food also tasted good, and could be celebratory. Christmas time found fudge stacked up in tins on the kitchen counter, popcorn strung on the tree, and a flaming plum pudding—often slipping and sliding off the plate—burning an indelible mark on the family soul.

But cooking was also a chore, something that bound us to routine and duty. And, cooking made us "nervous." We knew we could do it, but we knew others could do it a lot better, with a lot more success and flare. Unlike our German-American neighbors, who loved to pour all their troubles and frustrations into their bread kneading and found a real outlet for their creativity in their *Pfeffernüsse* and *Lebkuchen,* we found cooking only an added stress.

My mother used to recall a story of herself at five, seated at the kitchen table for a light supper, my grandmother having spent the week canning hundreds of quarts of tomatoes, corn, and beans, the steam from the pressure kettle still clinging to the already damp walls in the 95-degree Iowa summer heat.

As my mother finished the sandwich on her plate, she turned to her mother and asked, "What are we going to have for dessert, Mama?"

"Tomatoes," my grandmother spat.

When I reached my adolescence, my mother, who had her kitchen counter converted to a desk, where she much preferred to write letters, told me she was concerned that I took so little interest in cooking.

"Don't worry," I used to joke, "I can always open a can of tomatoes."

Once in college, I was the only one I knew on my dorm floor who thought the cafeteria food a treat. And later, when my mother was in a nursing home, I took one look at the bland and mushy meals on her tray and offered to fix her something else.

"That's okay," my mother said and shook her head. "The cook must be Irish. I feel right at home."

I, like the rest of my ancestral cooks, understood my obligation toward food, but would have just as soon walked away from the fuss and muss of the stove altogether. In the back of my mind, at the end of a stick a knapsack dangled seductively. My alarm clock had been set for a midnight exodus, when suddenly, at the age of thirty-three, I was forced back into the kitchen corner with a skillet and spoon to settle into a servitude of my own.

FOR THE FIRST six weeks of my illness, I couldn't eat anything. I lay in a hospital bed with an IV line into my arm, nurses depositing test trays of food by my side three times a day, one item at a time. I lifted the lids from stainless steel serving dishes, then nibbled bites of a single solid food—having a breakfast, say, of bananas, a lunch of carrots, and a dinner of beef. When I failed to tolerate bananas, carrots, and beef, my doctors advised testing strictly organic foods, ones grown without pesticides, herbicides, or drugs, ones that I had eaten only infrequently or never at all. In a few days, I'd picked up frog legs, lobster, duck. And so began a ten-year journey of searching out items from the top to the bottom of the food chain, from the top to the bottom of the world.

I ate wild blueberries from Washington state, salmon from Alaska. I tried taro from Hawaii, dates and figs from Arizona, yucca from Texas, papaya and pomegranates from Mexico, mangoes from Puerto Rico. I boiled quinoa from Equador. I ordered fifty-pound bags of cashews from Brazil. I combed through the Chinese grocery stores and bought squid, umeboshi plums, kombu, dulse, and kelp. Closer to home, I planted bok choy, yow choy, and choy sum in my own garden. I scavenged sumac for tea, milkweed buds and cattails for fritters, plantain and pigweed for greens. I gigged frogs; I studied the local newspaper and found a turtle farmer with snappers as big as hams. Hunters brought me partridge, quail, and coon. I signed up on a list at the Iowa Department of Transportation and put my name in for fresh road kills from Interstate 80, for venison.

When my quest began, I ate to survive, trying merely to stop my stomach from growling, my head from spinning in dizziness. Suddenly twenty pounds lighter, I was weak and faint, and it took all the strength I had just to procure three meals a day. I lived and ate alone, and although I tried to add variation to my diet by eating my mono-meals in a number of forms—an apple could be transformed into raw slices, a baked bundle, or a bowl of sauce, for example—I mostly just bore my way down and through another bowl of boiled parsnips, another dish of sweet potatoes. I clicked on the radio news and propped up the paper at the table, simultaneously blocking two senses, my lunch of steamed chard disappearing on my plate.

During that time, I was at once obsessed with finding food, and tormented with withdrawing from it. While I bought organic turkeys from a farmer and drove them in the back of my pickup to slaughter, their wattles bobbing and flapping in my rearview mirror, I passed a bakery, the smells of cookie and cake dough filling my cab. Since I couldn't eat sweets of any kind, I forced myself to close down to them, to make them, like the rest of the food from the "outside world," unreal. In my imagination, I cast them into cardboard. All restaurants were out of the question, so I pretended they didn't exist and blanked out their space, their very names from existence. Their street-front facades turned into black holes. Literally, my vision narrowed. In the food co-op, I wheeled my cart down the produce aisle, picking up the few things that I could eat and tried not to look at anything else. I circled round the store in a mazelike configuration to avoid going past the deli counter. Even tofu lasagna made me drool.

Since I was so thin, I was suddenly attractive in the classical American sense. My clothes were the latest fashion because I had to buy a whole new wardrobe. My old outfits hung limp in great wads of cloth from my body. Friends rushed up to me on the street and asked me how I'd ever managed to lose so much weight so quickly. They wanted my magic diet. Men began calling and asking me out to dinner and when they found out I couldn't go to restaurants, soon lost interest. Or, the few that stuck around expected me to cook normal meals for them while I sat down to my bowl of lamb's-quarters. During those years, I was so reactive that even if I'd been madly in love and wanted to do all the cooking for two, I couldn't even have kept an onion in the refrigerator.

Sometimes guests passed through, and since they'd learned of my malady only from a distance, had a difficult time adjusting to my new regime. I looked and acted normal—better than ever—a little weak and spacey, maybe, but didn't we all? So it was strange for them to see me breakfasting on steamed frog legs. They tried to understand, but the whole scene was just too weird. Many were very kind and said it didn't matter, they didn't need to eat either. They'd just have an apple, thanks. Others laughed and poked fun at my food, becoming offended I didn't offer to do more cooking for them. When I did try to scrape together some semblance of a meal from my foods for them, they joked that it was better suited for the dog and whistled out the door for him.

"Here, Bill," they called.

They went into fits of addictive withdrawal when they found my household contained not an ounce of caffeine or sugar.

"How can you live without pizza?" they asked.

"I'd die without coffee," they said.

I was raised a strict Catholic, and from my convent school days was practiced in the rigors of self-discipline and denial. Fasting and abstinence were familiar rituals. As small children, during Lent we routinely gave up candy, soda pop, and junk food. Sister Mary Rita, the midget nun, locked up her concession stand to the lunch hour crowd and instead of pumping us full of Baby Ruths and Butterfingers, sat us down at our desks and unjangled the stories of the lives of the saints. Sister Rita, barely taller than the third graders, relished the martyrs who slept on spikes, who had their toenails pulled out by heathens, and tongues cut off for singing the praises of Jesus Christ.

"Whenever you crave a Milk Dud, offer it up. If you're tempted to taste that piece of chocolate in your mouth," Sister Rita instructed us, her tiny hands fingering the rosary beads that hung from her side, "think of what it would be like not to *have* a tongue."

The nuns themselves ate as they lived, in silence. In fifth grade, the year I thought I'd heard the call to join the order, I used to wander away from the crowded winter noon-recess-filled gym and peer through a window on one of the stairwells that looked out on a courtyard and into the cloistered convent. Through another piece of glass, I could see the nuns in their dining room, seated around a long wooden table, the skirts of their black habits sweeping the floor, heads bent over their food, their veils falling down smoothly around their shoulders. Respectfully, rhythmically, as if in slow motion, they lifted their forks in the air, the utensils becoming wands vanishing into the whiteness of their wimples, casting a charge across the table that seemed to connect these women not only to one another but to something more powerful, personified by the picture of the Madonna and Child that hung, just a bit askew, on the wall. Transfixed, I stood at the window caught up in the mystery, the pure aesthetics of the moment, until the mother superior caught my far-off gaze, rose, and yanked down the shade.

Our religion was centered in eating. In death there was life. Our Communion—the bread and wine, the body and blood of Christ—was literal, uncomplicated by symbols or metaphor. Transubstantiation was a dogma we learned early in Catechism class and no more of a question than Sister Rita herself, who drilled us in our lessons spelling-bee fashion, our backs up against the blackboard. Our key sacrament, the Mass, was celebrated in style, the gold chalice lifted to the ringing of brass bells, our young girl voices chanting with the rising of the incense up along the stained-glass windows toward the chapel dome. But it wasn't the Mass that became my beacon during my food quest. Unable to ingest either wheat or wine, I could no longer receive Communion, and my already torpid Catholicism went into a deep sleep when I found myself sitting in a pew alone, unable to approach the altar. Rather, it was the memory of my voyeurism on the stairwell, those black ghosts bending over their plates in harmony, that came back to sustain me.

I now know that the nuns in their dining room were eating the same tuna-noodle casserole that we girls were served in the hot lunch line. Nothing sacred about the product but something hallowed in the process. One day I turned off the radio, put down the paper, and began eating as an act of meditation. I brought a plate of yucca to the table and sat with it for five minutes, focusing all my attention on the vegetable, clearing my head of any other thoughts. I blotted out everything in the room and took in its aroma, its white color, its texture.

I'd purchased this yucca, a kind of cactus, from Texas. But I flashed back in my memory to the same plant growing in the Loess Hills near my childhood home, a windblown region of the Midwest unique to North America, its only counterpart found on the plains of China. There in the midst of rich, lush flat corn and soybean fields, the Loess Hills rise up to present a totally different topography, spawning a surprising array of unexpected flora and fauna. I remembered driving to Omaha past a patch of native prairie in the Hills and spotting yucca, its rigid leaves and panicles of white, waxy flowers freaky among the low-key, less-showy indigenous wildflowers. Yucca looked like something that should be on the altar on Easter morning, like something too exotic for Iowa, with our work ethic values and temperature extremes. And here was part of that very plant in front of me. It tasted much like a potato, but tougher, more bitter. Still, in my famine, it was the closest I could get to my "roots."

My feet on the floor, back pressed against the oak dining chair, I stared at the chunks of yucca and took delight in their simple arrangement on the royal blue plate, the noon light bouncing off the snow outside and streaming through the window. I picked up my fork, and slowly, pleasurably, watched it glint in the sun. I lifted the vegetable toward my face.

A piece of yucca floated in my mouth, a steaming, plump fiber waiting on my tongue, its threads sliding down my throat. I brought my teeth together and chewed and chewed the slice, doing nothing, thinking nothing else until the last vestige of food dissolved. Then, and only then, I forked another section, and trancelike, began another round of chewing, taking the time to allow the liquefied yucca to pool in my cheeks, press against the roof of my mouth. My stomach filled with the vegetable, my body enjoying its fleshiness and, at the same time, lamenting its passing. Enchanted, I remained with my cactus, those ten or twelve chunks of vegetable, for nearly a half hour, and when I was finished, I seemed to be in a different realm, as if I'd had a good long visit with a treasured friend I hadn't seen in many years, and would never see again.

Primitive humans recognized spirits in plants, and engaged in rituals and ceremonies devoted to the first fruits and the last sheaves of the harvest. Harvest has not always been a joyous occasion, as we might assume, but also filled with mourning, as the body of the spirit was reaped. Anthropologists have speculated that agriculture may have originated as an out-growth of a religious concept. As an appeasement to the spirit, humans might have returned to the ground a token offering of the seeds collected, removing a taboo and making it safe for mortals to eat the plant, and at the same time assuring the growth of the next year's crop.

There in my dining room, on my own, I'd tapped a prim-itive spiritual power, one that offered an explanation of birth and death, that found meaning in their continual cycle, one that stretched back and connected me to ancient life—from *Australopithecus* and the Olduvai Gorge, to the Yang dynasty, to the medieval convents of Europe. After that, I tried to eat all my meals with similar concentration, aware of the signifi-cance of the act. I felt less deprived and more full of wonder as I began to experience the essential nature of each substance. Foods seemed vibrant and alive, to take on personalities that I'd never noticed before when they'd been combined with other ingredients or smothered with sauces. I approached them with a fresh respect. I acknowledged that their small deaths in my kitchen were keeping me alive, but looked forward to their consumption for reasons above and beyond the mere satisfac-tion of hunger. Alone on my tongue, new foods rested in splen-dor, old foods with majesty. In front of my eyes, the portion on my plate, like the midget nun of my past, reminded me that I was, indeed, very happy to have a tongue.

Over the next eight years, I ate ritualistically, almost al-ways by myself. Gradually, my list of foods expanded from thirteen to twenty to forty, and I was able to eat two and even three things at a time. Any more than that overloaded my physical and emotional systems. Gradually, my body became nourished by the healthy food it consumed. My strength began to return. My hair stopped falling out and began to shine. But I never lost touch with the cave woman at my table. Since all my foods needed to be organic, they either had to be shipped in at exorbitant cost or grown at home. So I learned to raise most of my own vegetables, and nurtured them from seedlings under grow lights, through the delicate swipe of my harvesting knife, to the last whirl of my dehydrator's fan.

Every spring, I carefully planned my plot, making certain I included enough space for my "safe" foods yet allowed room for "test" rows. On my safe food list, I experimented with different varieties. For example, I planted four kinds of chard—green, red, tough, and tender-stemmed. Once I'd passed "squash," I planted zucchini and yellow bush scallop, spaghetti, and cushaw. Through my membership in the Seed Savers Exchange, a network of home gardeners who work to preserve disappearing heritage varieties, I multiplied my possibilities a hundred times from what I could obtain in the normal catalogues. Once I passed "peppers"—oh, hot, spicy, what-a-perk-to-my-life peppers—I cultivated Sunrise Tequilas, Hercules Sweet Reds, and Bird's Eyes.

Through my gardening, I began to invent combinations of foods. I cut my zucchini into thin slices, dusted them with cayenne, and spread them out in my dehydrator, then picked up the crispy pieces several hours later and ate them, getting more enjoyment from them than from potato chips. I blended tomatoes with fresh basil, then scored and dried this concoction to make another heavenly chip. Living close to my foods, I found different modes of preparation had dramatic effects on the way I felt. I experimented with macrobiotic and raw foods regimens. I learned to control colds with juices and herbs. Feverfew stopped any headache, slippery elm any round of stomach flu.

I built a greenhouse and cold frames. I built raised beds and trellises. I talked to old-timers about their successes and failures. I received gifts of deer-tongue lettuce from my Amish neighbors, tips on how to plant by the moon, samples of fish emulsion and kelp fertilizers. My safe food list doubled from forty to eighty, and I even saw the return of the white potato. I began to feel that I had enough variety then, that I was coming out of my cave.

Oh, there were things I still craved—coffee, for instance, or chocolate, even that pizza no one could live without—but I'd resigned myself to wiping them forever from my list. Even if some day I could tolerate eating mocha ice cream, I'd lived so long on pure food I couldn't imagine endangering my health with junk. I'd become so used to the freshest, most delicate-tasting kernels of home-grown sweet corn that I wondered how anyone could put a greasy, preservative-ridden, three-month-old corn chip in their mouth.

At the end of my eighth year of illness, I ate a whole meal for the first time with others. Moses and Miriam insisted that we could work out the situation. They pulled a bear roast out of their freezer and picked fresh beans from their garden. I brought a salad from mine. The gray linoleum floor scrubbed to a sheen, and the matching linoleum countertops spotless, without a sign that a meal had just been prepared, the family gathered in the huge kitchen around the table, the place settings neatly arranged, paper napkins folded underneath the forks. A kerosene floor lamp lit the scene and threw more heat into an already warm mid-July room. From the living room, an old oak grandfather clock ticked the seconds, and when its hands reached seven o'clock, *bong, bong, bong . . . ,* we all bowed our heads over our plates for the blessing, locks of our hair falling in front of our eyes, the Amish with their bowl cuts and buns, me with my fashionable asymmetrical do. Glasses were filled with cool well water, salt and pepper were passed around the table, no one saying a word about my "problem," no one pressing me to "just try" this or that.

Tears of joy welled in my eyes as I realized we were about to "break beans" together, and as soon as we lifted our forks to our faces, a feeling of community, of love, and of thankfulness to these people who made this effort to include me shot through my body. I was "English," someone from their "outside world," a potential threat to these people's simple life. Yet I may have been one of the first English they'd met who, on at least one level, lived a simpler and more difficult life than they did. As we spooned more beans onto our plates, passing pleasantries with restraint and gentle humor, I wanted to leap up, rush around the table, and kiss each of these people. At the same time, a profound loneliness swept through me. While I'd been eating in isolation, the world had gone on, people had linked up, started families of their own, children had grown, and like those seated around me, taken their places at the family table.

Coming out of my cave had its complications. I was almost blinded by the "new light" and had an urge to rush back home to my own dark recesses. I ate much more slowly than my neighbors, and had a hard time talking, passing bowls, and chewing all at the same time. I felt disoriented and confused trying to talk about the summer's drought and at once balance a platter of bear and swallow a bite of salad. Even though the Amish are a quiet people, having five other voices at the table seemed deafening. The taste of the food faded in the wake of the conversation.

Now, my safe list has grown to around two hundred. Once in a while, I can eat out in a restaurant. Slowly, I've learned again to eat and socialize at the same time, although as much as I love the company, it still feels as if I'm activating one sense to deaden another. For the past year, I've been able to eat ten or twelve foods at once, and my menus have grown much more exciting. Instead of eating a meal of sliced tomatoes, I can make a spaghetti sauce with bear or venison and pour it over whole wheat pasta. I've learned to have fun cooking with what I do have, take pleasure in finding new textures and colors, and often wake up in the middle of the night with ideas for recipes. *I could blend those figs and dates, add a little carob and agar, pour the batter into a walnut crust, and have a pie!*

Now, I look forward to company and spend days inventing meals that are acceptable to my "outside world." My most understanding and adventuresome friends actually ask me for recipes and invite me to parties, where they try to fix things I can eat. *How much carob do I add to that fig and date batter?* But sometimes, even now, almost ten years since the onset of my illness, I'll find myself gravitating to an occasional mono-meal. A plain piece of yucca on a plate can be just enough to pull me back closer to the "spirit world," just enough to again narrow my vision to ultimately expand it, just enough to take me beyond the mundane to know that we and all life is one. And sometimes when I walk home on the gravel road from visiting my neighbors on a cold winter night, another package of bear meat tucked under my arm, I look up at the stars and realize how far I've traveled, how much farther I have to go.

WHEN I BOUGHT my home, one of the last functioning one-room public schoolhouses in the state of
Iowa, the stars were with me, even though I went through one
of the more complicated real estate transactions in the history
of the United States. Off and on throughout the years, I'd lived
in towns near the Amish settlement and had always enjoyed
driving down to the area to buy organic vegetables or goat's
milk from farmers, or stop in the spring at the Amish greenhouse for a few asparagus shoots and some cabbage seedlings.
Then, one day on the way back from the greenhouse, I wound
back past the General Store, took a wrong turn, and ended up
on an unfamiliar road. Meandering and enjoying the day, I
kept driving, fairly unconcerned. In this region, where the "Jeffersonian grid" has been superimposed upon the land, country
roads have an orderly pattern that I've learned to intuit. Just
when I was beginning to get my bearings, there before me was
an old, sturdy-looking one-room school with a FOR SALE sign
in front.

In Iowa, when a one-room schoolhouse is closed, the building reverts to the farmer whose property originally included

the land. Real estate rarely comes up for public sale at all, and when it does, one neighbor or family member buys from another. Even though I was a native Iowan who had lived in the area most of my adult life, my offer to the Mennonite farmer who then owned Fairview School was viewed with suspicion.

Once I'd made a bid, the owner's nephew Ron, a real estate agent, went around the corner to visit Moses.

"You better bid against that girl who made an offer on the school," Ron said.

"Why?" Moses asked. He stood outside his large red barn, the sheep in the corral poking their noses through the fence boards and bleating for food.

"That's a nice little chunk of land."

"Too hilly to farm."

"Make a good pasture, though."

"Got enough of that. Besides, trying to cut back on the livestock."

"Well, the schoolhouse would be just the place for your granddaughter and her husband to live."

"You think so?"

"Sure. And you want to keep control of the neighborhood. Don't want a bunch of hippies moving in."

"Hippies?"

"Yup. That's what's on its way."

Moses leaned back against the wall of his barn and grinned, his long beard bobbing and catching the rays of the early morning sun. "I know how to get along with hippies."

Moses was one of the first to greet me that first winter when I finally moved into Fairview School, a jar of Miriam's home-canned pickles in his hand. As the days of renovation began, he kept daily watch over and gave final approval of the carpenter's installation of a kitchen sink and cabinets, of the addition of a hot water heater, and of the plumber's conversion of the little "Boys" and "Girls" bathroom stalls into one, larger room. But he was stumped by my addition of a sleeping loft.

"What're you going to keep up there on that shelf?" he kidded. "Your boyfriends?"

He wasn't kidding one day the next winter when he phoned me from the Sale Barn.

"You better get down here right away," a voice said on the other end of the line. With no exchange of niceties, I was taken aback and didn't recognize his voice, nor was I expecting it, as we'd never before spoken on the phone.

"Who's this?"

"You better get down here right away and take a look at this buggy. I think it's just what Donna and Stu want."

Donna and Stu's acreage is adjacent to the schoolhouse, and "as the crow flies," their property lies between Moses and Miriam's and mine. They, too, moved to the area because they'd always liked the feel of the place, and because they enjoyed horses. Every day they harnessed up Emily, and drove her in their two-seater cart to town, where hitching posts are provided just off Main Street. Yet with friends, children, and grandchildren all wanting to join them in the trip, they soon found themselves longing for a larger wagon.

"Stu's are gone for the week, ain't they?" Moses' voice came back on the phone. "I tried calling them, but nobody to home. You know what they want. You come take a look at this."

I hopped in my truck and drove to the Sale Barn, the first-Monday-of-every-month horse auction already in progress— saddles, blankets, tack, and old buggies all waiting to find new owners. The cold air was filled with the jingle of spurs, the snorts of quarter horses, Morgans, and Appaloosas. My nose tingled from the smell of manure and new leather, of hot dogs, hot coffee, and popcorn. Clusters of men dressed in black and blue, their collars pulled up to their chins—the Amish in straw hats, the others in seed caps and cowboy hats—gathered around the canteen, milling together near booths selling whips and harnesses, pressing in around the auctioneer. I spotted Moses next to a homemade black cart covered with dust, its shafts worn smooth, wheels sturdy, two long bench seats nailed in place.

"Think it's big enough?" Moses asked.

"This'll hold four people, maybe six," I said.

"At least. All it needs is a good coat of paint," Moses said, and we agreed to get a number and bid up to $150.

"Twenty-five-dollars. Who'll give twenty-five?" the auctioneer chanted, his nasal twang broadcast through his megaphone, his ten-gallon cowboy hat nodding back and forth between the two bidders—Moses and another, younger, beardless Amish bachelor. Moses stood still, his face expressionless, his arms at his sides, only his left eyebrow rising ever so slightly to register a bid, the price climbing quickly and steadily by increments of ten.

"One-ten, one-ten, I got-one-ten-now-who'll make-it-twenty?"

The bidding was creeping dangerously near our limit.

"One-twenty?" The auctioneer glared at Moses.

I bit my lip and thought we were doomed. Moses lifted his eyebrow.

"One-thirty?" The auctioneer turned to the bachelor. "One-thirty?"

The bachelor hesitated.

"One-thirty?"

With ever so slight a motion, the bachelor shook his head "No."

"Sold to Moses for one-twenty!"

A rope was found, and Moses hitched the cart to the bumper of my pickup. We started out on the five-mile trip home together, Moses' horse Willy soon fading in my rearview mirror, the highway turning to gravel, the Amish children in galoshes running to the edge of their yards to watch the strange sight of a truck towing a buggy.

Once we joined up again, Moses and I raised Donna and Stu's garage door. Both of us leaned our weight into a shaft, rolling in the cart, its body just fitting next to their second car. Then I followed Moses around the corner to his place, where he wanted to show me the quilt Miriam had been busy making and have me meet his two daughters and their families, who were visiting from Indiana.

"You bought a buggy for Donna and Stu?" Miriam asked.

"Yup."

"And they're not even home?"

"Nope."

"Well . . . let's have a look."

Doors opened, doors closed, tailgate down, eight of us—Moses, Miriam, their daughters and children—piled into my truck, and off we drove back to Donna and Stu's. We stood in front of the garage, the children wiggling in excitement, then pulled up the heavy garage door.

"Mmm, this'll be all right." Miriam pressed her cane into one of the tires, the rubber flattening. "Just needs some air."

"But is it big enough?" Moses asked.

"Let's try it out and see," Miriam said, hoisting her foot up into the cart. The others followed, the buggy tilting and swaying, the children sitting on their mothers' laps, Moses taking up an imaginary set of reins.

"Gitty-up, Emily!" Miriam called and pantomimed a flick of the whip.

"Whoa, not so fast now," Moses said, jostling his torso back and forth to imitate the rhythm of the ride.

"Hee-he-he-he," one of the children whinnied.

Sitting there in the garage, we trotted down the road for a test drive, laughing and cheering on the horse, a family on an evening's outing together, our collective imaginations playing off and feeding one another, the sun just beginning to go down on the farmhouses, not one of which sported a TV antenna or satellite dish. Our capability for fantasy still very much our own, we abandoned ourselves to the game and one another.

"DO YOUR HORSE and donkey get along?" Joe, the Amish lumberyard man, asked Donna when she approached him about building her a new barn.

Donna and Stu wanted a new home for Emily and Katie. Their old barn, a tiny 8-by-15 structure no bigger than a garage, stood on top of the rise, housing all their animals and leaning into the wind like a drunken sailor. Weathered and aged, the doors no longer closed, the metal roof was beginning to rust through, and snakes had taken up residence in the foundation cracks.

"Let's pull the thing down and build a new, bigger barn—one that will have room for the hay and all the critters," Donna said.

"No, no, no." Stu pleaded for a reprieve, enough time to see if they could fix up the old place to become serviceable again.

They compromised by leaving the old structure solely as a coop for their chickens, ducks, and geese, and building a new barn on the other side of the pasture for hay storage and the housing of Emily and Katie, their two sheep, and Scalawag, my wandering pygmy nanny goat.

Once the plan was set, Donna spent days on the phone calling the local discount lumberyards, trying to get estimates for a small barn. Some sold kits with flimsy materials. Others sold ready-made buildings but without concrete floors. Still others sold standard two-car garages close to her specifications but without plans for expansion or alteration to create a hay loft or horse stall. Then she drove to town to Payless Cashways and typed in her own dimensions in a computer that spat out a blueprint that looked something like what she had in mind but cost twice as much.

At last, one Friday afernoon she drove down the road to Joe's Building Supplies, the lumberyard nestled on a few acres just off the highway. Stacks of plywood and lumber were piled in clusters at the gate, and rows of small freshly painted hog sheds lined the lane. The constant noise of hammering emitted a steady rhythm from the barn, where two Amish men in button-up denim pants and jackets were building a chicken coop, their heads down, arms swinging hammers with smooth, even strokes, sending the nails deeper and deeper into the wood. They cut boards with Skil saws powered by hot air pressure. Outside, a five-year-old girl in a stocking cap and blue coat, the hem of her dress trailing below, swung back and forth in the old tire that hung from the oak tree in the yard next to the two-story white farmhouse.

Joe's office crouches between the house and barn. The one-room building, adorned with porch and railings, looks like an old motor court cottage from the Bonnie and Clyde shoot-out era. As you approach, you expect to find bullet holes in the walls, but instead, a little OPEN sign in the window welcomes you inside, where Joe, a lanky man in his late fifties with a scraggly black beard and a wide smile, glances up at you from behind his desk, papers strewn across the top.

A small propane heater is wedged into one corner of the room, and if you decide to sit—most people don't—you need to clear off piles of receipt books from an old easy chair shoved into another corner, bits of stuffing spilling out from the holes in its worn cover. Often the wait for Joe's attention takes fifteen minutes to a half hour, with two or three other customers there before you, squished into the office, Joe thumbing through one of his inventory books for the price of a particular brand of fiberglass shingles for one, the others discussing the crops or telling stories while they wait.

"Did you hear about the woman who went with her husband to the doctor's office?"

"No, what happened?"

"Well, the doctor checked the husband over for a long time, then took the wife aside and said, 'Unless you do certain things to help, your husband will lose the will to survive and surely die. Each morning at five A.M., before your husband goes out to milk the cows, fix him a big breakfast with pancakes, sausage, and freshly squeezed orange juice. At noon, make him a big lunch with roasted meat and potatoes and homemade freshly baked pie. And make sure the hammock is set up under the shade tree so he can rest before going back into the field. Then no matter what time of day or night he gets in from doing chores, serve supper with a smile. And don't burden him with household problems. After supper give him a nice bowl of popcorn in his rocking chair.'

"So on the way home the husband asked his wife what the doctor had to say. 'You're going to die,' she said."

Donna leaned closer over the piece of ledger paper Joe was using to draw his diagram of the barn.

"Now if we build this thing about twenty-four by twenty-four," Joe said, working the carpenter's pencil across the page, "we'll have four quadrants. The animals and hay'll take up three fourths of the space, with one quadrant left over for miscellaneous. You'll be glad you have that miscellaneous," he said.

Then like a good director directing a play, Joe launched into a discussion of entrances and exits, and took down the exact measurements of Donna's garden cart, so that the swinging doors on the south would provide clearance. Next, he quizzed Donna about extras.

"Will there be any other critters in this barn besides the horse and donkey?"

"Oh, half the year a couple of sheep. And then Scalawag, the little goat, comes and goes. She usually sleeps in the manger."

"Ah, the manger. Now again, do the horse and donkey get along?"

"Oh, yes."

"Enough to eat together or does one grab all the food?"

"No, they seem to share pretty well."

"Good, then we'll need only one manger," Joe said, sketching in the feeding apparatus on the plan. He turned the paper upside down so Donna could get a better look, and she nodded her approval.

"And do you keep the manger filled all the time, or do the animals get restless and hungry?"

"No, we keep it filled so they can have as much to eat as they want."

"That's fine. Then we keep the wall at five feet and won't have to build it all the way up in case they try to get to the hay. Some horses leap right over a short wall when they're hungry." Joe marked the dimensions on the paper, and drew in the vents he'd put in each gable to prevent moisture condensation.

"Otherwise water can build up and drip back down on the critters."

"Oh, we wouldn't want that."

"No. Now, when the horse and donkey are in the barn, do they stand with their heads by the other's tail, swishing the flies away?"

"Yes, they do that."

"Okay, then we won't need a dividing wall in their stall." Joe leaned back in his chair, inspecting his diagram to make certain he hadn't missed a consideration, then scrawled a column of numbers on another slip of paper.

"And, one more question. Do you clean your barn regularly?"

"Yes."

"That's good."

Donna glanced up at Joe with a quizzical look.

"That makes a difference, you know, in how high we build the roof. Some don't shovel out the manure much in the winter. That stuff piles up and the animals can end up bumping their heads on a low ceiling."

Flipping through his price lists, Joe tallied and figured, and figured and tallied, everything done in his head or on paper without the aid of a computer, calculator, or even a hand-crank adding machine, until he came up with a precise estimate: $6,153.65.

"Now, that doesn't include painting," Joe said. "You'll have to do that yourself."

Customarily, the Amish rarely do anything alone. When they gather to build a large barn or house for one of their own, they rattle their buggies and buckboards into the farm lane, thirty or forty men assembling at once to construct a building that would take a normal crew ten times as long, the women congregating in the kitchen to cook a big lunch of roasted meat and potatoes. One man takes charge of the "frolic," the others falling into a division of labor, sons working at the elbows of their fathers—elbows bending and straightening with each blow of the hammer.

The men pound with joy when they build a new house or an addition for a family so rich in children that they've outgrown their smaller home. The men pound with grief when they build a new house and barn for a family whose whole homestead burned to the ground when a kerosene lantern got too close to a hay mound. But whether in delight or sadness, the walls go up straight and true, the buildings finished off to perfection down to the last shingle, the last piece of shim.

Like a well-made play, Donna and Stu's new barn was executed in three stages, or acts. On Monday morning, Joe's crew arrived to pour the concrete floor. On Tuesday the cement dried, and on Wednesday the barn went up, three Amish men working in sync in a mini-frolic, each anticipating the others' movements, each with his lines and actions well rehearsed.

"I'll send Mahlon and his boys to build your barn," Joe had told Donna, and she had been delighted to be hiring the services of one of our nearest neighbors. Mahlon had learned his trade from his father, Joshua, a man who had held the reputation as the best carpenter in the country. Mahlon sawed, fitted, and hammered with the finesse of a master, each movement swift and efficient, each movement learned through years of apprenticeship and passed down through the family from one generation to the next.

By late morning, the barn frame was in place, the skeleton of the gabled roof branching up into the air, patches of crisp blue sky showing through the two-by-fours. In the afternoon, when Mahlon and his sons returned from dinner, clopping back down the road in their buggy, the walls were nailed on, plywood covering the rough pine studs. Next, the roof was shingled, Mahlon unrolling the tar paper, one son hammering the pieces of asphalt into place, another son climbing up and down the ladder. Then the doors were hung; with all the men lifting the great sliding front panel onto its track, the barn looked complete from the outside. Inside, the hayloft, manger, and gates were crafted, and by supper time had been fastened into place.

On Thursday, Donna painted the barn, and by Friday Emily and Katie had taken up residence, sniffing the new gates, which still smelled of freshly sawed pine. By Saturday night, their new home already had that lived-in feel. With manure covering the floor, and a tiny goat asleep in the manger, the lights went down, the stars up, on a production that by all counts should have a long, long run.

DOWN, DOWN, hammering and pounding, pounding and hammering, I worked on building houses for my animals—a doghouse for Bill, a cat house for Hilda and Doolittle, a coop for Ruby and Groucho, the geese, and a goat shed for Scalawag. Hammer, nails, screws, a measuring tape, a power drill, and saw—I pulled out scrap boards from the woodpile, fit one together with another, piecing and fitting, squeezing and planing off ends to at least an approximation of evenness. An evenness of temper followed, guiding and lifting me through the task. Was this just a balm, a trick to see me through a job for which I'd had no instruction, no apprenticeship?

If you can make a bear stew, if you can make a dress, you can make a goat shed, I told myself. On the whole, fewer parts to cut out, fewer mistakes to be made. And mistakes I made on this one-woman frolic, this event so akin to yet so opposite from my Amish neighbors' endeavors. How often did I make a dress anymore? Sewing, just like cooking, was a chore designed to make a person nervous. But this hammering and pounding, these big muscular strokes, the biceps moving in unison with the hands, the wrists holding firm, then bending at just the right moment—there was something bigger and bolder in this hammering, this outdoors work, the air still condensing with each breath. There was something calming.

You hold the hammer in your hand, fingers wrapped around the handle—not too loosely, not too tightly. Not choking up too far. The sensuousness of wood against palm. Ash. Your hand feeling the movement of hammer sail through you, never forcing, but letting the weight of the metal do the work, falling down through the air, down, down. The music began, all the tiny hammers pressing down, piano strings sounding their pure notes, holding and sustaining. The pedal pressed to the floor. Forte. Fortepiano. The music, the ash sailing through you, building and lulling, building to let the world know that for now you were flesh. Not ash. From dust you are made and to dust you shall return.

Who cared if the first building wasn't a work of beauty, that one wall slanted too much? The power was in the process. The power was in figuring out how to join two walls, to drive that first nail into the wood without assistance. The power was in the sawhorses and vise grips and the satisfaction that no one else had to be called or consulted. The power was in the head hitting the nail, the shingles now in place, the freezing rain pounding down, hammering the roof, and the roof holding, Scalawag inside perfectly dry.

Down, down, down, the nail and hammer on the ground, the post pounder went up and down, up and down. Fences began to form. One around the garden, one around the goat shed to make a pen, four-foot-high wire. And more stakes bought for a song from Wilbur, the Amish welder and junkyard man. Now a pasture, now a horse and donkey grazing, a lamb, two lambs, a goat, three goats. Good fences make good neighbors, and Donna and Stu and I decided to share our pastures, the critters moving back and forth from their side to mine, the grass always greener, always higher. Good fences do make good neighbors, and in tending them, mending them, I unrolled the coil of wire. Snip and cut, the clippers biting down. The power is in the palm and thumb, the fingers stretching round the stakes. The power is in hands joining hands, the neighbor holding the wire in place, the horizon stretching clear and wide.

DOWN, DOWN, DOWN, drifting and floating, floating and drifting, listening only to the sound of my voice, letting any other noise in the room or outside the window drift and float away. Going deeper now. Five . . . four . . . three . . . two . . . one. Just listening to the sound of my voice, deeper and deeper still.

Eyes closed, muscles relaxed—several winters ago I left Fairview School and sat in the middle of a room in a hypnotherapy school in Oakland, California. The words of the hypnotist drew me inside myself, into a calm and restful state freed from self-consciousness, from the gazes of my nine classmates. We had already spent two intensive weeks together, learning techniques—induction, deepening, creating suggestion—and knew all about one another's image and weight problems, stage fright, phobias, and attempts to quit smoking, but I had never been the "demonstration model" before, the focal point of the day's lesson.

Turning your attention now to today's lesson, to pain control, to your pain. Imagining its site, imagining its color. Getting a clear sense in your mind of exactly where that pain is located and what shade it appears. You have all the colors in the rainbow available to pick from, and one precise color, one hue, will match.

My pain was rust brown and located in both my wrists. I had carpal tunnel syndrome, a crippling arthritic malady related to my Environmental Illness, which had put me out of work for the previous six months. With CTS, the wrist joint swells and exerts pressure on the ulna nerve, which runs from the hand all the way up the arm to the spinal column. In my case, the swelling was so severe that it not only pinched the nerve but cut off the flow of blood into my hands. They were constantly cold, blue, and in spasm.

My pain was dull, heavy, decaying. My wrists ached all day, and whenever I tried to open a door, roll down a car window, type a page on the computer, the ache turned to a sharp stab. Then, at night, even with my arms at rest, the stab settled in for good and shot up to my elbows and into my shoulders. My ulna nerve, or "funny bone," zinged in a rhythmical pattern, the pain unrolling up my forearms all night long. To sleep, I wore splints that reached from my knuckles to my elbows and immobilized my wrists so they wouldn't bend and further exacerbate the situation.

Rust brown, rust brown. Your pain is rust brown and you imagine it at its worst—ten on a ten-point scale. Go ahead and feel the twinge, the ache, the stab, your nerves zinging up and down your arms. Feeling your pain with all its problems, very intense now. That's right. At its worst.

My wrists, my elbows, my shoulders throbbed with a hot burning sensation that sank into the very marrow of my joints. My nerves felt squeezed, stretched tight. The pain heated up further still, then leveled off to a steadiness that kept my whole body focused on its presence, my stomach turning sour, nauseated. Tears pooled in my eyes.

You're at ten now, ten, ten, ten, and you bring your pain

down. Nine . . . diminishing with each number . . . eight.
Going down, smaller and smaller, less and less. Seven . . . six
. . . five. Halfway there. Feeling your pain recede, going away.
Four . . . three . . . two . . . one.

With each count, each suggestion, I followed along and felt
my pain cooling to the seven or six range, but no further. I
wanted the pain to go away, to be gone altogether. I knew the
power of hypnosis. I'd seen the weight roll off one of my fellow students, day by day, the pounds melting away. I'd seen
another student, her bridge phobia having nearly paralyzed
her travel plans, sail across the Golden Gate Bridge in a con-
vertible, top down, singing to rock music on the radio. I
wanted this to work, but no matter how strong my desire, I
retained a lingering doubt that I'd ever be able to use my hands
again.

IN MY CHILDHOOD rural Midwest, you found your
place in the world through your hands. I loved to trot along-
side my grandmother as she wrapped her liver-spotted hands
around her corn knife and walked beans on her farm, the
cockleburs no match for the blade that careened down through
the air with a sudden whack. The same hands and the same
knife decapitated chickens, ducks, and geese, cut off their feet,
and carved them up into familiar parts: legs, breasts, thighs,
backs, and wings. I imagined that the birds' clipped wings,
their lack of hands, was what doomed them to the life of prey.

We lived with my grandmother in her large, white Victo-
rian turn-of-the-century house, which was in constant need of
maintenance and care. I was entertained by a steady stream of
helpers, who arrived at the back door with toolboxes and baskets full of implements that assisted in a morning or afternoon
of work on the house. There was Ott, the electrician, whose
eyes were crossed but whose hands were so deft that he didn't

need to focus to splice and string wires, installing the circuit breakers, intercoms, and dimmer switches my father requested. There was Bill, who hunted squirrels in our backyard with a homemade slingshot and helped mount our heavy wooden second-story storm windows, tapping them into place with one blow of his rubber mallet. There was Olga, the seamstress, who in her youth had been my great-uncle and aunt's hired girl and sewed the family's Sunday dress-up clothes, and, in her old age, made the heavy draperies that hung from our living-room picture and bay windows. There was Bud, our neighbor, owner of the feed and seed store, who brought over daylily and tulip bulbs, to be planted in our flower beds.

And there was Rudy, the carpenter. Rudy wore overalls, with a pencil—thick, flat, and yellow—perched in the smallest pocket. Around his waist, he sported an apron with larger pockets, which hid nails, screws, and a wooden measure that folded accordion style into sections. I'd sit for hours and watch him lean his whole weight into his hand drill, his left palm flat against the oak knob, his right gyrating the handle around and around, always exerting just the right amount of pressure, his movements steady, practiced, efficient. Once the hole was made, the screw floated in with a couple of quick pumps from his Phillips, his hand twisting with force, his biceps flexing.

One winter, Rudy repaired our staircase, a beautiful, ornate structure that had been imported from France during the more elegant beginnings of the house. On hands and knees, crowbar and hammer working in unison, he excavated worn and rotten boards on the landing, then measured replacements. The teeth of his saw bit into the hardwood tongue-and-groove boards that were braced between his sawhorses, sawdust trickling to the ground. He sanded off the edges until the boards fit perfectly into their slots, the nails driven at angles to render them invisible.

Once the job was finished, Rudy whisked the area clean

with a tiny dustpan and broom, items I thought belonged more in my dollhouse than his toolbox, then untied his apron and laid it carefully in his metal chest. Then his saw was in his hands, plying and bending, the steel beginning to whine and wobble out a sound so mysterious, so scratchy yet melodious, that I was mesmerized by its power. Rudy threw back his head and sang.

Ist das nicht Dein Schnitzelbank?
Ja, das ist mein Schnitzelbank.

We laughed and sang and sang and laughed, the saw buckling and glistening in the late morning sun that poured through the stained-glass window onto the landing. We stomped our feet and beat time, the saw adding another voice to ours, an animal whine akin to Happy's, our beagle's, on a full-moon night. My mother came down from an upstairs bedroom and my grandmother rounded the kitchen corner, drying her hands on her apron, positioning her dentures in her mouth. We all clapped, Rudy sweeping a bow, his hair flopping down in front of his face like Leonard Bernstein's, his yellow pencil spilling onto the floor.

HAIR SLICKED BACK, my Amish neighbor Joshua, a carpenter, lay in a coffin, the cherry wood hand hewn and polished to a sheen that matched the brass hinges and handles. In my adult rural midwestern life in Fairview School, work and hands are again synonymous. Thirty-five years removed from Rudy and his saw, I have lived in cities, traveled around the United States and Europe, and brought myself through an odyssey of higher education that valued mental over muscular might. I have come full circle, and my present life among the

Amish has allowed me a return to my original schooling and the lesson that work with your hands opens your heart.

So, it was only fitting to find Joshua, a man who had sawed, sanded, and planed wood his whole life, carried to the cemetery in a box that was beautifully made and showed all the care and craft of a Steinway piano in Carnegie Hall.

"This way, come." During the day of the home visitation, Mahlon had led me into the dining room, where Joshua lay. "You'll want to see the body."

Actually, I hadn't wanted to see the body. I hadn't wanted to make a scene, being the only English in this farmhouse filled with benches full of black suspenders, black shawls and bonnets pulled tightly around chins. I'd picked a large watermelon from my garden, walked quietly down the gravel road, offered it to my neighbors as a sign of respect for their loss, then had hoped to slip back home. I hadn't wanted to invade this religious ritual, nor face the stark reality of this home death. I've been to quite a few funerals in my life, but never to one outside the sanitized atmosphere of a mortuary.

"Here, we'll go through the back way." Mahlon guided me through a kitchen pantry door, depositing me in the dining room right in front of the dead body.

No flowers or wreaths prettified the room. Instead, the cherry coffin, lid open, its lines simple and sleek, was shoved up against the plain white wall. Silk lined the cavity of the casket, and against the cushioning lay Joshua, the grandpa, or "Grossdadi," dressed in a black suit, his beard fading into the whiteness of his shirt and death mask. His face hadn't been fixed up, doctored with makeup to look alive. Rather, it was colorless, almost translucent, and clearly evidenced passage into a different state, the cheeks limp, mouth drawn. But Joshua's hands dominated the physical and psychic space. Big veined, knuckled, and knotty, they lay crossed and flat against his chest. The skin, dry and dabbled with freckles, was spread over the surface like a canvas paint tarp, heavy and creased here, bulging there. The fingernails, stained the same tint of yellow that ran through the old man's beard, were ridged, scored into tiny prisms that reflected the late August light. The nails, immaculate and scrubbed clean, were longer than normally expected for a man who worked so intensely with his hands. They chronicled the last couple of months of his illness, confined to bed rest and inactivity.

During the same time, the events of the household had been anything but quiet. Nightly, buggies paraded down the gravel road, pulling into the lane, couples and often whole families with six or seven children making their way into the house with Bibles, casseroles, and cookies. Sometimes as many as twenty horses were tied to the hitching post, their tails swishing away flies, their heads bobbing, waiting for their owners to complete their prayers and visit with the dying man, who was propped on pillows in the front room next to the open window. Each night for a week before his death, a chorus of young girls, bonneted and barefoot, appeared before the screen, singing hymns, the notes light and pure, lifting the heaviness of the tempo and melodic line into another realm, drifting through the wire mesh and enveloping the old man in comfort.

The young girls sang again when the two draft horses pulled the wagon that hauled Joshua's coffin the half mile to the cemetery. There, the hole had been dug, adjacent to the last burial site, by two men with shovels. The Amish, one large family, bury their dead efficiently in a land-saving configuration, in neat rows in chronological order of the deceased. Uniform, small white stones mark the graves, the slabs often nameless, with only the death date engraved into the limestone. I've heard that in the old days, the Amish wrapped their dead in rolls of sod for burial. Then, no box, no artifact, no ornamentation stood between the dead and their return to the earth. Dust to dust, they made what they could of their lives while they had them, retaining the final goal of disappearing back into the ground in the end.

"LIE FACE DOWN on the table and cover yourself with the sheet," I said when I began with a new client.

I washed my hands in the other room while the person in my therapeutic massage studio undressed. I returned to find an elongated form on my table draped in white. Sometimes, even to me, the scene looked clinical, but once the woodstove that warmed the space caught hold, the flames inside expanding the cast iron with a low moan, once I lifted the sheet from a client's leg and began stroking the calf with my palms, the body under the covering came alive, my connection to it intimate, unique. I loved the physical and emotional release of massage, my hands, slick with oil, sliding up and down muscles, finding definition, working down and around bones and ligaments, smoothing out spasms, pressing and targeting pressure points along meridians.

In my early thirties, after I'd spent most of my adult life in academic pursuits, I learned massage therapy, a craft that disappeared the moment you practiced it. I went off to school in California and came back with a list of French terms—*effluerage, petrissage,* and *tapotement*—that embody Swedish massage, and with a skill that supported me for years. I began my practice in the living-room of an old house I'd bought from the son of an old woman named Ida who loved to garden and had ringed the place in flowers. Surrounded by beauty, I carried out what I'd been well taught, that the human body is a work of art and that my job was to engage in safe, modest, nonsexual body work.

"Do you ever massage anyone really fat?"

People frequently asked me this question. Yes, I massaged

fat people, and skinny people. I massaged Olympic wrestlers and professional football players and dancers. I toured with the Royal Winnipeg Ballet as its therapist, my table set up in the stage wings. I massaged polio survivors with shriveled legs and accident victims with no legs. I massaged cancer patients in the last days of their life, rape victims hours after attacks, babies weeks after birth. I massaged a quadriplegic who communicated yes and no through forward and backward movements of her thumb.

My hands glided over truck drivers and bank presidents, plumbers and stock brokers, all on the same table, all of different sizes, shapes, and colors. Against my palms, my fingertips, the human body took on a dignity, a mystery, and a force I'd never known before. All the people on my table were beautiful, no matter how fat or thin. Rather than flaws to be concealed, cellulite, saggy breasts, bulging bellies, wrinkles, and birthmarks appeared natural and right.

In my Catholic upbringing, I'd been taught that the human body is a temple of the Holy Spirit. At that time, the phrase was used almost solely to deter us from "the sins of the flesh," but years later, it came close to capturing the reverence I felt for the people I touched. Through contact with so many bodies, I could sense the presence of something deeper, more mystical, more everlasting than just muscle tissue and bone.

In massage school, our instructors constantly referred to sensing the client's "energy." I tuned out the term as a vague, nonscientific New Age coinage and went through the motions of the exercises designed to sensitize us to the idea. While we pulled our hands apart, then brought them back together, slowly and rhythmically, many of my classmates delighted over the feel of the electromagnetic field that they experienced.

"My hands are magnets!" they exclaimed.

I felt nothing. Not a spark. Not a flicker. I dismissed this activity as a flaky California component I'd just have to tolerate and get through before I could learn the more technical aspects of therapeutic massage.

When I graduated and became certified, I returned to Iowa, hung out my shingle, and soon the phone began to ring. I saw an average of twenty clients a week, and with that large a practice, my hands began to "tune in" on their own. After only a month of practice, I saw a spunky, elderly woman one Saturday afternoon, a complete stranger and referral from the local women's health center. I took a medical history, screening for diseases and past injuries, then began my routine, which still found me glancing up from time to time at the list of strokes I had tacked to the wall.

As I massaged her face and moved toward her scalp, an area near her right temple seemed different, physically colder, inexplicably "off balance." Something bigger, more dramatic than I'd ever expected or felt before seemed to be radiating from her head.

"Is there something I should know about this part of your skull that you didn't tell me in your history?"

My fingers hesitated to dip into the disturbed area.

"Oh, that," the woman scoffed. "That's where I was shot in the head doing peace work in Africa."

Over the years, my hands sensed no more bullet wounds, but they did key in to other physical and emotional wounds. It wasn't long before they awakened a sensibility in me that even the most skeptical part of myself could no longer deny. One of my teachers, a learned Chinese acupuncturist, had told me that a good practitioner should be able to reach a relatively accurate diagnosis of his or her patient even before sitting down for a history. In Chinese medicine, more reliable information is gained through carriage, pallor, and smell than the patient's own words.

I was not in the business of diagnosis and never reached the level of the acupuncturist's expertise, but after my hands began to pick up the unmistakable tingle of my client's "energy," my heart and mind developed their own intuitions. I sensed pregnancies, addictions, and emotional upset before my clients even climbed onto the table, and once there, the center of my palms seemed to have a radar of their own.

The holy cards of my youth had provided me with images of saints blessed with the stigmata, spontaneous sores in their hands and feet that imitated the wounds of Christ. Often, the artists depicted these saints performing healings, rays of light beaming from their palms. I am no saint, but after I began practicing massage, this old image took on new meaning and power. I read through literature on both Eastern and Western religions and became fascinated when, again and again, I found the same image of the hand and the special radiance— call it grace, chi, or chakra—that it emits.

YOU FEEL A HEALING light pooling in your hands, soothing and lifting the pain, sinking down into the muscles, the bones, working its way around your wrists, healing and soothing, soothing and healing. And while that light remains with you, get a sense of what your pain feels like. If it had physicality, if it were some sort of tangible object, with size, shape, and texture, what would it be?

"A sharp piece of metal. A hook."

A hook?

"Yes."

Now where is that hook?

"Buried."

Buried in the ground?

"Buried deep in the ground."

How can you get that hook out?

"Dig it out."

Go ahead and do that now.

"It's very hard to find. Very far down."

Call in any aid, any help you need, to assist you in the dig.
Call in any people, animals, tools, that would help you dig.

Suddenly, they were all there, standing in my front yard—
Olga and Ott, Bill, Bud and Rudy, Joshua and Mahlon, even
Ida—all the handy people from my youth, all the handy people
of my adulthood, every craftsperson I'd ever known who had
helped me string a wire, hem a skirt, or hammer a nail. They
huddled together in a pack, visiting, introducing themselves to
one another, shifting their weight from foot to foot, not knowing exactly what to do, wanting to work but waiting for orders
from me.

"I can't use my hands," I explained, "but need to dig out
a piece of metal buried in the ground. It's down deep and
should be about here." I indicated a spot with my foot.

Shoulders hunched, the whole crew took up shovels and
garden spades and began to dig, their palms gripping the handles, their work boots caked with mud and pressing against
the blades. The sod opened with a rip as if Olga were pulling
out a seam, then shovelful by shovelful, small piles of dirt
accumulated on the lawn, little dribbles of topsoil, then clay.
Sweat rolled down the helpers' faces and Rudy fished into one
of the pockets of his overalls for a red bandanna to mop his
forehead. Bud dabbed at his bad eye, and Ida wiped her brow
with her apron.

What's going on now?

"They're digging."

Deeper and deeper. You're going deeper now, deeper and
deeper.

Deeper and deeper, but getting nowhere. The mounds were
growing, but slowly, the additions, small morsels, dollops of
dirt. The ground was getting harder and harder, ungiving. Bill
flexed his biceps and stabbed the shovel into the soil. He
turned up only a handful of dirt. Joshua jumped on the blade

of his shovel with both feet, all his weight driving the metal into the ground. He rocked back and forth to wedge the tool into the clay and loosen more soil, but the ground resisted.

NEITHER OF MY PARENTS was good with their hands. My mother loved to read, write letters, play sports, dance, go to plays, the ballet. She loved to dress up in nice clothes but didn't like to sit down at the sewing machine and make them. Nor did she like to knit, crochet, tat, quilt, garden, or cook. On Saturdays, we cleaned the house together, a drudgery for both of us; then, when other mothers and daughters were baking bread or cutting out a new pattern, my mother and I would go outside and shoot a few baskets in the driveway hoop. Or, she might buy tickets to see Nureyev and Fonteyn dance *Swan Lake,* and we'd hop in the car and drive to Saint Louis for the weekend.

She had been a small child—only a few pounds at birth—and all her life she had to be prodded to eat. She found cooking a chore and throwing dinner parties hell. She had ten or fifteen basic menus she could do well, and didn't like to stray from that format. Nor did we encourage her.

One Christmas Eve, she tried to make a fancy dessert topped with meringue. In the kitchen, she stirred and scraped, poked and pecked at the ingredients, then brought out servings of an elegant fruit and liqueur concoction perched on our best Haviland china. The table was adored with a linen cloth, candles lit. *O Holy Night.*

"Oh, Christ almighty!" my father yelled when he stuck his fork down into the meringue and it flew up into the air and across the room.

My mother laughed and warned the rest of us not to eat what was on our plates lest we chip a tooth.

My father was not only klutzy with his hands, but also

with his feet. He tried to take care of the yard, but bought an electric lawn mower and repeatedly ran it over the cord, slicing the thing into a den of thin, black snakes. He tried to wipe out the dandelions with an application of spray from a huge metal tank he'd slung over his shoulder. For some reason, he performed the dandelion execution in his swim trunks and thongs, and when he dropped the tank on his toe, it washed him up on a rocky shore. For days he lay adrift in his bed, his big toe turning purple, swelling up bigger and bigger, unable to bear any weight, not even the pressure of a sheet.

Finally, the doctor came and drilled a hole through the toenail, and my father paid my brothers and me a nickel for every bushel basketful of weeds we could dig out of the lawn. Stabbing and gouging, stabbing and gouging, inching along on my hands and knees with a small version of a corn knife, I used up most of the summer to make some loose change.

YOU'RE MEETING RESISTANCE *now and need to relax down deeper. Going down, twice as deep, twice as deep as I lift your arm, loose and limp, that's right, limp and loose, and let your hand fall into your lap. That's it. Twice as deep. Going down. Ten . . . nine . . . eight . . . seven . . . six . . . five . . . halfway there . . . four . . . three . . . two . . . one. Twice as deep.*

What's going on now?
"Stuck."
Stuck?
"Can't go any further."

HANDS FLOATED TOWARD ME—large hands and small, smooth and calloused, manicured hands with long red fingernails, grease-stained hands with layers of dirt worked in and around the cuticles. The precise, quick hands of my grade school piano teacher, the nun, dashed over the keys, easily, fingers arched, fingers stretched to encompass the octave-length chords, demonstrating the new sonata I would labor over for weeks, plunking out note by indecipherable note. The clean pudgy hands of the priest raised the Host, white and round, above my head, and held it there—*This is My Body;* my own hand curled into a fist, striking my breast. *Mea culpa.*

We sin through the senses, the nuns told us. *Especially the hands.* What crimes, what crimes resided in our childish fingers, those midget digits. Not just the little pieces of penny gum snitched from Woolworth's and stuffed down deep into our pockets. Down deep, we knew the stuff of hands, how without even looking they found what they were looking for, the crevices and cracks of our most private selves, the shift in temperature, in texture of skin, in thought and desire. This is my body, temple of the Holy Spirit. The thoughts were often more exciting than what we were doing with our hands, the surprise and pleasure we found in them between our legs, opening, squeezing back closed together. Surely, this wasn't wrong. On fire, we knew we wouldn't burn.

Mea culpa. Bigger sins. My father's hand on my bare bottom, whacking over and over again. My father's whip on top of the refrigerator, the handle that just fit his grip. My mother's hands folded together on her deathbed, the fingers thin and squared off at the ends, the fingers longer than mine, always longer, always larger, the hands I used to measure mine against until I stopped growing and realized that I would forever remain smaller, never reach an octave. "I like to watch people's hands more than their faces," my mother said. My own face is nondescript, another midwestern Mick Kraut. My own hands are fine-boned, still a child's, petite, out of proportion to the rest of my body. Delicate freaks. My legs, arms, torso grew in adolescence, my feet gaining another half size every six months, but my hands stopped.

It was as if my hands were still stuck in that car door, and never grew again. I was five, maybe four, climbing in the back-seat, the driver's side of our old Studebaker, my parents getting in the front, my father at the wheel, my mother beside him. I remember the cloth seats, the way they slanted back toward the trunk, the hard center hump. I remember the hot summer light slicing through the window, dust particles swimming in the beam, dust particles swimming in my nose and lungs. I remember coughing from the smell, the mustiness, the closed-up feeling of the sedan, the seat bent back for me to crawl in.

The seat sprang forward. I pushed it there with my hand, and my hand was brushing against the cloth, my hand was brushing against the door, and my hand was caught in the door when it slammed, my father never noticing how it hung there near his shoulder, my mother's eyes on the road. The pain seared through my fingers, but I didn't cry. *Mea culpa.* I thought it was my fault, I thought I had been careless, I thought my father would scream or explode and the lashing from tongue or hand would be worse than the crunch of my fingers between metal. Little Spartan, I rode the eight blocks downtown without a word, waiting for my father to park and swing open the door.

"Your hand is stuck in the door again," my therapist said once when I was emotionally numb. Your hand is stuck in the door. She was right. I have a hard time admitting pain, phys-ical or mental, and tend to push it down, wait for it to pass. It comes out of my dreams. Wild nights, wild nights. The nuns are Huns and the Huns have horns and guns, and their bullets lodge between muscle and bone. What I've learned: pain never moves through, never passes, just grows fainter, and even when the throbbing has calmed, even when the swelling is down, you still carry the bullets encased in your skin, the imprint of that door latch across your palm, intertwining, merging with your life line.

YOU CAN CALL IN any help you need now. Any people, animals, or objects that would assist in the digging, any help you need. Let the assistance come. Let the aid arrive. That's right. Five . . . four . . . three . . . two . . . one. Let the help arrive. . . . And what's happening now?

"More help."

What kind of help?

"More diggers."

More diggers.

Yes, all the handy persons had invited relatives, friends. There were hundreds of people in my yard now, digging together, in unison, and those who weren't digging were hauling dirt in wheelbarrows, pitching and piling it up into great mounds. The crowd worked as if it had performed this job many times before and knew every step, was anticipating and prepared for each task the way the Amish are for a frolic. Suddenly, they took up a song, a call and response, Rudy down in the pit accompanying them on the saw:

> *Ist das nicht Dein Schnitzelbank?*
> *Ja, das ist mein Schnitzelbank.*

The workers dug and sang, excavating little shreds of dirt, then digging more. And more.

"The workers. They're digging but not getting anyplace."

Do they need more help?

"They need a backhoe."

Call in the backhoe.

A backhoe appeared, putting around the corner and up onto the lawn. Joshua guided the driver into position, signaling him to advance, swing to the left, then halt. The backhoe bit down into the dirt with an energy that shook the yard. Stunned by such force, the rest of the diggers stopped, circled around the machine, and merely watched, leaning against their spades and shovels, the backhoe's blade slicing deeper and deeper.

"WHY ARE YOU here?" the young resident asked me in the neurology clinic of one of the oldest teaching hospitals in the country.

"I have carpal tunnel syndrome. In both hands. And want to get it verified for my records." Self-employed, I had no disability insurance of my own and planned on applying to the government for assistance.

The young doctor took down my symptoms, asked me to squeeze his hand ten or twenty times from different angles, poked my skin with a safety pin, then left me for an hour in the little white examining room while he consulted with the staff physician.

"We're certain you don't have CTS," the resident said when he returned.

I was perplexed. I'd researched the symptoms myself.

"So to find out what's going on, we're going to send you down for some tests."

Down for some tests. Why are tests always down? But down in the basement past the morgue I went for an EMG/ NCV. In the waiting room, a blue cloud of cigarette smoke hung in the air and a brochure on the coffee table explained that the tests I was about to have determined muscle and nerve problems and were no more painful than getting a shot. Something told me otherwise when I saw patients coming out of the testing room with tears streaming down their faces.

First, I was shocked up and down my arms and legs with

an electrode. Then another resident stabbed me in several places in both hands with a heavy-gauge needle attached to a computer.

"Right hand," he said and stuck the needle into the fleshy pad beneath my thumb. Apparently, the needle didn't find the proper depth because the computer screen remained blank. The resident bopped the needle with a book and drove it deeper into my hand. He busied himself scribbling numbers in my chart, adjusted the current several times, then withdrew the needle. "Left hand," he said.

I carried the test results back upstairs and waited another hour while the neurology team analyzed them.

"You have bilateral carpal tunnel syndrome," the resident announced. "And we have scheduled you an appointment in the hand clinic for surgery."

The hand clinic was in yet another wing of the hospital, its entryway graced with a large display case. From far down the hall, I thought the glass encased bowling trophies, bronze statuettes shining behind the panels. But walking closer, I found the trophies were hands, castings of famous men's hands, palms outstretched, fingers splayed in the air. Gilded and unpaired, Wilt Chamberlain's hand was nearly a foot long while Louis Armstrong's was tight and compact. John Glenn's hand was solid, wide, Lyndon Johnson's deeply lined.

I stood in front of the case, caught in the glow of the hands, riveted to every heart line, the smooth lanes and the gutters of the palms. The more I studied, the more I stared, the more intimate these hands became, even though they were all male, and but for Joel Grey's, much larger than my own. They beamed and flared. The custodian ran the vacuum across the carpet behind me, and the hands shook on their tiny stands, moving on their own, their fingers parting the air.

Silently, the hands were applauding, welcoming, beckoning. But surgery meant anesthesia, and I am sensitive to all such drugs and could have gone into shock or even died from the operation. Too, I'd researched the CTS surgical success rate and found it quite low. Surgery seemed to help for a while, then the patients often relapsed. Or worse. Some found themselves permanently damaged, with less movement than before. I even discovered a department at the Mayo Clinic specializing in CTS surgical failures.

I turned around, left the surgery wing, the glass case of golden hands, and found my way down the long corridor to the cashier's office. I paid my $300 bill for the day and walked home in the September late afternoon, the air just then growing cooler, the days darker.

Surgery terrified me, but regular M.D.'s had nothing else to offer but pain pills, which, again, produced severe reactions in me. So I tried alternative routes and took rounds of vitamins, especially niacin and B_6, which had completely eliminated the CTS symptoms in a half dozen people I'd known. The vitamins weren't supposed to have an effect until after six weeks, so I kept up my hope until week ten, then began to realize they probably weren't going to work.

I went to a Rolfer, who deeply massaged my arms, bearing down with his whole weight, his hands and forearms pressing into mine. His sessions gave me relief for three or four days, then the dull, heavy pain set in again. I went to my acupuncturist teacher, who also was able to provide only temporary relief. I went to chiropractors and even a psychic healer, but my hands only got worse, turning blue, each day the circulation diminishing. I went back to church and got down on my knees and prayed. I joked with myself that maybe the pressure on my knees would alleviate the pressure on my wrists.

But when I left my pew, I wasn't amused. As the months stretched on, I knew that if I didn't improve soon, I was in for a lifetime of nerve damage and would be forced to risk surgery. I knew I might also be falling into a lifetime financial abyss. I had had to close my massage practice. I had applied for disability and been denied. The state had sent me to a nephrologist rather than a neurologist for my physical, and this kidney specialist determined that I could find other work, in which I didn't need to use my hands.

THE BACKHOE CUT through the compacted dirt, driving deeper and deeper still. Then, finally, it unearthed the small piece of brown metal and brought it to the surface.

Take the hook away, far away. And again, use any help you need.

The diggers backed in a dump truck, its bed open and wide. The driver tilted the bed toward the hole, and ceremoniously the diggers reached for the hook and carried it on a pillow to deposit in the truck. The diggers quickly filled in the hole, and I laughed when Joshua signaled the driver to pull ahead, directing him toward the street, where his tail lights faded away into the distance.

That's right. Let yourself register the scene. The hook is in the dump now, in the dump, and your pain, too, is going far, far away.

The hook was far away, the diggers were celebrating, throwing their hats into the air, dancing and doing jigs on top of the ground to stomp down the dirt. But my pain remained in my wrists. Didn't budge.

The instructor counted me back to normal consciousness and reiterated, for the class, the steps of the sequence. I quickly slid back into my role as student, returning to the knowledge that this exercise was only that, and attempted to toss off my disappointment that the demonstration had done nothing to relieve my predicament. Yet, as the instructor reviewed the session, she spoke as if my pain relief were a given, that I had been freed from my malady.

"But I don't feel any change," I said finally, half in protest, half in apology.

"You will," the hypnotist said. "You now need to practice that same sequence over and over in self-hypnosis."

THE DAY I gave up my massage practice, I completed my last Saturday morning session, stuffed the sheets in the washing machine, stamped the client's check for deposit, and sat down on my stool and wept.

"Stop your practice immediately," my acupuncturist had warned me when I told him how in just a week my pain had progressed from a sting in the end of my right thumb to an electrifying jolt through both wrists.

My tears weren't from the physical pain but the knowledge that I was losing my job, my income, my business, a career that I loved and had worked for years to train for and develop. My acupuncturist told me I needed to take six weeks' rest, away from my practice, but I knew my condition was so severe that I would never return to it again. I could no longer deny it. My hands were crippled.

That Saturday I estimated that I had given over three thousand massages. In the early days of my practice, I stuck to the routine I'd learned in school. As weeks, months, years went by, I needed my wall chart less and less, and I added moves I'd learned in extra classes, techniques I'd picked up from other massage therapists, innovations I'd invented myself. Over time, my hands knew instinctively what to do on which client, where to linger, to lighten my touch, to delve deeper into the muscle tissue. My hands were birds with hollow bones, small, common, but beautiful birds, goldfinches that dip and dive over the garden.

Yet birds don't automatically know how to fly, but have to be nudged out of the nest to imitate the opening and closing, the launching and take-off of a parent. That day in hypnosis school, I realized that I would follow the instructor's directions, practicing the pain control sequence until I felt some results. Hypnosis was probably going to be like massage, I decided, a skill that had to be acquired slowly, methodically.

So, I was startled that afternoon when I sat in the lounge on break from class and closed my eyes for a self-hypnosis practice session. We were told we had only five free minutes. I induced myself as deeply as I could, then ran my pain control tape in fast forward, skipping right ahead to the backhoe. Again, I watched the dump truck drive into the sunset, then counted myself back up out of my trance, and walked into the other room to begin class again. That's when a rush of blood flooded into my hands, turning them back to their natural color. I dismissed the sensation as a change of air temperature from one room to another. I sat quietly listening to the new lesson. Then my wrists began to tingle and be soothed.

Again, I thought this only a fluke. I'd felt so many strange sensations in my hands over the last few months that it was difficult to distinguish this new feeling as one of relief rather than just one more layer of pain. But over the next three hours, my discomfort began to diminish, to slowly ease, first lessening in my fingers, then up to my elbows. The tingling intensified and felt similar to the energy I'd sensed emanating from my own clients. By that evening, the energy could no longer be ignored. My palms were warmed by the new flow of blood. My hands were alive again. Not merely hanging limp and useless from the ends of my arms, but there to reach and hold and grasp. I rubbed them across my corduroy slacks and took in the soft polish of cotton. I ran them over my face, up my chin to my lips, up over my nose, across my eyelids and through my hair, parting strands, as if I were blind and feeling my own head for the first time. All night long, the energy wrapped around my arms, fingertips to shoulders, radiating, pulsating, as if all three thousand of my massages had focused and pooled their power into my wrists, as if my hands were canonized with their own tiny halos.

What I was experiencing was rare and wonderful, non-religious but surely divine, linking me to whatever it is that links all spirit, all flesh. I was graced. I was blessed. I was lost but now found. When I had volunteered to be the demonstration model for the pain control exercise, I'd thought the lesson would be just that, pain *control*, that the hypnosis would function like an aspirin dulling the hurt for a limited amount of time. This event was different. The hypnosis was facilitating my body to release its own hold on my wrists. The pain was actually leaving me at the site of its origin, moving out of my body through my fingertips. This was a healing.

Ja, das ist mein Schnitzelbank. Ja, this was a healing. These were my hands attached to my body. I was in my body and my pain, the pain I'd grown so accustomed to, was gradually lifting from me, was spiraling out somewhere into space. I had passed into a different state. I was an astronaut free-floating in the atmosphere, looking down on the planet Earth, thinking how limited we are, how attached to our small visions. Physically, emotionally, I was opened to a realm of new possibilities. I realized that our knowledge of the body is so small, so narrow, that there are mysteries I hadn't even begun to probe. I wanted to drop down and kiss my instructor's feet, thank God, the Goddess, or whoever else might have been involved.

I wanted to parade the Oakland streets and thank every yuppie, every street person, shaking their hands, throwing my arms around them. At the same time, I wanted to keep the event entirely to myself for fear it was just a cruel tease and I would relapse in a day or two. My cure had no physical evidence. No crutches hung up on the walls of Lourdes. I feared no one would believe me, that if I exuded my joy, my delight would be met with blank stares.

I had no proof. I'd be dismissed as a fabricator, a kook. After all, where were the measurements, the double-blind tests? Or even the bill?

"I think my hands are better," I said tentatively the next day to a classmate at lunch.

"Really? The pain is gone?"

"Not totally, but it feels like it's moving out."

"Listen to you," he said.

Still, I wasn't ready for a public announcement. I went through the day euphoric but still guarded, taking in the next lesson, on hypnosis and childbirth, reading my texts, doing the exercises. But on the third day my classmate couldn't contain himself when he watched me throw open the heavy glass door to the school's entrance.

"Look, everybody," he shouted. "Look what Mary just did with her hands!"

Ja, a door had been opened.

2

To Plant
from Branches

TO PLANT FROM BRANCHES

Make an incision in a branch of a fruit or other tree, then wrap around the limb where the incision is made a quantity of matting, and hang a leaking vessel over the matting; keep supplied with water, let the water continuously drop on the matting, and a root will form. After the root is well formed the branch may be cut off and planted, and you will have a tree of the same fruit or blossom. This can be performed on quite a number of fruit and garden trees.

—Stringtown Grocery Calendar

L ONG BEFORE THE grass begins to green and the first buds appear on the tree branches, long before the time and temperature dramatically change and the days stretch out into luxurious evenings, the more subtle signs of spring arrive. While the snowbanks are still pressed up against the garden fence and a fire roars in the stove, the environment slowly, almost imperceptibly begins to shift like tectonic plates.

"You have to be aware of the small things," Donna said when she hitched up Emily to the cart and we rolled down the gravel road for a ride. "Have you noticed that the animals are just now beginning to lose their winter fur?"

Emily's gray coat, still bushy and full, shed a few strands at every brush with the harness, every turn in the road. Occasionally, hair flew back into our faces.

"Small things? I need a set of windshield wipers," I said.

"Come on, Em." Donna snapped the reins to prod the horse into a faster canter. Emily is not a natural at cart pulling, and her pace is always too fast or too slow. After three or four sessions at the horse trainer's, Emily still either lopes along nonchalantly, her gait equal to a good power walk, or bolts down the road at a fierce gallop, kicking up her heels. She doesn't flinch at a car speeding along at fifty-five miles per hour, but a piece of paper in the ditch makes her shy into the center of the road, and a truck or combine drives her into a panic attack.

"Oh, that's nothing," Donna said, restraining the horse from a sudden surge toward the ditch when a tractor sputtered by. "She's so much better. She used to run the other way. Once when a semi-truck passed, she charged right toward it!"

The buggy wheels teetering on the edge of the road, the ditch dropping off five feet straight down into the creek below, the horse righted herself again, and I relaxed against the back of the seat, thankful that Emily's blinders kept other sights from view. In the adjacent field, two draft horses pulled a man sitting atop a manure spreader, the fertilizer spitting out from the implement and spilling into the air. The sweet smell of dried cow pies wafted toward me, an odor that had permeated the whole area during the previous week.

For those who farmed with horses, manure spreading had been done with relative ease, the animals stepping gingerly through the wet soil, but for those who used tractors, the task had become a night job. They waited until the sun set and the ground froze up again with the falling temperature so their heavy tractor wheels could roll over the fields without miring down in the mud. These more "modernized" folks worked the graveyard shift, their headlights beaming through the dark.

Fresh cow pies graced the other side of the road, two-day-old Holstein calves standing on their wobbly legs in separate sheds, their faces peeking out, their black and white markings still brilliant and clean. When we reached Wilbur's junkyard, lambs leapt and bounded over stacks of old buggy wheels, rusted pipe, and scrap metal. A sow, her teats swollen and dripping with milk, rolled on her side in a mud puddle, her shoats, skins caked with dirt, scrambling through the slop with abandon, clamoring over their mother, snouts routing for the plumpest nipple. Farther up the road at the Shady Grove, the private Amish one-room schoolhouse, apple trees were wrapped with damp matting to force the growth of roots. The sugar maples that lined the lane dripped sap into white buckets suspended from the trees.

Plip, plop, plop. The sound of the sap carried across the valley like the ticking of a huge clock.

Plip, plop, plop. Now in my forties, I've come to a peace and acceptance about the ticking of my biological clock. In my thirties, my single, childless state often found me awake in the middle of the night with tears rolling down my face. Now, I've learned to relish my life of solitude. On my own, I have the freedom to experience and enjoy my world in a different way than I would if I was trying to raise a family.

"Oh, you're the school marm," many Amish men have said to me when we've first met. We've exchanged a few pleasantries, then the inevitable question arises. "And you're not married, then?"

"No." I reply and allow the silence that usually follows to assume its own weight.

The man blinks or stares at me.

Then his wife's gaze inevitably meets mine, her eyes filled with empathy for the moment but also with a kind of knowing. Women, no matter what the social or religious differences, seem to always understand the situations of other women.

"That way she can do as she likes."

And I do. Make my own plans, spend my own money. It's not that I set out in this world to be alone. I love people. I've had relationships, and would like them again, but I've always relished the space I've had and valued it over being in a bad relationship just for the sake of being coupled. Then, illness forced me into a social isolation incomprehensible to most people. There I found terror. There I found self-reliance and knowledge. There I found a broader vision than I would have had if I had been cast into the traditional roles of lover, wife, and mother, each often formed to empower someone else. Linked too young even to the "right" person, I would have turned into Emily, happy to be out for a ride, but grudgingly trudging along too slowly or hysterically bolting through the ditch. Either the whip hitting my side, or the bit yanking back in my mouth. In desperation, I'm afraid I would have headed straight toward a semi, head on.

But in the spring when those white buckets hanging on the maples are filling and the quarter horse stud swishes his tail at Emily when she trots by, sometimes I long for some "action."

"Just look at the ducks, if you want that," Donna said, pulling back into her drive.

There, Magic, the big mallard drake, was mounting one of the hens, the bulk of his large body flattening hers to the ground. Her mouth in the dirt, eyes dark and wide, she lay under him in submission, his flesh thrusting into hers, his beak biting her neck, plucking out a feather. He shimmied and shook his tail, slid off his mate, then within minutes waddled toward another hen, his bright yellow penis, over an inch long, erect and dragging on the ground.

"Now there's a small thing to be aware of," Donna said.

One, two, three, four. We watched Magic mount each one of the hens in as many minutes, their neck feathers yanked out with a high-pitched squeal of victory from the drake. In between conquests, Magic pranced and danced, chest out, his head held high.

"By the end of the summer, a couple of those hens are always bald," Donna said, but had to concede that, although the ducks had no finesse, they at least accomplished the task efficiently.

"Those geese are another story." I pointed at Groucho, who wandered toward the road, removed by a dozen feet from the rest of the flock by the two exotic African ganders. "Now, if you want to see something pathetic, watch them in their spring ritual."

The Africans, who had been introduced into the barnyard as goslings the previous summer and raised as if they were their own by Ruby and Groucho, had matured into aggressive birds. They got along peacefully at first, but in early spring, they absconded with Ruby and kept Groucho distanced from his lifelong mate.

"Oh, Ruuu-by," Groucho seemed to bellow, his head thrown back in woe.

Oblivious to his lament and the mores of the Anatidae family, the Africans pecked and prodded Ruby until she was cornered against the barn. Then they both bred her, jumping onto her backward one after another, sliding off, then trying again and again in awkward stabs at the act, groping and thrusting like nervous adolescents going at it for the first time in the backseat of a car.

Meanwhile, on the sidelines Groucho cried, and cried, his plaintive honking lasting into the evening and often waking me at six in the morning.

After a couple of weeks, I could no longer bear the emotion or the racket. I sent away for two "mail-order brides" for the Africans.

"I'm coming to your part of the state next week," a friend had written. "Is there anything I can bring you?"

"Yes," I responded immediately when I thought of her excessively large flock of geese.

She pulled into my drive in a few days with two beautiful geese in the back of her station wagon. One was a rather ordinary gray and white bird we named Maggie, the other a magnificent white-throated beauty we called Lucy Goosey.

"Ruby ought to get a restraining order on those Africans," my friend said, unloading the new arrivals into the barn, where they would be imprisoned and acclimated for four or five days. "But maybe these brides will deter their attention."

Once Maggie and Lucy were out on parole, my hopes were high that the Africans would mate them and let Groucho return to his beloved. But no! The Africans herded these new females next to Ruby, waddling along in a flock, Groucho again on the periphery honking and crying all the louder. The Africans' aggression only seemed to intensify, and any motion, any indication Groucho made toward inching closer to the females, was quickly rebuffed with a nip of the tail. Yet each day Groucho tried a little harder to come into the fold, and each day the Africans became a little rougher. Finally, I came upon the three of them early one morning, the Africans batting, almost clubbing Groucho with their wings, feathers riddling the air, floating down into the yard, the squawks of the three males high-pitched and frenetic.

Battered and beaten, Groucho slumped for the rest of the day near the coop, his energy drained but his eyes still following the flock. With their competition quelled, the Africans became bolder, widening their territory and herding the females around a larger area. Always together in a tight unit, they marched down toward the garage, up past the garden, and into the farthermost reaches of the pasture. By late afternoon, they had gone all the way down the road to the creek, swimming for a while in the cold water, then trudging home, their feet nearly in step in the middle of the gravel road.

Just as they were nearing the mailbox, I glanced out the window and saw Lucy lagging behind, dawdling in the weeds in the ditch. Hidden in a clump of big bluestem grasses was Groucho. He stood still and let Lucy approach, then bobbed his head to her in greeting. She bobbed back. They circled each other, silently, the Africans disappearing down the road.

Groucho sidled up to Lucy, tentatively at first, and after a few minutes with more authority. Before long, she was his, and as hard as she tried to return to the Africans, Groucho forced her to stay at his side. For the rest of the spring, Groucho mated Lucy. So much for devotion and monogamy. Even in an Amish community!

"Ah, well," I said one day, helping Donna pull the cart out of the garage to harness up Emily. "It's either the buggy whip or the bridle."

L AST NIGHT A big storm blew up and a huge branch from the cherry tree cracked, careening to the ground, crashing down into the coop with a *thwack* and sending Magic, Ruby, Groucho and Lucy, Maggie and the Africans into a frenzy. Inside the schoolhouse, I flew down the steps and sat in the cellar on an overturned bucket I keep in the furnace room along with a battery-powered radio, a book, a lantern, and a blanket. Spring is tornado season and warnings were out for all over the state, but when I went to sleep the sky was still calm, the trees swaying gently in a slight breeze. A couple of hours later, the winds were upon us, hammering and forcing their way across the plains, the rains driving into the window glass with insistence.

Living in Iowa, I've come to know storms, when to be leery, when merely to be alert, when to relax. Last night's blow fell into the leery range. Without even turning on the radio, I had a sense of the scope. "There's a tornado close by, maybe five miles away," I told Hilda and Doolittle, the cats, who had come to huddle at my feet at two A.M. "We'll be all right, but we're on the edge of it now."

I wrapped myself in the blanket, both felines in my lap, and read by lantern light, the power lines down, centipedes crawling across the cement blocks in the furnace room. Next to me, my set of four grow lights dangled from chains, eerily creaking back and forth when Doolittle tapped them with his paw. About three o'clock the rain and hail began to subside, and I went back upstairs to bed. The next morning while sawing up the fallen limb, I waved at Mahlon, who'd come to use the phone.

"Had a little wind last night," he said and grinned.

"Where'd it touch down?"

" 'Bout five miles south."

"Any damage over at your place?"

"Oh, not too bad. Blew part of the roof off the barn, but the house is still standing . . . yeah, we had us a little wind."

Night winds and storms are one thing—sometimes severe —but you usually sleep through most of them. The day winds are often the most wearing in this part of the country. They begin in the morning, mercifully often after chores are done, quietly at first, swirling the water in the puddles on the road, sending the clothes on the lines into a slow dance—leading with the right sock, the toe floating up, lifting a pants cuff, elevating a shirtsleeve ever so slightly. Then as the morning comes into full adolescence, its dance card fills, the wind its steady partner. The steps become swifter, more complex, the left sock pivoting, dipping and diving in a smooth tango with the right, the pants legs looping one over another. By ten, it's on to the rumba, the jitterbug, and the wind spinning still faster and faster, by eleven rock-and-roll. Shirtsleeves snap and pop. Sheets tangle and bunch. By noon the scene is wild, out of control. Underwear leaps off the line and is gone.

At Fairview School, on the top of a hill, the vista clear and clean on three sides, the wind is especially strong. Moses and Miriam, Mahlon, and all the other neighbors have a windbreak of pine trees planted near their houses and barns. Year round, the conifers soften and slow the wind's path, creating a sheltered cocoon for their homesteads. Their houses, square, two-story white boxes, protected and hidden from the road, make claim on the land. They seem to understand that they are there "for good." Although dwarfed by their companion barns, they exude a confidence in their solid stance toward the landscape. My place, on the other hand, has a more precarious character. Vulnerable and starkly exposed to nature's full forces, Fairview School takes the brunt of whatever weather comes our way. And once the snow stops, the wind comes by itself again, and again and again.

Friends in town never understand. Buildings, trees, and cars break the wind in cities, and although gusts carry away hats and turn umbrellas inside out, city gales are tamer than those that rush over the plains. Here, shingles stand on end, the wren house swings on its little wire, doing a complete double back flip. The grass mats down, the goats' fur collapses against their backs, the trees creak and groan. I hang on to the flagpole and fence posts to make my way from house to barn, little bits of hay stubble flying up into my face. Inside, dust whirls through the cracks, and the relentless, pounding blasts against the outside walls keep up a steady pulse, drumming louder and louder, the rhythm a constant beat. You continue on with your day as if nothing is happening, but your movements become more deliberate, lapsing into slow motion, your muscles meeting resistance with every contraction and expansion.

Yesterday I knelt in the garden, thinking I'd transplant seedlings early in the morning. At that time, the wind was still a waltz, but I knew its possibilities for the day and the days to come, so I carried out my boxful of wooden shingles to pound down into the ground—individual windbreaks for the cabbage, broccoli, and tomato plants. "Sick bays," my friend Carl, who also gardens atop a hill, calls them. I dug holes, fertilized and erected the bays, but just when I was about to transfer the seedlings into the ground, the tango began. Not the day for this job, I thought, and looked up just in time to see Duane, the Amish painter, balancing on the scaffolding on the north side of my house. Wind or no, Duane has been in slow motion on this project, working now for almost two full years on my small place.

"Duane ever get your house painted?" the horse trainer asked in January when we stopped at his place on New Year's Day.

"Not yet," I replied. "Maybe he'll finish this year."

"What'd he do last year?"

"I'm not sure."

"Oh, yes, that's right. Last year he was mixing the paint."

Errands, illnesses, deaths in the family, and gossip with others in buggies passing by on the road had all slowed Duane, but yesterday found him hard at work, a twelve-year-old apprentice Amish Tom Sawyer at his side in a straw hat and suspenders. Brushes in hand, the two painters inched along the scaffolding, dipping and dabbing at the trim around the bank of windows that line the north side of Fairview School. Then came the wind, blowing the paint rags and can lids across the yard. Each time Duane reached into the bucket, the brush brought up a sprinkling of paint that rained down his arm and blew back into his face. The boy tried not to laugh, his hands gripping the windowsill for support, but soon his face, too, was freckled from the wind-blown paint, and Duane decided it was time for a coffee break.

When the wind stops suddenly you feel the difference, like wearing a pair of shoes that don't fit for months. You don't notice the pinch in the toe, the rub of the heel until that day when you slip your foot into a more comfortable pair. Ah, the comfort, the letup, the relief that pervades your body.

"The wind has stopped," I say to Hilda and Doolittle. "Hooray. The wind has stopped."

I know that no wind isn't good either. Here, the wind still turns windmills, pumping water up from deep within the earth. The wind carries pollen and fertilizes the flowers and the fruit trees. With windows open for cross ventilation, the wind cools down the house on a hot day. What worries me most is that still day, that very muggy still day without wind when the air quickly becomes humid and warm, too warm for the time of year. The very calmness of the atmosphere is a giveaway.

Young people or newcomers to the Midwest rejoice in these days, going outside in shorts to wash the car or toss Frisbees across the lawn. Storm veterans know better and keep their jeans on, standing in their doorways with an eye on the horizon. They lean against the doorjamb and make a mental count of loved ones, mapping out their whereabouts in their minds. They know that clichés are based in truth. Calm before the storm. Any minute a tornado could reduce their house to kindling.

This is no cause to panic, though. A hint of disaster brings out a calmness in midwesterners that matches the weather. Psychologists say we're in denial when we wander out into the yard from that doorjamb, the skies darkening into a purple bruise, and chat with our neighbors, pulling a dandelion or two before heading back into the house to the cellar. Psychologists say we're in dissociation when we sit right on the river in the local tavern during floods and toast the rising tides, the water lapping through the door. I say we've merely grown used to the situation, and in a region that the rest of the nation views as a flyover zone, we don't expect every day to be "beautiful."

We even get a perverse pleasure in seeing a newcomer's eyes widen with fear when we say the word *tornado*. Once years ago, I had a friend from the East Coast who hitched a ride with an Iowan driving across country in his Volkswagen bug. On the trip, the friend kept voicing her reservations about moving to this state, how it was flat, provincial, how she might die without a particular brand of coffee beans believed to be found only in New York City. "And the weather, those tornadoes," she exclaimed.

The Iowan listened to these complaints for nearly a thousand miles, then just as they were crossing the Mississippi River at the Iowa-Illinois border, he pulled his car over onto the shoulder of the interstate and said, "This is it."

"What?"

"A tornado. See, those white clouds are a sure sign. Quick, the only thing to do is get under the car."

The friend dove down into the dirt and scrunched herself under the bug, scraping her rear end on the tailpipe. She stayed there for a good fifteen minutes, oil dripping onto her head, traffic whizzing by around her, before she caught on.

When I was eighteen, a real tornado roared straight toward me, sounding like a big semi-truck, and I didn't have time to duck or dive under anything. I was sitting in a restaurant on Rock Island in the middle of the Mississippi River, eating brunch with my mother and some family friends, sipping a Bloody Mary and stabbing my fork down into a piece of bacon when I heard a churning, racing noise.

I looked up and there was a perfectly formed funnel cloud, something right out of *The Wizard of Oz,* charging across the water toward the plate glass window in front of us. My body paralyzed, my fork stopped in midair. The adults kept right on eating. Are they already too soused to notice? I wondered. Finally, I uttered one word, "LOOK!" At that moment the funnel cloud, a mere one hundred feet from our table, hit the bank of the river and dissipated. Poof. It was gone.

"Oh, yeah. A tornado," one of the men at the table said.

"Something about the water always makes them disappear," another said.

"Isn't that strange."

When I was in my early thirties, I spent a week's poets-in-the-schools teaching residency in a town that had been flattened ten years before by a tornado, then entirely rebuilt on the same spot. The downtown, the schools, the churches, and most of the houses were new, the whole place taking on the look of a shopping mall. This town had lost not only most of its physical possessions but its architectural history and the memories, the landmarks—both real and psychological—that accompany a sense of place. The trauma of the event still lingered. Children who hadn't yet been born when the tornado hit had nightmares about the disaster. They wrote about them in their poems. If the adults had nightmares, they kept them to themselves.

"Their hands are stuck in the door," I thought, then realized how this midwestern stoicism could be both a virtue and a vice. While I felt that the townspeople tamped down their emotions, I also admired their pluck in being able to brag about their new, brightly lit café. These people knew how to handle stress, big stress, and go on with their lives.

Whether they come by day or night, whether in stillness or turbulence, whether as an invisible but steadfast force or a twisted-up concentration of quick destructive energy, the midwestern winds are a key character in our landscape, and a key to our character. They are "strange," irritating, comforting in their predictability, and eerie in their maverick behavior. We stand up to them, we blow and bend with them, our cats tucked into the folds of our laps in fear. They teach us to blow and bend with whatever else comes our way. In the folds of our minds, we know they keep us in check, keep us closer to the earth, closer to death, and so closer to the preciousness of life with their constant threat of lifting us up—not so gently —to the heavens.

"**I**F A TORNADO comes up, I'd go lie facedown in the pond," May Chadek, my old neighbor, said.

The pond? I thought, the pond? Well, I'd heard the pioneers had jumped into ponds to escape the flames of advancing prairie fires, but in all my years in the Midwest, I'd never heard of a splash in a slough as an antidote to a tornado. Then again for May, a woman who was nearly phobic about the sun and kept the windows covered with heavy awnings and draperies, perhaps drowning was better than being hurled forever into the sky. But the pond? At the time of our conversation I'd lived at Fairview School for a year and thought I'd explored every inch of the nearby environs. I hadn't seen anything that looked like a body of water.

"What pond?" I asked.

"Oh, up there by the barn," May said.

"By the barn?"

"Yeah, since we was here, darn thing never did hold water."

The pond, a twenty-foot-in-diameter depression grown

over with grass, was only a dip in the earth during the fifteen
years that the Chadeks owned their place.

"Never was dug right," Moses told me later.

When Donna and Stu moved in, they tore off all the awnings and draperies from the house and filled the bottom of the
pond with chunks of concrete. Then during wet years, the
spring rains crashing down, the water laps at the edges, even
spilling down the slope toward our gardens. Groucho, Ruby,
Magic, and all the other waterfowl dive and plunge into the
human-made wetland, honking and quacking in delight in
their desired habitat. During drought years, and my stay at
Fairview School has swung back and forth between deluge
and drought, the pond regresses to its original state, a mere
puddle, the grass inching over the cracked cakes of clay. Up
and down the water levels have gone, keeping me in tune not
only with the cycling of the seasons, but the rhythms and ca-
priciousness of nature. Up and down the water levels have
gone with my health following suit, this hole in the ground
becoming my wheel of fortune.

In the pre-settlement days, Iowa was filled with such
ponds, created not from the force of a backhoe but from the
movement of the glaciers over bedrock. When Marquette and
Jolliet first glimpsed this land from the banks of the Mississippi, the territory was a maze of prairie grasses, savannas,
and sloughs—marshland so impenetrable that the pioneers
were forever finding their wagons mired down in the muck.
Farming brought dikes and tiling methods, an underground
drainage system that created thousands of additional cultiva-
ble acres and a decrease in the wetlands needed to sustain the
lives of native reptiles and amphibians, water-dependent mammals like muskrats and beavers, and migrating fowl like ducks
and geese.

You can still find lagoons in this part of eastern Iowa,

where the land is hillier and poorer than in the central corridor, and tiling, though pervasive, hasn't been carried out with quite as much zeal. The day I first spotted Fairview School, I was on a research trip with a writing collaborator, and just as we rounded a curve in the road that would lead us to the greenhouse, we came upon a pothole, the water dark green and murky but sporting five brilliant great blue herons. They perched on their long legs, their beaks stabbing down into the water spearing minnows, their eyes always alert to danger. A year later, in the midst of a drought, we tried to find that same pond again and spent one entire afternoon driving around and around on the gravel roads, the dust kicking up, creating a trail of what looked like fog that followed us everywhere in our quest. We drove north toward the greenhouse, then rounded the square mile and headed south again, questioning our own memories, questioning our own sanity, the sun beginning to go down, young Amish girls hoeing in their gardens looking up perplexed when we passed by for the third or fourth time.

"Oh, you must've meant the lagoon by the Sunday school," Moses said when we came back that night without reward.

"But where's the lagoon?" I asked. "I drove by the Sunday school a million times today."

"Right there, north of the building."

I was stumped.

"Course, it's dried up now. Nothing but a bunch of weeds."

The first time I saw Walden Pond, I was surprised by its size. Such a great and far-reaching piece of literature was spawned by such a tiny body of water. In my Iowa high school imagination, all things eastward had to be better and wetter, but when a college friend took me to Thoreau's sanctuary for the first time, I was astounded by its ordinariness. Of course, then I realized that was exactly the point. Thoreau went there to recapture and search out the simple life, to live self-sufficiently to enable himself to find his own center and balance:

> I wanted to live deep and suck out all the marrow of life, to live so sturdily and Spartanlike as to put to rout all that was not life . . . and, if it proved to be mean, why then to get the whole and genuine meanness of it, and publish its meanness to the world; or if it were sublime, to know it by experience, and be able to give a true account of it in my next excursion.

I came to Fairview School to also find balance and re-awaken myself to a life of simplicity, and it's curious how much grounding I find near Donna and Stu's pond. I've found refuge in that spot the way the animals have found a haven there. On warm May nights, when I sleep on the porch, I drift off to the sound of the chorus frogs, the first to call in the spring, their sounds raspy like someone dragging a fingernail along the teeth of a comb. When the temperatures rise, so does the pitch of the gray treefrogs, a bubbly musical trill that sounds as if the creatures are under water rather than clinging with their suction-cupped toes to wet leaves or stems. One evening Donna and Stu glanced up from their TV to find hundreds of treefrogs covering their picture window, staring in at David Letterman with their bulging eyes, a flash of orange on the inner surface of their back legs lighting up the dark night.

Sometimes when I can't sleep and lie awake staring at the eastern star shining brightly over my head, I'm comforted by the late-night-show cavorting of the ducks and geese in the pond. *Splatter, splash, dash.* I hear the geese dive down into the pool. Lifting themselves up momentarily from the surface, they spread their wings, playfully pitching water all over their bodies in cooling refreshment. Other times, in a sound slumber in the middle of the night, when the frogs have quieted, and the chickens are sleeping safely on their perches in the coop, the moon risen bright and bold in the sky, I wake to a cacophony of alarm sounds, the ducks and geese bellowing out their warnings to the hungry fox. The fowl swim out into the center of the pond, these birds who refuse the protection of the coop, and elude the desires of their non-aquatic predators. During droughts, the absence of the pond water is witnessed almost every morning with the disappearance of yet another bird, its ravaged carcass sometimes appearing on the road later in the afternoon.

Mornings, too, find the pond a watering hole, for Emily, Katie, and Scalawag. Gingerly, they approach the pool, their hooves sinking down into the damp banks, their tongues lapping the liquid. Still in my pajamas, I like to walk up to the pond at dawn and watch the early sun rays warm the water, the robins and wrens, the sparrows and jays filling in the void in the air left by the frogs. When the water begins to disappear during dry spells, the animals stake out their dominance over the pond, nudging one another aside to vie for the best position. Once, when Scalawag beat Emily to her favorite drinking spot, the horse simply reached down and picked up the small pygmy goat by the scruff of the neck and deposited her back on top of the bank.

When I was small, I lived in an extended family, with my parents and grandmother, in western Iowa. Although we resided in town, my grandmother owned two farms and drove out to the country daily to attend to their management. Old enough but deemed too immature to begin kindergarten in a time and place before day care, I was allowed a year of freedom to ride along with her to the farms in her 1942 Ford, the trunk fastened shut with baling wire. On the farms I rode on the hayrack and in the oats wagon, sat on top the pony as she trotted through the pastures, and picked up the broken egg shells when the goslings hatched. There, I watched the ducks waddle across the barnyard and swim in puddles. There, I pulled bluegills out of the creek with a cane pole.

I wandered for hours in a tiny grove that seemed like a vast forest. In late April, I watched the bloodroot blossom forth, the first flower to curl out of the soil in the spring. Spring beauties, rue anemones, Dutchman's-breeches, and mayapples followed. Bluebells and jack-in-the-pulpits swept through with regularity, and after that, if I was lucky, I might see a shooting star, its pink clusters of flowers arching away from the stem, nodding, seemingly floating in the air. Sometimes I'd sit on a fallen log and listen to a flicker drill holes in a tree or a garter snake slither up on a piece of bark. I loved worms and snakes, any creepy crawly thing, and had a coffee can filled with a collection of the reptiles.

"You can go to the farm with me anytime," my grandmother said when I walked to her car with a box full of salamanders I'd caught by the creek. "But let's leave the lizards here."

Other times, I'd sit on the log and stories would fill my head, fantasies of cowboys and cowgirls in boots, galloping away on their slick, fast horses, lassos twirling high above their heads. The grove became my sanctuary, my place during my year of wandering, and when it was time to go home, to hop up onto the dusty seat of my grandmother's Ford, I felt whole. Even at five years old, I recognized this emotion.

At forty-three years old, I experience the same feeling on those mornings by the pond near Fairview School. In the early morning light, I sit on the bank and catch a glimpse of Moses' grove just on the other side of the fence. Occasionally, I climb over the cattle panel, making my way through the soy bean field to listen to a flicker or watch for a snake. My Amish neighbors have told me that as children they, too, would climb the same fence during their morning recess in the spring and fill their May baskets with wildflowers from this grove. One adult experience recaptures the security and safety of childhood and becomes healing. One childhood memory links with another's to create an expanded consciousness.

"Morning is when I am awake and there is a dawn in me," Thoreau said. "The man who does not believe that each day contains an earlier, more sacred, and auroral hour than he has yet profaned, has despaired of life, and is pursuing a descending and darkening way." Each morning, my way is well lit. The frogs finish their serenade. The pond waters go up. The pond waters go down. The pond waters go up again.

THE SPRING I was thirty-three, I paid Johnny the neighbor boy a quarter for every frog he could catch. The amphibians arrived on my porch in coffee cans, Kermits squiggling, croaking, and hopping against the round metal sides. Inside my house, quickly and as painlessly as I knew how, I smashed the frog's head with a hammer, cut off its legs, and broiled them for dinner. Johnny laughed when I wrapped my hand around the frog's neck and readied it for execution.

"Ooh, look at its eyes bug out!"

I trembled and gripped the hammer hard. Johnny thought this all great fun and more profitable than a paper route. I found it repulsive but cheaper than spending twelve dollars every week on the delicacy.

Why so much trouble for frog legs? I desperately needed them, not for gourmet pleasure but for survival, as they were one of the few safe foods I could tolerate in the early days of my Environmental Illness. Since I'd also become sensitive to chemicals, most of that first year was spent in my house isolated from people with their cigars and cigarettes, their scented, formaldehyde-based lotions, their hair sprays and colognes, which gave me raging headaches and crippling double-over stomach pains. I avoided going anywhere where I might come into contact with moldy basements, new carpet and its glue fumes, fresh varnish or paint, fresh tar, gasoline or diesel exhaust, insect or yard sprays with their 2-4D, office machines with their inks and alcohols.

After a long confining winter, a spring frog gig became one of my first ventures into the outside world. Before I struck my deal with Johnny, I tried to catch the amphibians myself.

"No big deal," a fisherman had told me. "You just dangle a little piece of red cloth over their heads on the end of a pole. They jump for it and you've got 'em."

Seemed easy enough, so one cool, wet evening, pole and flashlight in my backseat, I ventured out of my house and drove to my friend Peggy's farm. We waded toward the squishy edge of her pond, pushing away the shoulder-high weeds, our sneakers, covered with stick-tights, sinking into the mud. Frogs sang and jumped through the reeds. Slowly, deliberately, I inched toward them with my pole, a tiny piece of a bandanna stuck to the fish hook. But just when I got in position, the crunch of a bur oak sapling gave me away, and the frogs fell mute, diving down into the depths of the algae-filmed water, fanning out for safer ground.

"Hey, they're over here now." Peggy waved on the other side of the pond. I trudged in her direction, the sun fading, the mosquitoes buzzing and bombing my ears. I tried again, crouching in the weeds, my pole shooting out over the bank. Peggy stood ready with the flashlight in hopes of stunning the frogs into submission with its glow. But the creatures only fell silent and eluded us. I moved again and again, until the darkness engulfed us and my line became bound up, tangled in a willow branch, and we finally had to cut off the hook to free it from the leaves. At last, we groped our way back to Peggy's farmhouse, laughing and croaking our own frog imitations. "Rivet, rivet," we called, giggling at our failure, joking and telling fish stories until I found my way to my car.

"Well, no frogs for you tonight. You'll just have to eat lobster," Peggy cracked.

I pulled out of the lane and headed home, leaving Peggy on her front porch still with tears in her eyes from the fun, then nosed through the dark night, tears streaming down my face in frustration and rage. Suddenly, nothing was funny.

Emotionally that spring, I became both predator and prey. While "on the hunt," I felt like one of those frogs, operating at some base level, completely on instinct, displaying raw, gut reactions. If something poked me one place, my whole being retracted, drew in. If something poked me another place, I'd gather up all my strength and leap away. My days were spent hopping from one task to another, searching out, preserving, and cooking my organic foods, fighting my insurance company, trying to keep my therapeutic massage practice going to make enough money to pay for air, water, and furnace filters, drops, drugs, and vitamins, special clothes, bedding, and soaps. I felt the constant presence of a human inching toward me, a creature who might lift me out of the pond and gobble me up. I stroked through the water, trying to keep just a few inches ahead of my descent into the great beyond.

I plunged through the stages of grief, swimming from one to another in a matter of weeks. At first, I was stunned by what had happened to me and couldn't visualize my future life without Christmas dinner, or ever again tasting a single bite of bread. I raged against smokers, who kept almost every public building, site, or private home inaccessible to me. I sank into despair when I opened my closet door and realized I'd have to give away most of my clothes and rid my house of any synthetics. I made a bargain with God to keep me alive long enough to complete my new book of poems. I was ashamed my affliction was so big and such an inconvenience to others.

"I'm sorry to have to ask," I said, "but when you come to my house, could you not wear perfume?"

I was ashamed my affliction was so small. How could I complain when I still had a roof over my head and could get up and down the stairs alone? Finally, I accepted my problem and buckled down to gig frogs. What I never did was deny my illness nor its seriousness. I didn't have to. Everyone else did that for me.

Most disabled people fight to let the able-bodied world know that they are not their disability, that they are capable of normal activities and functioning. I wanted the able-bodied to grasp that I was different, very different, and couldn't "function normally," couldn't eat, sleep, dress, work, or socialize the same way they did. I tried to get my point across, but couldn't. Even most traditional M.D.'s deny Environmental Illness exists, and explain it away as "depression." So, how was the lay person going to understand? I was locked inside myself, and grew to resent even the majority, the supportive people who tried to understand.

When my hands became crippled and I had to close my therapeutic massage business, friends and even other disabled urged me to go underground with my condition. "Don't tell them you're ill," they said as I set off for job interviews. "Just sign the contract." The advice, as wise as it may have been at the time, made me crazy. Even if I had wanted to pass as able-bodied, I couldn't. I couldn't work in an air-tight building. I couldn't attend smoke-filled meetings seated next to perfumed colleagues. I couldn't travel to conferences. I couldn't "do lunch."

I couldn't get anybody to get it. I applied for disability compensation and was turned down because they didn't have a code number for Environmental Illness in their books. I went to Social Services for help to pay for my prescription drugs and was advised to emigrate to a country with socialized medicine. I joined support groups, but no one had ever heard of a situation like mine. I read through women's health literature, and even in books like *Our Bodies, Ourselves* couldn't find one line on EI—an illness whose population is 90 percent female. I subscribed to magazines for the disabled, but never saw a single article addressing autoimmune diseases. I took my accessibility problem to my city's Disability Rights Commission, and was waved away with a laugh and shrug.

I went on TV to fight my insurance company to pay my hospital bill. I sued the doctor who had given me the vaccine overdose, and couldn't get my own lawyer to understand I couldn't fly a thousand miles on a smoky plane to a highly polluted city for a deposition. I contacted my San Francisco specialist, the man who had analyzed the contents of my vaccine and told me I was lucky to be alive, but couldn't get him to testify on my behalf. Then, a month before my trial, I couldn't go on any longer.

I cried for two weeks. Every day, I worked and functioned for three to four hours at a time, then put my head down on my desk and wept. I dug organic carrots out of my garden, washed and juiced them, then ranted at anyone, anything around—the plumber, the dog, the petunia planter—collapsing into bed in a heap. Night after night, I dreamed of chocolate cake, a luscious piece of dessert, deep, rich, and swirled with frosting, on the end of a fork, just about to glide onto my tongue. My watering mouth hung open, the cake approaching ever so closely. I wanted to eat it, how I wanted to jump at the bait, take just one bite of that cake, but knew I didn't dare close my lips around it. I woke wild and weepy. Psychically, I was leveled, back on Peggy's bank on my hands and knees, hunting for sustenance, my fishing line hopelessly wound up in the willow tree. Something had to change. I needed to set myself free from the tangle.

One night, cake poised in front of my face, I said to myself, "This is only a dream. You can forget the frog legs for now and go ahead and eat the dessert." The fork rose to my lips. I hesitated, staring at the chocolate. "That's right, go ahead. This is only a dream. You have permission." My teeth parted. "You'll be all right, really." My mouth closed, encircling the tines. Oh, the sponginess, the delicate texture, sweet taste of the cake against my tongue! I savored the first bite, then taking my time and enormous pleasure in the sight and smell of the dessert, the way it was arranged on the china plate, the gleam of light bouncing off the silver fork drifting down into the frosting, I ate the entire slice.

I woke up smiling, understanding that my life was reality —not a dream—and even if others denied it, I could find a way to live with its consequences more peacefully. After that, in my nighttime fantasies, I gobbled up elegant entrees at the best French restaurants, toured the globe to sample full-course Indian, Bulgarian, and Moroccan dinners with wine, candle-light, linen tablecloths, with violinists serenading, cadres of dancers swirling and twirling past in long flowing black dresses, clicking castanets. In the morning, my cravings were satisfied, my stomach full.

Then I discovered ways to find satisfaction in my waking state. First, I found my meditative eating method, with yucca. Then within my isolation, I found I had the time and space to read hundreds of books—poetry books, novels, travelogues, natural history narratives about deserts and wetlands, about yucca and frogs. I wrote three more books of my own and learned to build glass-enclosed cases to shelve my books away from dust. Within the confines of my diet, I developed exten-sive gardening skills, not only branching out into heirloom varieties but experimenting with designs, shapes, and configurations, adding fruit trees, prairie grasses, and flowers to my yard. I learned to distinguish between a black samson and a prairie coneflower, between a pipevine and an eastern tiger swallowtail butterfly, delighting in the insects' paths as they glide and dip over the wild cherry tree. My world was small but well explored.

And the exploration turned inward.

"What can we list as losses?" my lawyer had asked me before we filed the suit. "You didn't have much income to begin with. You had no spouse, so we can't sue for loss of affection. See, if you could no longer have relations with your husband, we could get money out of that for him."

Once again, I tried to explain to him my circumstances.

"You're condemned to a life of loneliness," he said at last.

"Yes."

"Going to be hard to pitch. You don't have any burn marks or a missing leg. That's what a jury wants to see. There's where you get the big awards."

The big awards, or rewards, I finally discovered were going to come from turning my life sentence around into a life passion. The Bird Man from Alcatraz. The Frog Woman from Iowa. Why not? Loneliness became solitude, with time to sort through the chain of events that had led me to Fairview School. Solitude gave me time away from the noise of the world, the constant croaking of other people's needs and desires, to mourn my losses—even though I had no missing limbs. Then, as if I'd spread myself in a dissecting tray in a high school biology class, I probed and poked at my soul to try to better understand the strengths and weaknesses of my character, the intricacies of my relationships to others, and my connection with my spirituality.

The country roads became my nerve fibers, and up and down the hills, over the gravel, through the old railroad beds I bicycled, building up my strength, observing the exotic environs of my own neighborhood. I raced Amish buggies and whizzed by farmsteads with rag dolls, white and faceless, pinned to the clothesline, tumbling and turning in the wind. Their small owners, barefoot and aproned, tumbled their own turns on the trampoline in their yard, flipping over in somersaults in midair. While my friends showed me slides of their latest trip to Tahiti, their grass hotel hut crammed full of tropical fruit, I showed them slides of Esther Chupp's root cellar, her fifty canning jars of peaches lining the far wall.

When things weren't peachy keen, I learned to confront the gigglers, the eyebrow raisers. "You've never *heard* of Environmental Illness?" I asked. Little by little, I became a more assertive, more political animal, recognizing the ripples that emanate from the plop of my illness in the pond. I had a problem that was part of a much bigger pattern of disregard for our environment, for the invisibly disabled, for women. I began to write letters, editorials, become involved in environmental causes larger than myself.

Within my circle, my individual case became educational. I've read that frogs are very sensitive to polluted water, and will die from chemical contaminants long before fish in the same pond. Dozens of people have told me that they would never have given a thought to problems like pesticides in the food chain nor indoor air pollution if they hadn't known me. Sure, they understood things on an abstract level, and although they still weren't real certain about the validity of my illness, they began to entertain the thought that there might, just might, be a link between their sudden headache and their new carpet glue fumes.

Daily, my health is improving, the environmental and disability rights movements gaining momentum. Women's physical problems are at least beginning to be discussed. But losing my health has made me question not only the goodness of doctors, but every principle, every custom and mode of behavior I once took for granted. It has made me critical of the whole American way of life, and thrown me back to a more primitive existence. I have enough foods in my diet now that I don't have to eat frog legs, but it would be nice to go down to the local café once in a while for pancakes, sausage, and a cup of coffee.

Instead, every spring when the leaves unfurl with their sudden burst of energy, and when tadpoles transform themselves to full-grown adults in just a few short days, I take my breakfast to the pond and eat on the picnic table. Chewing slowly, I remember the anniversary of my illness, thankful I've seen another year. Above me, the sun shines down, beginning to warm the surfaces of things—my skin, the ground, the ripples in the pond. Next to me, the frogs burrow out of the deep mud where they've hibernated for the winter, hop from log to lily pad, singing out over the water one of their first tunes of the season.

BONG, BONG, BONG. The sound of the bullfrog, the deep, single, reverberating strum of a bass fiddle resonates over the pond. A single song with a single note. Old-timey music with a back-up band from the wood duck and green frogs, whose calls sound like loose banjo strings. *Twang, twang, twang.* Bullfrogs, hunted for their big, fat legs, are the largest frogs native to the United States. *Bow to your partner.* Bullfrogs with their big, fat legs are voracious predators, eating insects, fish, snakes, even small birds, and other frogs. *Bow to your corner.* Their large size and proportionately huge mouths permit them to consume a wide range of foods. *Do-si-do-and-around-we-go.*

One male may mate with several females in a single breeding season. *Ladies star in and men stand out.* Then after breeding in the spring, frogs spend the remainder of the year feeding and gathering enough energy for another reproductive season. If they survive that long. Most frogs live only a few years. Many become food for other animals—an important intermediate link in the food chain. *Swing your partner and bring her on home.*

Bullfrogs like quiet, deep water, deep enough to support tadpoles through the winter. The tadpoles hatch from eggs, their growth sped up by the warming effects of the sun on the water. Then the transformation begins, of these small, sleek slimy creatures that survive by internal gills, by internal will. At first they are buds, slick with rain, their eyes mere dots covered with the film of the morning dew. Each day their eyes grow bigger, faces changing, changing the face of the pond, the face of the earth. By June, they have sprouted legs, little weak spindly legs soon to be bigger and better. The better to jump with, the better to hunt with.

The better to grow up and begin the cycle, the song again, fiddle and banjo strumming the same tune. *Froggie went a-courting and he did ride.* The better to swim across the water with those oh, so webbed feet, the web that spins so deep. The adult frogs' bodies are bullet shaped. *A sword and pistol at his side.* Frogs need clean, pure water to survive. The lack of frogs in a pond can indicate high levels of toxic chemicals, harmful also to humans. Like the canary in the mine, frogs can alert us to danger. *Uh-huh, Uh-huh.* Without frogs we're sunk. *Uh-huh, uh-huh, uh-huh.*

ON ONE OF the first days of spring, the ground still frozen but the snow cover melting, I raise my binoculars to my eyes and spot a bald eagle, a bird brought back from near extinction, flapping and soaring above Fairview School, circling the pond, a fish in its talons, its seven-foot wing span nearly blotting out the sun. In that small eclipse, I take a breath, a second to ponder what changes the sun and moon play upon the face of the earth. Here in the midwestern countryside, the land wears many masks. The seasons are dramatic and extreme, the twenty-below-zero temperatures of January seem distant and remote just six months later, when the one-hundred-degree days of July make us long for just one gust of cool air. I sit at my desk inside my house and watch the fields glass over and cover with snow in winter, wake to their deep, rich black underpinnings during spring plowing, pop with the sound of corn growing in summer, and bow to the swipe of the combine in fall.

Today, the sun so bright it lit up both inside and out, I worked at my desk in a pair of dark glasses, my newly acquired reading spec's perched on top of those, riding piggy back. Wearing these double lenses, my face hidden from even myself, I thought of all the masks I've worn in my lifetime and how they've had their own seasons, one blending into and continuing on the energy of the other, the way nature cycles round and round.

Imagine the scene: ten years ago I am just out of the hospital, wearing a thick, padded paper charcoal-coated mask. It filters out pollution, dust, cigarette smoke, and strong smells like perfume. At first, I have to wear my mask just to go out of my house, for even the smell of my neighbor's dryer exhaust, with its heavily scented fabric softener, is enough to make me ill. I stay away from any place like a restaurant or bar where I know I'll encounter heavy fumes, but keep my mask dangling from the strap of my backpack for use whenever I know I won't be able to avoid pollutants.

Soon, I'm in O'Hare Airport on my way to see my doctor in New York City, winding my way through the United Airlines terminal, the air filled with jet fumes and cigarette smoke. My face covered with my mask, I glide along the moving sidewalk in the underground passageway, the blinking neon lights of the artwork lulling me into a trance. I ride forward on the conveyor, with a disembodied voice chanting over and over, *You are reaching the end of the moving sidewalk, please watch your step.* Suddenly, a little boy of about five points up at me, his eyes wide.

"Mommy," he says, grabbing his mother's hand and reaching at her skirt as they coast by in the opposite direction. "Mommy, why does that woman have that mask on her face?"

"To help her breathe," the mother says, then disappears from view down the walkway. Behind me, I hear the boy burst into tears.

In a few minutes I am on the escalator, riding up to the gates. Two college-age men in Hawaiian shirts descend on the adjacent stairwell. They spot me and begin laughing and jeering. Everyone on the two escalators turns around and stares.

"You," one of the Hawaiian shirts calls. "Are you so ugly you have to wear a mask?"

Now *my* eyes fill with tears and I want to vanish down into the building with the collapsing escalator steps. Instead, I simply walk toward my gate, find my seat in the plane, and wait for takeoff.

"May I ask, why do you wear that mask?" the flight attendant says once we're in the air and the seat belt and no smoking signs have been turned off.

"The cigarette smoke makes me sick," I say, my voice muffled through the layers of filters.

"What?"

"The smoke makes me sick," I shout.

"That's funny," the attendant says and turns away. "It doesn't bother me at all."

Then why did my mask bother her? Why did it bother anyone? What was so frightening? What hit that deep chord of fear in people when they encountered this wad of paper strapped to my face? Masks have been worn by all peoples in all cultures throughout the centuries, for protection, make-believe, social acceptance, disguise, amusement, or religious devotion. Any alteration of the face is a mask, and most of us, both women and men, have engaged in some alteration, whether through raising a pair of binoculars to our faces, putting on a pair of dark glasses, applying eye liner, or growing a beard. Our physical appearance as a whole could be considered a mask of our individuality, the expression of our inner being, the image of what we want to be—at least for a moment.

Perhaps that's the scary thing—to give form and shape to those inner urges and display them up front there on the face, the center of all emotions. We identify each other, after all, through our facial characteristics. We make connections through our eyes. It's the protruding eyes of the frog, the sharp, alert eyes of the eagle that make those species real to us. We communicate through our mouths and ears. We are seduced and form lasting memories through our noses. So, in contrast to the standard definition of the mask, as a cover-up, the power of the device and the very word itself come from its opposite meaning. The mask doesn't hide but reveals, and revelation of self, confrontation of ourselves face to face, is something most of us want to run away from with a childlike fear or dismiss with a macho bravado.

Certain "primitive" peoples understood the power of displaying emotions through their use of masks. Eagles, bears, rams, goats, dogs, antelope, elephants, snakes, and frogs all figured into the masks of Native American and African ritual, each representing a slightly different aspect of the personality, each invoking a different god. In masks, these people changed from human beings to animal spirits, and once a spirit, the masquerader had both a new authority and a new freedom. Shamans, witch doctors, and ritual dancers were invested with powers of influence over others. Through the use of the mask, they became raw feelings frozen in time and space. Their animal selves healed, blessed, summoned up courage for battle or abundance in drought. In mask, they were possessed by spirits and no longer constrained to act according to human convention. They shook, giggled, danced, and pranced, twisting and bobbing their heads, arms, legs, and torsos in stances outside the world of standard body language.

Imagine the scene: my plane finally lands at La Guardia. A friend picks me up, an oxygen tank tucked in the trunk of her car just in case I need help. Then we are driving into the city on an overcast spring day, my mask still covering my face, protecting me from the exhaust fumes of the hundreds of cars that speed around us on the freeway. Now we are walking down East Fifty-eighth Street, heading toward the office of the costly specialist. My friend holds my arm. I'm exhausted and dizzy from the pollution and dust sweeping up from the street, seeping into the folds of my mask.

We wait at the crosswalks, hordes of people on the sidewalk pressing round, some staring, some trying to look away, most looking past me with the polish of city dwellers experienced in avoiding eye contact with the bizarre and insane. Above us, the buildings rise up forty to sixty stories in the air. We pass a gap, a blank space in the architectural mouth where one building has been pulled down and another is just beginning to fill in the place. The new tooth is just three stories high, men balancing on scaffolds, driving rivets into steel. *Rat-a-tat-tat.* The sound pierces my skull like a dentist's drill.

"Miss," one of the construction workers yells down at me. "Where'd you get that mask?"

I keep on walking and don't even look up.

"Miiiiisss," he bellows again, climbing down off the scaffolding.

I pick up my pace.

He scurries after me, shouting, "I said, 'Where'd you get that mask?' "

I hurry on, my street-wise New York friend at my elbow. "That's right, just don't answer," she advises.

"Miiiiisss." He keeps it up, the sidewalk population parting for him to make his dash. "Miiiiiss, stop."

Finally, keeping my vision straight ahead, I raise my hand into the air in a power sign and flip him the bird.

My friend's grasp on my elbow tightens. "Now, we better get out of here fast," she says.

I break into a trot.

"Oh, I'm sorry. Please stop, Miss." The man's voice has immediately softened. "I'm so sorry." His voice is almost in my ear now. "Please turn around and talk to me."

I stop and hesitantly crane my neck in his direction.

"Forgive me," he says, removing his hard hat and slicking back his hair. He stands before me, a big bear of a man in jeans and a white T-shirt smeared with dirt and grease, his belly protruding slightly over his belt buckle. "I don't mean you any harm. That was awful of me. I just wanted to know where you got that mask."

I look at him perplexed.

"See, I work up there in those fumes all day and have never found a mask that really works. I've tried all sorts of different kinds and the one you're wearing looks perfect. If you could tell me where you got it, I'd like to buy one for myself."

My clenched fist loosens and I fish in my backpack for the name of the mail-order company where I purchased my mask. I jot down the address on a slip of paper and hand it to the man while we discuss the intricacies of the devices—their straps, fit, and filters. After a few minutes, we part, he slipping the piece of paper into his wallet next to the picture of his spouse, me feeling at once empowered, humbled, and connected to another human being.

After that, I looked on my mask with both a new sense of liberation and a new respect for its strength of communication. I'd been harassed by construction workers on the street many times before, but never would I have even entertained the idea of giving one the high sign. Behind my mask, I suddenly felt my anger in a more clear-cut and dramatic way. My face hidden, my speech eliminated, I discovered the gestures that have become symbolic of any minority group finding its power. Suddenly, I had authority. I had freedom. And, oddly enough, I had a new friend.

A few days later, on the airplane home, I thought back to my use of masks with young students when I'd conducted writing workshops throughout the state of Iowa. Traveling around to elementary and junior high schools for one-week residencies, I drove into town like Meredith Wilson's music man, trying to find a hook into the community—common material that the students might explore in their work. We wrote collaboratively, interviewing and gathering folklore from the town storytellers, piecing together histories of local sites, creating plays from snippets of conversation from the regulars in the Main Street cafés.

During the fall of one particular year, I arrived in a Mississipi River town that had plunged into a week-long celebration of Halloween. Witches perched on brooms atop the residents' rooftops. Front porches were decorated with life-size puppets of ghosts and goblins. Large, homemade papier-mâché masks, painted boldly in blacks, greens, and reds and adorned with teeth, hair, and nose rings, hung near the doors. On Halloween night, a parade wound its way along the snaking river bend. Shriners in red fezes careened down the street in go-carts to the rhythm of ten or twelve different marching bands with tinkling glockenspiels and booming big bass drums. Santa Claus rode through the night in the gas company's cherry picker, followed by a mile of costumed children. And no ready-made, prepackaged skeletons did they wear, but inventive, free-form guises that had me laughing with the passing of each new school banner, each new blast of the tuba. One of my students proudly strode by dressed as a voting box, a huge cardboard carton engulfing his tiny frame, a slit for ballots near his buttocks. Another student posed as a toothache, her whole body wrapped in poofy white fabric.

Early the next morning, I ran into the farm store to buy some extra batteries for my radio and there, next to the hog pans and Hav-a-hart traps, was a display of masks, big plastic masks in primary colors to cover the whole face and molded into big primary expressions. I picked out five—sadness, hapiness, anger, fear, and pride—and carried them with me to class. I covered my face with them, one by one, and moved about the classroom, asking the students to write poems that approximated the feelings they registered in response to the mask. Soon the room was transformed. The students poured themselves onto paper, concentrating as they had never done before that week, their pencils dancing across the page, hands waving in the air, begging to read their poems aloud, volunteering to slip into the masks and become the very essence of their own creations.

After that, I carried the box of masks to every school I visited. I watched big, tough, hormone-hardened eighth-grade boys in southern Iowa soften into tender pups behind the mask of fear. I watched shy fourth-grade girls in central Iowa come in touch with their own power behind the mask of pride. I watched hunched, withdrawn, learning disabled students in northern Iowa straighten with a new carefree sense of themselves behind the mask of happiness. I watched the same students pick up the metal wastepaper basket and use it as a drum, four of them donning different masks at once, linking arms and skipping around the center pole in the room. Faster and faster they spun, reciting their poems, feet bouncing to the beat, heads back, arms flying, the other teachers finally coming to the door to investigate the racket.

I thought that one of my most successful teaching exercises. The teachers thought otherwise. They scowled at the students and directed them back into their seats, the children collapsing into their previous selves. The teachers rushed to the principal's office and wrote negative evaluations. Oh, to stir up the students, to get them involved, excited. The school had gone to rack and ruin!

Why did my mask work cause such a commotion? Sure, we got a little loud, but the students had become so enthusiastic about their material. Some of their poems were even published eventually in a reputable children's magazine. What really caused the problem? Authority and freedom, the current of the animal spirit. Even the suggestion of witchcraft. There I was, a single woman, overseeing a bunch of children who were suddenly dancing with relish and release around a pole! The suggestion of paganism. Of matriarchy. Women's power and sexuality. It's one thing to allow this energy to have an outlet for one day on Halloween, but I was tapping this sap in the spring of the year. Not the time of falling leaves and the Day of the Dead, but of lilac blossoms and living. The time to deny our mortality.

When I arrived from New York, another friend, Marie, a puppeteer, met me at the airport, and when I recounted to her my mask escapades there, she went right to her workshop and transformed my paper mask into the face of my big brown dog Bill, his tongue sticking out. His expression was at once friendly and defiant. Now, I could slip on my mask and feel powerful, angry, affectionate, and loyal all at once. Now, I could laugh at myself and be as outrageous on the outside as I felt on the inside. Here was my animal spirit blatantly displayed on my face. Now people really stared in airports and pointed. Suddenly, with just an alteration of the mask, I changed from a pathetic creature to a celebrity, children running up to their mothers, wanting to know where they could buy a mask like mine. Marie could've made a fortune.

Again, I felt a surge of power and control. Again, I felt a change in my concept of womanhood. I found myself wishing I could maintain the same sense of confidence without a mask, but knew that throughout the ages, to attain autonomy, women had appeared in different guises. Heavy makeup has always been the realm of prostitutes, who up until modern times were often also actresses, adept in applying face paints. Akin to my situation, a prostitute's mask became both her defense and badge of honor. She could function independently and usually illicitly in a male-dominated world behind her mask. Like prostitutes, women herbalists, or "witches," lived outside the system, and threatened the status quo through their economic independence and the control they lent other women, who not only healed but plotted love affairs with the aid of their potions. Witchcraft provided medicines, abortions, paints, and powders—the here-and-now needs that the male world dismissed or forbade.

In 1770, Parliament heard a motion that women who wore "cosmetics, scents, paints, washes, artificial teeth, false hair, Spanish wool, iron stays, hoops, high-heeled shoes, or bolstered hips" and seduced men into matrimony would be subject to the laws of witchcraft. Certain death. But such alterations have given life to women through the ages and provided a kind of psychological distancing that allows them more space to function. City dwellers have always worn more makeup than their rural counterparts. Cosmetic masks would seem to help compensate for the intensity of living in close proximity.

When I became ill, I could no longer wear makeup. I reacted to the chemicals and broke out in huge hives all over my face. At first, when I looked in the mirror, I felt naked and frightened, so accustomed had I become to my mask. Since I have moved out to the country, to Fairview School, I've lost that fear, surrounded as I am by the makeupless faces of my Amish women neighbors. I've noticed a directness and lightness to their countenances, although they aren't entirely without masks. All keep their heads covered in some fashion, with a bonnet or scarf. Many wear large, thick-lensed glasses, and most have spent a lifetime outdoors, with the sun and wind brushing and weathering their skin. Many are classically beautiful. Often a buggy will roll by, and for a moment I'll think I have been watching a movie, with Liv Ullmann portraying an Amish woman. Others can only be characterized as homely, with asymmetries and rough-cut features. Yet underneath these incongruities and accessories, their faces, "pretty" or not, have an openness not unlike the land itself that comforts me.

What accounts for the uniqueness of their faces? Diet, exercise, a strong social and spiritual connection. But also the starkness of their existence. Educated only through the eighth grade, they look at things straight on, without intellectualizing their problems. Not that they don't have stresses and anxieties—for honesty can also be a mask—but these people are stripped of a layer of complication and pretension that most of the rest of us, whether consciously or unconsciously, walk around with every day.

Imagine the scene: one day in May, the season just turned to shirtsleeve weather, Donna, Stu, and I have walked into the back parlor of one of our neighors' houses. Another funeral. Another Grossdadi in a handmade coffin. Oren lay shriveled and tiny in the box, his hands crossed, his legs, twisted from living for over sixty years—his whole adult life—with the effects of childhood polio. His head propped on a small pillow, Oren's face was almost the same color as the case, a cloudy white. His beard, a thin, straggly clump of hair neatly combed and groomed, fell from his chin down toward his chest, white against his starched white shirt. The only dot of color came from Oren's lips, drawn tight and in a straight purplish line.

We bowed our heads, acknowledging the passing of yet one more human in our midst. Oren's face was without makeup. No powder, rouge, or lipstick kept us from the bald facts of his demise. No cosmetic mask covered his visage. Instead, we were confronted with the stark spookiness of unadornment—something very uncommon these days in the funereal kingdom. A death mask. After we'd wound through the front parlor, offering our condolences to the relatives who perched on the hard wooden benches, the immediate family against the back wall, the aunts, uncles, and in-laws squished into the center, holding babies on their laps, after we'd visited with Moses, who sat on a folding chair on the back porch, his legs crossed, black jacket unbuttoned at the collar, a house wren trilling from the tree branches, we climbed back into the car and pulled out of the lane in silence.

"Now, that guy really was dead!" Donna said at last.

Stu and I laughed nervously, but we understood her remark. Even though all three of us had seen our share of death and been to many "viewings" before, these Amish ones were a kind of initiation rite. When you peel off one mask, you find another, the second even more revelatory and disturbing than the first. If even in death we wear a mask, where does the real person start and stop? Is the human body and face only a social shell and we just masqueraders, mere layers of pretense? Can we ever get to the self—whatever that is? Can we ever get to our own hearts?

Examine this photo: I am five years old and sitting on the living-room couch with my two older brothers, ages eight and ten. One has his hands over his eyes, the other over his ears. Mine are placed across my mouth. See no evil. Hear no evil. Speak no evil. We've been posed that way by our photographer father, who thinks this is cute and funny, our hands becoming masks transforming us into monkeys. The picture is haunting. Three middle-class children suddenly leap into the primitive, our bodies becoming animal spirits, our faces like the masks of ritual dancers, driving away evil spirits.

My mask is especially appropriate, as I am an extremely shy child who has a hard time saying anything, whether good or evil, in "public." I literally run and hide in the closet when someone comes to visit, and loud voices and laughter from strangers make me flee behind doors. I am a connoisseur of woodwork, a mistress of concealment among racks of winter coats. My problem is so severe that finally in the second grade, in consultation with my teacher, my mother gives me a choice between going to a psychiatrist or children's theater classes. I choose the latter and take on the role of the little toy kitten, part of the cargo of *The Little Engine That Could*.

Whiskers drawn on my face, a little wad of cotton pinned to my derrière, and my hands shaking in fright, I can and do make it up the mountain, even if it takes one spill off the stage to get me there. Yet my voice gets no louder, my social interactions no bolder. A wise director throws me into the part of the wicked queen in the next play, forcing me to stomp my feet, pound my fists, shout and yell, bossing my subjects around until I am exhausted from my own outpourings. In rehearsal, at first I am a complete failure in this role—so bad that the other little thespians complain that they want someone else to play the part.

Then, as we go over and over the show, my wispy voice begins to take on some resonance, my fists slamming harder and harder on the arms of my throne. I get more and more boisterous. My voice rises, louder, full of anger. I am nasty, evil, and I enjoy it. The show opens with me dressed in dark blue with thick, ominous-looking eyebrows painted on my face. I never look twice in the mirror. I never turn back. From then on as I grow up, I still have trouble showing my anger, but learn to fake a kind of confidence, and soon faking seems real, almost more natural than my wimpy self. No matter how scared, I am able to muster up the courage to talk in class, to get up in front of an audience and speak, to eventually teach a class. This facade becomes another mask. Throughout the rest of my life, in one way or another, I pursue theater, and one role is superimposed on top of another. Throughout the rest of my life, one emotional mask masks another.

My theater classes were held in the building that housed the Lend-a-Hand Club, a home for unwed mothers. Built on the Mississippi levee, it was a dark brick structure that reeked of mold. Almost every spring the flood waters of the muddy river spilled over the banks and down into our basement "studio," which served as both a cafeteria for the "mothers" and rehearsal space for us. The current carried away some of our costumes and sets, leaving yellow water marks on the walls every season, one higher than the next.

"You'll arrive for the performance on time," our indomitable director shouted one spring through her megaphone at dress rehearsal. "Come hell or high water. And last year we had high water!"

The water was so high we watched King Arthur's magic sword float out and an upright piano in; we canoed through the Lend-a-Hand that year, waiting for the raging river to subside. When it did, it did gradually, the lapping waves outside our window always a threat. After we cleaned and tuned up the piano, we still could not relax, as the streets and sidewalks were full of dead fish, frogs, and salamanders. The sewers boasted even stranger creatures. We kept a brick on the toilet to keep the muskrats from making their entrances into our quarters.

By this time, I was a teenager and had several princesses, a fairy godmother, and a string of wicked queen roles in my credits. Good or evil, I had become adept at displaying a public front to hide the private self, and could swim in and out of personas on demand. In my dreams, however, I couldn't fake it. During the day, my face may have been stony to mask physical and mental pain, my face may have been smiling to conceal deep anxiety, but when I put my head down on the pillow at night, my animal spirits came out to claim their own reality.

And so it found me—the muskrat—in my nightmares. It grew larger and larger each time it appeared, and it appeared off and on for the next fifteen years. It was wet, smelly, scary, its claws sharp. It chased me, gliding through the river, water whisking off its back. It dove down into the depths and took me with it. At once it was my evil spirit, my power. It was my primitive, base self, with all its inhibitions, all its desires and sexuality, growing larger and larger as I learned to hide myself more and more.

In my thirties, my illness forced me to wear a literal mask again—the padded charcoal-layered one used to keep away pollution, perfume, and germs, a direct descendant of the carved, wooden face shields worn by witch doctors while exorcising the demons of disease. As I struggled to regain my health, the muskrat grew into a bear, wrestling, smothering, and consuming me completely. The muskrat became King Kong, roaring with a deafening din. The muskrat became a dragon breathing fire. The muskrat became a huge white bird rising up off the roof of my house, an angel, Saint Michael, slayer of dragons.

Now, more often the muskrat is a cat stretching on its haunches, exercising slowly. Yet sometimes whole nights are spent still searching for food, running up and down the basement stairs, stalking, being alert to the smallest micromovement. And sometimes whole mornings are spent with the image of a mouse between my teeth, its tail hanging out of the corner of my mouth. Then sometimes even more horrifying nights are spent with the muskrat a winged hyena, flying toward me looking for its own dinner, fangs out, fur fanning away from its body in an aura of psychedelic colors.

Often I wake from these wild nightmares, shaking and sweating, only to be calmed by the sound of a buggy rolling by my window. I look out onto the predictable, solid blackness of the vehicle and its occupants, their faces tranquil in the morning light, eyes wide open to the sun, foreheads shaded by their black bonnets or straw hats. I think back to the year I was ten years old and dressed up as a witch for Halloween, my hair powdered and pulled back in a bun, age lines drawn on my face. I wore my great-grandmother's dress, which I had found in the attic, a frock—long, black, and plain—that buttoned straight up the front like those of my Amish neighbors. One Halloween night, I went to a party at a friend's house and we roasted hot dogs around a huge bonfire, the flames crackling and dancing in the air, near the wooded ravine that rose up to meet her backyard.

I stood there next to the blaze, my prepubescent body already filling out the dress of my tiny ancestor, my impersonation of a witch more closely aligned with my role model, my great-grandmother, than I knew then. For in that dress, my great-grandmother had made rounds from house to house in the pioneer Iowa countryside, nursing the sick, bringing herbs and potions to those who suffered from typhoid fever and diphtheria, the plagues of her times. When she exited the houses, her poultices and teas left inside to do their work, and returned to her farm, she built a big fire under a cauldron, stripped down, and boiled her dress, the steam rising up into her face, before entering her own gate.

Witch, witch doctor, healer, healed—today they all seem part of the same fabric. They all seem part of the same authority and freedom of the human spirit to realize its own power. The most powerful bird in the sky circles one more time above the schoolhouse, then is gone out of sight. Soon, the spring fields will flame, farmers burning them clean of stubble. I'll stand at my window and watch the blaze roll over the hill, reminiscent of the old prairie fires. I'll feel the same excitement and fear the pioneers must have felt when they saw the fire grow closer and closer—concern for where its awesome leveling force might stop. In just the course of a month, the fields will turn from white, to brown, to black—three quick costume changes, three different masks. Then the real magic will begin. The inner urges of plants will be given shape and form, displaying themselves upon the face of the land. The rains will fall. The branches will bud. The gods will be evoked.

"FIRE! There's a fire in Mahlon Bender's hog house," a man yelled and ran around me, disappearing into my neighbors' garage. Mahlon, who at that very moment was ten feet away, grading the yard with his small bulldozer, heard the call and rushed in after the stranger.

Most mornings when I make my way back from Donna and Stu's barn with hay for my goats, I run into Mahlon coming out of the Amish phone booth that's located in the back of their garage. The letter of the law states that Amish people can use a phone but can't have "lines from the outside world" running into their own farmstead. So, families from the surrounding area pull their buggies up into this cooperative English couple's yard, wind the reins around the hitching post, and make their calls in the little three-by-three room with a single bare electric bulb hanging down from the ceiling.

A set of emergency numbers is penciled onto the wall: the local Mennonite doctor, Yoder's veterinarian clinic, the county sheriff, the volunteer fire department, and the chiropractor, who, once a month, comes to Max and Fannie's farm down the road, sets up his table in their dining room, and helps patients from all over the area. Graffiti covers the rest of the phone booth: a picture of a beautiful young woman in a bonnet, a picture of a barnyard, a split rail fence encircling a stallion, its tail held high in the air, a balloon caption pointing to its body and holding a single word—"STUD."

Kind is the one word that describes Mahlon. He is in his thirties, with six children; his masculine yang qualities seem to be in perfect balance with his yin. Standing only about five foot seven, his legs slightly bowed, his muscular arms hanging a bit too long for his torso, a fringe of red beard ringing his round face, he becomes the spirited troll every morning when he drives up in his buggy with his border collie, Phantom, on the seat beside him. Phantom, who lost his testicles and part of his right hind leg in an accident with an auger, would have been shot by any other farmer, his gait too slow to herd sheep. But Mahlon leans in the doorway of the phone booth, one hand holding the receiver, the other reaching down to pet his dog, talking, conducting his business, and smiling at the goings-on of the English.

"Eeeey-aaaaaw," Katie brays, and Mahlon doubles over in laughter at the sound.

"Now what earthly good is that donkey?" Mahlon often kids Donna.

"Oh, you wait and see at Christmas time."

Mahlon is good all year round. It's Mahlon who plows my drive at six A.M. after a huge snowfall, and it's Mahlon who gathers up the whole neighborhood—Amish and English alike—to surprise his wife with a party for her thirtieth birthday. It's Mahlon who goes off to work with the Mennonite Disaster Service, rebuilding houses demolished by tornadoes or pumping out flood-ravaged houses around the state while his own fields lie muddy and fallow, too soggy to even grow hay for his milk cows. It's Mahlon who offers to grade Donna and Stu's backyard when the run-off from the heavy spring rains has cascaded down the hill and rushed into their kitchen. And it was Mahlon whose hog house was going up in smoke.

Donna, Stu, and I were all in the car waiting to go when Mahlon ran out of the phone booth. We sped the one mile down the gravel road to his farmstead in minutes, but already cars lined the lane, volunteer firemen pulling on their rubber boots and yellow coats—Frank from the hardware store, Ted from the lumber store, and Henry from the gas company. The fire truck's siren blasted past, flattening Phantom's ears with its wail. We jumped out and Donna drove back down the road to pick up more neighbors.

Hoses were unreeled from the truck, water spraying hard and fast on the hog house, a low-slung shed clustered close to the farmhouse and in between the milk house and shop, in a picture puzzle of structures—large and small, wooden and tin—that created the homestead. The chicken coop with its incubating chicks, the machine shed with its 1940s tractor, the tool shed with lawn mowers, sledgehammers, rakes, and hoes, Phantom's doghouse, the barn filled with draft horses and hay, all wedged together, one next to another, to create the perfect pastoral scene. But if the winds started up, we all knew that this bucolic dream could turn to ashes in seconds, fire leaping from shed to shed, barn to house.

Flames crackled through the roof of the hog house, smoke pouring out of the row of five small windows, the squeals of 130 pigs carrying over the countryside. Water gushed over the shingles, cascading down the walls of the hog house, splashing and spilling onto the ground, forming deep, muddy puddles. Soon, the flames smoldered down and went out, the last snapping embers punctuated by the slamming of Donna's car door. She had returned with more helping hands.

A division of labor was immediately established, the men rushing into the hog house, still black with thick smoke, to pull out the pigs, the women forming a line to transport them across the barnyard to a smaller, dry shed, and a middle-class dapper-looking couple wandering around in the middle of the whole scene doing nothing. The woman wore a purple hat with a fake yellow flower pinned on the side while her husband sported a matching yellow bow tie.

"Who's that couple out there?" Frank asked Ted, his face black with soot, searching inside the dark farrowing pens for the pigs.

Ted shook his head.

"Who's that couple there?" Donna asked Fannie, who "works like a man" and has biceps nearly as big as those of her husband, Max. Donna reached down with both hands to grab one of the forty-pound pigs by its hooves and hoist it over the gate. The animal, too stunned now to even squeal, was covered with manure, its pink skin blistered from the fire.

Her overcoat smeared with mud and knee-high rubber work boots mired in muck, Fannie worked twice as fast, picking up one pig in each fist, tossing them into the shed. "I don't know who that is," she said.

"Who do you suppose?" Max asked Stu, pulling pigs out of the manure pit of the hog house.

"Put on your Easter bonnet," Stu sang and rolled his eyes.

Mahlon slapped a piece of plywood over the shed door, trying to block the wind, and called to his six-year-old son to bring some nails. The boy ran past the unknown couple and soon returned to his father's side with two small tacks and two bent finishing nails in his hand.

"No," Mahlon said, stooping down to put his arm around his son. "Those won't work. Run and find some larger ones."

A fireman quickly produced some appropriate nails from his coveralls, and instantly the shed was boarded up, but twenty of the pigs had already died in the corner of the building. The men searched the hog pit for a few remaining pigs that had squeezed down between the slats and hidden in the manure. A couple of the women held the surviving pigs in their arms in the shed, trying to calm them and clear their air passages.

Then Mahlon was in the middle of the crowd with a large stainless steel bowl full of oranges. He handed a piece of fruit to each of the workers—even the mystery couple.

"Thank you for coming," he said. "Take a break now and eat something. Thank you for helping."

"Don't mind if I do," the woman in the purple hat said, and brushing soot from an old tree stump with her glove, sat down to peel her orange.

Slowly, painfully, the remaining pigs gasped for breath. They lay on their sides, their snouts in the air, their hooves quivering. The crowd stood there together for a few minutes, some digging their thumbs down into the orange skins, tearing off sections and plopping them into their mouths, the juice cool on their tongues. Others simply slipped the oranges into their jacket pockets. At last, the crowd drifted away, realizing the fire was out, the rest of the buildings spared, and that nothing more could be done for the animals. The firemen rewound their hoses, and others fanned back across the township by car, on foot, and by buggy. The mystery couple drove away in a dark blue Buick, flicking an orange peel out the window.

At five that afternoon Mahlon was back at Donna and Stu's on his bulldozer.

"Mahlon, you can let this grading go," Donna said.

"No, I want to get this done before we have another rain. You don't want that water in your house again this spring," he said, working into the night to finish the job. By seven he was home again, checking on his pigs, only ten of which survived the week.

"My father said them ten pigs will never grow right,"

Mahlon told me one morning at the phone booth. "That they ain't going to be worth nothing."

"What will you do with them?"

"My father wants me to kill them."

"Now?"

Mahlon nodded and his eyes met mine. "I just don't know if I can, though," he said. "I don't have any trouble killing an animal that's been raised right and fed well for slaughter. But to kill an animal just because it won't grow right . . . I just don't know."

Mahlon straightened in the doorway, then whistled for Phantom. The dog, who had been lying in the sun, his eyes fixed on a mother rabbit just leaving her nest in the tall grass, five or six bunnies hopping after her, hobbled out to the driveway. Then the two of them rode home together, side by side, sharing one last orange in the black buggy.

MY GARDEN WAS growing right, the peas just beginning to push out of the earth and sprout tendrils to climb the fence, when my plot caught fire. It was a late spring evening, the end of a long windy day, an old feed sack tumbling over the fields and plastering itself against the side of the house. With windows and doors shut tight against the force and coldness of the air, I had spent the entire day inside doing paperwork, but for early morning and late afternoon forays out to feed the animals. After supper, I washed my dishes, then changed into a spiffier outfit, for a night at the theater in town.

Just as I stepped out the door, I heard a crackling sound and turned around to see my garden mulch in flames. The fire had caught hold in the farthest corner of my plot, but with the wind still strong and blowing from the north, the flames were spreading rapidly across the garden toward the goat pen. Mac and Shenanigan jumped excitedly up onto the roof of their shed. A change of wind direction or an erratic gust could have sent the flames leaping from the garden to the schoolhouse in an instant.

I dashed back inside, kicked off my pumps, pulled on my

rubber boots, and thought about calling the volunteer fire department but hated to pull everyone away from their families for this small blaze. Instead, I called Donna and Stu.

"Could you come over right away?" I asked. "My garden's on fire."

Grabbing a rag rug from the floor, I raced back out the door and into the plot, beating back the flames. Arms raised high, I pounded the rug down into the mulch hay, the fire flaring, then smoldering under the weight of the cloth, the fire skipping down the row toward the plantings of turnips and beets I'd already sown into the ground. I knew help was on the way, and quickly I worked out a strategy of beating back the flames toward their point of origin. Down, down, pounding, pounding, I flung the rug into the earth, beat the ground with this weaving, strips of cotton shirts and dresses of my Amish neighbors. Down, down, hammering, pounding, the smoke rising into my face, into the sky, carried south by the wind. *Snn-ap.*

Donna arrived first, running to the side of my house to hook up my hose. Next, Stu appeared with a shovel. He went to work on the opposite side of me, tamping down the flames with the blade. Then Donna had the hose up to the garden, spraying water into the flames. The fire smoldered down, then with a blast of wind, skipped over to the row of lettuce. With his shovel, Stu beat one way. With my rug, I beat the other until we met in the center. Donna kept the hose nozzle aimed at the hay, dousing the corner of the plot. At last, all the flames were out, but the hay still smoked and popped. Back and forth, back and forth, with movements steady and sure, Donna and Stu soaked down the rest of the garden until every trail of smoke was extinguished.

"I thought you had to be crazy when you said your garden was on fire," Donna said when we finally rested for a few minutes by the gate, surveying the mess and watching for further eruptions. Smoke lingered on our clothes, in our hair, smudges of soot rubbed across our noses and foreheads. "I was sure you meant your house was on fire."

"How did it start?" Stu wondered.

"Maybe a spark from the chimney blew over here and lodged in the hay."

"Maybe someone tossed a cigarette out their car window and the wind carried it to the garden."

Maybe the elements—earth, air, fire, and water—just decided to join in the perfect union, converging in one tiny plot of land. For how strange to have the space that provides my food, the crux of my existence, on fire. How strange to use the hose that usually brings life to these plants to deaden flames. The elements twisted and flipped upside down. The elements taking a stance—all four together—and creating a sign. Maybe this wildfire was the perfect alarm, the jolt I needed to remind myself that I can try to change the face of the earth, I can try to tame the land, but a wildness is always inherent, smoldering somewhere underneath a mat of hay. Down, down, drifting and floating, floating and drifting, the earth in tune with itself spins through the seasons. The earth in tune with the universe chants its plainsong. I can dress up, go to the theater, cover my face with masks, but the elements still provide the real drama, the conflict at my door.

3

To Measure
a Circular Stack

TO MEASURE A CIRCULAR STACK

To get the number of cubic feet in a circular stack multiply the circumference of the stack by itself, then multiply this product by the height and divide this result by 25. This gives the number of cubic feet. Then where hay is being considered, by dividing this number by 500 if the hay is not settled much or by 422 if the hay has stood from 30 days and more, the result will be approximately the number of tons.

—Stringtown Grocery Calendar

S WEAT TRICKLED DOWN Emily's back, her
mane wet and limp in the early June afternoon sun, but
her ears stood up straight and alert when we passed the horse
trainer's and a sleek Arabian stallion dashed out toward the
fence, whinnying.

"Yup, Em's quite a looker," Donna said, clicking the reins.
She pulled back on the bridle and sent her filly trotting faster
down the road. Emily sneezed in protest and tiny droplets of
mucus flew back into our faces. Donna held firm, though, wiping off her face with the back of her hand and steering her
horse around the curve and on down the gravel road.

"Come on, Em. We have other things in mind for you
today."

We were on our way to see Perry Hershberger, a tall thin
Amish man who had stopped Donna several times that spring,
circling around her horse and cart without saying a word. He
glanced at her, then at the horse, again and again. "I couldn't
figure out what was going on," Donna said. At last, in the
spring, she pulled up next to Perry's buggy at the hitching post

in town, and he suggested a mating between Emily and his prize Morgan.

"So that's what he wanted," Donna said.

She protested that Emily was still too young to breed, but finally a month later Perry persuaded her to at least come look at his stud.

"One of my mares just had a foal by my Morgan," Perry told Donna one day when he ran into her at the General Store. "You come look."

"We'll just check this out. For future reference, you know. Find out what Perry wants for the fee," Donna said that day when we headed out of her drive in the cart.

The sun warm on our faces, the robins singing in the mulberry trees, the blackbirds diving over our heads, then back to snuggle in their nests hidden in the ditch grasses, we rolled by the Mennonite church, a wedding just letting out. The bride and groom were dwarfed in the entryway, the huge oak oversize doors casting them in shadow. The exterior of the church, with its big boxy lines and dark brown imposing brick, shed another layer of gloom across the scene. Yet I knew that the inside of this building was cheerful. Stripped of all decoration, the white walls shone out brightly, boldy, the exposed oak beams rising to a peak above the sleek lines of the pulpit. Light streamed in from the windows, the glass clear and unimpeded, warming the congregation, their bodies squeezed in next to one another in the wooden pews.

The bride and groom stepped from the doorway, bird seed showering down upon them, to find their black sedan completely sealed and bundled up in Saran Wrap, long strips of plastic wound around the windows and doors, the engine and trunk. Peals of laughter from the crowd carried over the fields, the corn just ankle high, the alfalfa cut and loose on the ground, waiting to be bound into bales or piled into stacks.

In the distance, two draft horses pulled a man in a straw hat and his combine, reins in his hands.

"Now look at that powerful pair," Donna said, and at first I didn't know if she meant the newlyweds or the horses. Here, June is the same as everywhere, a time of couples and nuptials. Traditionally, the Amish have a short period of engagement, just two weeks or so, but their celebrations make up in numbers anything that they might have missed in anticipation. Relatives from all over the country, three and four generations' worth, pour in, from Oklahoma to Ohio, for weddings. Buggies spin down the road and eighteen or twenty people at a time crawl out of hired vans with English drivers.

How do young couples meet? In church, in youth groups, during their service work in other communities. Often, an Amish youth will be employed by a family in another state to help out with chores, and there he will find a mate.

"I grew up in Wisconsin," Miriam once told me. "And came down here to Iowa to work when I was eighteen."

"Then I met her at church," Moses said. "And thought she was pretty nice."

Fifty years later, after eight children, and a lifetime of fortunes and misfortunes, Moses still finds her the same. One day when he came over to use the phone, he explained that he needed to make a series of doctor appointments for Miriam, her high blood pressure and leaky heart valves taking their toll at her advanced age.

"We've been married fifty years," Moses said.

"That's a long time. What's it been like?"

"Oh, we've had a few good days."

Moses stood on my front steps with his hat in his hands, his eyes suddenly spilling over with tears and, and as if it were a revelation to himself, simply added, "I love her. That's what I do."

Marrying at young ages without the option of divorce, the Amish grow to love each other, their bonds deepening over the years. Of course, these unions aren't without tension, and their sharp self-defining banter is almost nostalgic of a bygone era. The rest of us, engaged in serial marriages, usually never reach the longevity mark of comfort in conflict.

"I don't want that chocolate," Miriam told Moses once when I'd taken them into town for grocery shopping. She took the half gallon of ice cream out of their cart and put it back into the freezer unit.

"Why not?"

"Well, it tastes greasy."

"What kind do you want?"

"Neapolitan."

"Neapolitan?"

"Yes, Neapolitan."

"With all those stripes and colors?"

"There are only three."

"Well, all right," Moses said, opening the freezer door again and dumping one half gallon of Neapolitan into the cart. Then, as Miriam pushed down the aisle toward the orange juice, he turned back and grabbed the chocolate again, placing it quietly but firmly down among their other groceries.

In farm culture, there has always been more gender equality than one would assume. Men are clearly in a dominant position, and can and do abuse that status as frequently as anywhere else, but the family is an economic unit and both partners as well as the children know they have a job to accomplish together. Interdependence is a given. The home is also the family business. While Amish women are taught to "obey" their husbands, they are much more vocal than I would have guessed.

"I don't like that old chocolate," Miriam said once home and dishing up plates of angel food cake and ice cream. She put a big scoop of Neapolitan in each dish and set one down right in front of Moses. He ate it without a word.

Surrounded by a culture that may seem oppressive to women, I've learned some feminist lessons from my neighbors. Women are valued here for their cleverness, muscle, and hard-working nature more than for their looks. In the "English" world, femininity is closely defined in terms of facial beauty, a trim, lithe figure, dress, makeup, and passivity. While beauty may spark the initial attraction in the Amish culture, one searches for more in a good life partner. Fannie has silky blond hair accenting an exquisitely carved face with high cheekbones, full lips, and a delicate, fine nose. I've never heard anyone comment on her beauty, although her brawn receives many compliments.

"That Fannie is so strong," one family member bragged during a particularly pressing harvest season. "We don't have to hire extra help with her around."

"Oh, some women like to have their houses just so," Fannie told me once. "Me, I like to be outside working in the garden or choring. Let me slop my feet around in the manure and I'm happy."

In our urban, English society, a woman like Fannie would be considered an oddity at best. Here she's allowed to move closer toward an androgynous center. At the same time, the younger Amish men, the equivalent of our New Age sensitive guys, have acknowledged their responsibilities toward the household.

"Now, Fred," a thirty-year-old brother told his sibling from the pulpit on his wedding day at the ceremony I attended, "you're getting married today and you have to understand that you are there to help your wife. If she asks you to fix the washing machine, you hop right up and do it, not tomorrow or the next day, but right now. And pretty soon you'll have children and this creates a lot of stress for a woman, so don't you create any more by leaving a bunch of junk around. She's going to have to pick up after those kids, so you make sure she doesn't have to pick up your socks, too!"

"Pick up those hooves, Em," Donna said as we loped past the church. "I'd like to get home before morning." With Emily slowly pulling us uphill, then clopping down, the weight of the cart pushing her forward at a faster pace, we finally reached Perry's farm. Immediately, from the dark recesses of the barn, a chocolate brown Morgan, tall, proud, and handsome, raced out into the corral, his eyes flashing.

"There's his foal." Perry pointed to a sleek young horse, nursing at his mother's side. Then he led the Morgan around the lot, showing off his strong shoulders, short, sturdy legs, and crested neck, and vouching for his good disposition. It occurred to me that the animal world had the human one long beat. Rather than having equality of the sexes, the females of the barnyard have always been the valued gender; here we were with Emily, able to be choosy, eyeing this male to see if he was "good enough" for our girl.

Emily, tied to the hitching post, pawed the ground restlessly, her ears nearly turning around 360 degrees.

"Well, what do you think, Emily?" I asked. "Do you want this chocolate boy or would you rather have Neapolitan?"

SOCKS OFF, I leaned back in Esther Chupp's reclining chair, my bare feet up in the air, and looked out over her huge garden, the corn growing up, vigorous and strong, in perfectly weeded rows. Cockscombs and red cannas, their leaves large, flat, and bending slightly in the breeze, ringed the plot. Beyond the fence opened the river valley—the canopy of trees, dense and thick, surrounding the one-lane bridge over the water, the rows of peonies in her yard, the robin flying low with a worm trailing out of its mouth. Esther pressed her fingers deep into the webs between my toes, and my eyes returned to the room, taking in her reflexology certificates and charts on the wall next to a religious poster: *Slow me down, O Lord. Make me relish the day.*

I sensed Esther did relish the day but that she had probably never slowed down much in her life. A tiny, thin-boned woman in a brown calico dress with puffed sleeves and buttons down the front from neck to hem, she perched on a stool near my feet working with the quick, intensely alert movements of a bird caring for her young.

"Now there's the pituitary," she said, digging her thumb-nail down into the center of my big toe.

I winced in pain and pulled my foot back, but then relaxed again, surrendering myself to her skills. Her hands were steady, yet lithe, constantly searching with the precision of an animal who takes on the world by sheer instinct.

"You might want to try goldenseal, red root, or plantain for your problems today," she advised. "You know what plantain is?"

"Sure, I pull it out of my garden all the time."

Moses and Miriam had told me about Esther. Several years before, when Miriam had suffered from sneezing fits, they made the hour-long buggy trip to her house once a week, and swore that her services had helped. Quick to use modern medical services when needed, the Amish will not hesitate to go to an M.D. for a serious condition, but they still utilize folk remedies for more minor complaints. Foot rubbing, herbal cures, and the use of vitamins and minerals are all common practices, and like most folk medicines throughout the world, chiefly in the hands of the women.

Once, caring for the sick was an expected job of women, with childbirth, death, and dying all part of home ritual. My grandmother used mustard packs to "draw out the poison" on her swollen knees, watermelon as a diuretic, and a shot of whiskey before bed as a sedative. My mother blew cigarette smoke in my ear to ease the pain of infections and baking soda on bug bites and hives to eliminate the sting. Both my grandmother and mother stretched me across their laps and rubbed my back during my childhood growing pains. Healing knowledge was passed down the maternal line. Today, we go to doctors in mostly male-dominated clinics and hospitals for drugs for these ailments, and although the wonders of modern medicine are many, women have lost a certain identity with their knowledge of folk remedies.

"Boil the plantain up for a tea and drink four glasses a day," Esther said, rotating my ankle between her palms.

Esther had only an eighth-grade education, but she always exuded a confidence and decisiveness that I've noticed missing in me and my circle of highly educated feminist friends who are still searching for our power.

"Aren't the Amish women oppressed?" many of my friends have asked.

"Yes and no," I've replied.

Yes, they marry young and have large families. Yes, they live within a patriarchal system. In Esther's waiting room I'd picked up a book on attaining happiness in marriage, and, of course, the author advised the wife to "adjust" and become totally subservient to her husband. Yet, just footsteps away was an Amish woman who had been running her own successful business and office for over twenty years.

"I'd studied reflexology for a while," Esther had told me. "But to be certified you had to pass a test, and I didn't do well on tests, so I decided not to take it. But my husband urged me. He was sure I could pass. 'You might need a career one day,' he said. So I took the test and passed. He died in an accident three months later. After that, I raised and supported my five children on my practice."

In today's terms, Esther has done it all. She had a career and a family, in addition to being the quintessential single parent. And she held magic in her hands.

Germanic sects of all sorts seem to have had their women healers. They held their power in their hands and brought their centuries-old ideas and practices in their heads to the New World. The Russian Germans who settled North Dakota had a Braucher tradition, healers who concocted herbal potions. The Amish spoke of *Brauching* and the Pennsylvania Dutch, a group akin to the "plain" Dutch varieties of Mennonite and Amish, had doctors who knew how to fight off the evil eye with charms and spells, but could also cure dyspepsia with the proper herbs and stop a hemorrhage with a chant:

This is the day the wound was made.
O blood! Thou shalt stop and be still
until the Virgin Mary bears another son.

Discovering similar powers, the Pennsylvania Dutch healers became friendly with Native American shamans, or powwows—"dreamers" in the Algonquian language. Powwows knew how to enter and interpret the world of dreams, from which the ways of magic and healing derived their power, a territory familiar to the Germans. The history is unclear, but soon the German healers began calling themselves powwows, reaffirming the concept that healing is a cosmic affair, that charms and folk wisdom link us to a common culture in all societies. Folklore is the ultimate democracy. It helps the people have a hand in restoring order.

Once, when I was in an illness crisis, my circle of women friends gathered together for a powwow. Having followed the suggestions of doctors of all sorts and sizes without luck, I opted for a more mystical approach. So, they came, women from every one of my social groups, women who had studied and understood the traditions of healing and women who had not, women who knew one another well, and women who had just met that day but who decided to pull together for this occasion to reclaim their maternal powers.

I am a circle, I am healing you.
You are a circle, you are healing me.
Unite us, be as one.
Unite us, be as one.

We sat in a circle on the floor of Fairview School, joining hands and chanting, the windows open, the cool, fresh May air blowing through. On a small table in front of us, we had placed artifacts to symbolize the elements that we hoped to harmonize inside my body: earth (a rock), fire (candles), air (a feather), water (a glass filled from the tap). As we moved around the group, each member brought me a small gift of healing. Some were tangible presents—a basket of geraniums, a rose and a reading from an herbal manual on the flower's healing properties, a piece of quartz from a fellow gardener's plot, a small quilt, a tape of soothing music. Some were in-tangible presents—stories of memories from my childhood theater group, and finally a puppet show with a cast of my totems, all joined to help me: a goat, a frog, a cat, and a dog. The animals sang and danced and sent me get-well wishes.

Then I lay down in the middle of the circle and my friends gathered around me with a different kind of energy. They stretched out their hands over my body—my head, neck, torso, and limbs. With a strong, steady rhythm, their voices blended together in harmony in a chorus that began with a hushed quality, building into a larger presence in the room, then reaching a crescendo that poured out through the screens, spreading in every direction and sifting down to the valley below. *Oh, oh, oh, pur-i-fy, and heal us. Oh, oh, oh, purify and heal us.*

Eyes closed, I imagined a green light filling each cell and pore of my body, sinking and settling into my skin, seeping into my bones and all my internal organs. I visualized myself healthy again and able to do the things I'd longed for. I saw myself balanced and whole, my physical, emotional, and spir-itual selves fortified and combining in a perfect blend the way my friends' voices were mixing in the air around me.

May the circle be open, but unbroken.
May the peace of the goddess go in our hearts.
Merry meet and merry part and merry meet again.

We concluded our ritual and stood for a while in the dusky light, quietly visiting with one another, everyone feeling lighter, more in touch with something outside and bigger than ourselves, everyone feeling heavier, more in touch with something of solidity inside our beings. Slowly and then rather quickly, my friends filed out the door, hugging me good-bye. *You take care. Sleep well.* Their voices trailed off into the night, and soon the darkness found me deep into dreams of goats, frogs, cats, and dogs all scurrying around me, warding off all evil, even the thought of illness, coming to my aid and delivering me into the arms of a nurturing maternal figure. Call her Mary. Call her the Goddess. Call her what you will, but since that time I've carried her with me and felt her connect me to other women healers on my odyssey toward health.

"You might work over this area real good yourself," Esther told me, pressing on a point on my ankle.

"Okay," I said. I took a big, deep breath, feeling totally relaxed, and gazed out the window. "Your sweet corn is looking great!" I said.

"I had a mole that was destroying my patch," Esther said. "I contacted the extension agent and he said moles don't eat corn, must be a ground squirrel. 'Ground squirrels don't have tunnels, do they?' I said. 'Well, this critter is digging tunnels.' 'Moles don't eat corn,' he insisted. Then I remembered that moles are repelled by garlic, so I soaked the corn seed in garlic and minced some more and put it in the hills. Now I have a nice stand of corn. See, that agent might have book knowledge, but I have practical experience."

Then with me prone on a table, Esther kneaded my neck

and back, finishing off the session in a most uncharacteristic way.

"Do you want the vibrator this time?" she asked.

"The vibrator?"

"You know, on your back."

Other associations crept to mind. Women's power, indeed. Readily, I agreed.

With two hands, Esther picked up a huge, rubberized back massager that looked like a floor sander, and with a flick of a switch, a powerful rush of electricity swept through the machine. She worked the vibrator up and down my back. *Speed me up, O Lord,* I prayed when Esther revved the vibrator from low to high. *Speed me up.*

Make me relish the day, I recited on my way out of Esther's studio, my whole body calm, yet tingling and alive. In the waiting room, an Amish woman sat thumbing through a magazine, ready for her appointment. We smiled and nodded at each other as we passed, acknowledging that in this small way we were making that female connection and carrying on the folklore, the wisdom of the woman line. The circle was open, but unbroken.

"WHAT DO YOU do for grasshoppers?" I had asked Esther during one of my first summers at Fairview School, my feet up in her chair.

"Grasshoppers? Now that's a real problem. Maybe you should ask the extension agent."

The summer of 1988 had been sizzling. When the temperatures held the dust particles in the air so long that a blue haze hung over the landscape for weeks, I broke down and bought a small air conditioner. Not wanting to stir from the cool interior of the schoolhouse, I surveyed my garden out my window with my binoculars. It was then I noticed insects hopping all over my plot.

"What do you do for grasshoppers?" I had asked Mahlon one day at the phone booth.

"Well . . ." He leaned against the fence, the sun shining down hot and hard on his straw hat. "A person could get two blocks of wood, see. Two-by-fours . . ." Mahlon pressed his palms together, fingers outstretched, and hinged them open like a jaw.

"Yes?"

"Then smack 'em." Mahlon snapped shut his hands and rocked back in laughter, his suspenders rising with his shoulders, then puckering at his waist with the deep inhalations of his diaphragm. A smile rippled his face, his mouth widening, upper hairless lip curling, bearded chin dropping.

"I think I'm beyond the blocks of wood, Mahlon."

I motioned to my late June garden. Grasshoppers—infants, molting adolescents, and adults, short-horned and long, green, brown, white, and yellow—stripped tender green leaves from the lettuce plants, shredded the cabbage and broccoli down to the stalks, left nothing of the Swiss chard but its greenish-white stems. Grasshoppers jumped two feet in the air to riddle my young tomatoes with holes, the fruits, plump and succulent, just beginning to set and tug at their staked vines. Grasshoppers leapt three feet to chomp away at my Kentucky Wonder green beans that wound up and around the three-poled tepees I'd spliced together from downed tree branches. Grasshoppers perched boldly on the fence wire and clicked their legs together in mating calls. Grasshoppers dove over my row of squash, spitting juice, dropping their cargo on the baby zucchini and patty pan squash below.

I motioned to my pickup truck and house. Grasshoppers had devoured the nylon screens on both crank-out windows of the topper of my Toyota. On my porch, large, softball-size holes in my screen door let mosquitoes and other grasshoppers into my home. The flutter and flap of their wings created a steady background sound, a hum that put me to bed every night and woke me up every morning, a white noise that in a few short weeks I'd grown accustomed to, that I almost didn't hear anymore, as if it were jet traffic over a busy airport nearby.

"I guess you do need help," Mahlon said.

I asked if he was experiencing the same problem, if the grasshoppers were destroying his crops before the drought had a chance. The summers of those years had been especially hot and dry. The year before we measured the severity of the heat by the number of days over one hundred degrees, and had lost count somewhere in July. But that summer's heat had been the worst—in my memory anyway. Some said we were just going through a cycle, that every couple of decades or two Iowa has warm years with mild winters and summer heat waves and drought. Yet, most of us knew that this was probably just a taste of what was to come as we headed into a century of the greenhouse effect and global warming. Only Moses could remember a hotter summer. He sat in his porch swing in the evenings, circles of sweat under his armpits dampening his shirt.

"Guys who lived in town just walked out of their places and slept in the park at night. So hot inside you could scarcely breathe. Didn't have no air conditioner hanging out of the window then, neither. And now, some of us still don't."

That summer's heat stretched on without relief, the sun melting the patch of blacktop in front of Moses and Miriam's place, the gooey tar sticking to the horses' hooves when they trotted by. And the heat was intensified by the drought. The winter brought only a few inches of snow to scrape from the drive, then the spring rains never arrived, and in May, for the first time in ten years, I watered my garden with a sprinkler hose.

Every morning, I lugged my hose to a different row and stretched it along the path. The water spurted from the tiny holes, spraying higher and higher with the pressure, the well motor clanking *ker-chunk, ker-chunk,* the dawning sun already shining red and angry in the sky. A few drops of rain fell in early June, but not enough to even streak the dust that had collected into a gauzy brown film over the window glass. Then in the middle of the month, the grasshoppers started hatching, their eggs deposited in the topsoil the previous fall, dormant throughout the winter, and preserved into summer by the drought.

"Usually their eggs get drowned by the spring rains," Mahlon said.

But there was nothing usual about that summer. In February, I'd begun my gardening season with my normal routine of sprouting several hundred seedlings under the grow lights in my basement. Each week, I raised the lights higher on chains as the seedlings pushed, heads bent, necks strong and firm, out of the potting soil toward the light. By April, my trays of broccoli, cabbage, kale, lettuce, and chard were ready to be transplanted to the garden. The days were invigorating, balmy, but when I scratched the ground with my hoe to drop peas in along the fence, the earth was ungiving.

I predicted then that the season was going to be troublesome, and in May, when I went to the hardware store to purchase a soaker hose, my neck stiffened with tension as I waited in line with three others there on the same errand. *Ching-ching*. We stood in silence and shook our heads as the clerk made change from the old cash register, raising, lowering the weight in the dollar bill compartment, fingering out quarters, nickels, and pennies. I paid my bill and knew this hose wasn't worth a dime if we didn't have rain, for no amount of irrigation would ever compensate for the subsoil moisture we'd already lost.

When I expressed my worries, my city-bred friends stared at me blankly as if to say, "What's the big loss?"

If this drought did indeed point to global warming, the loss could be astronomical. It could mean major environmental changes, melting ice caps, widening deserts, famines, the extinction of whole species of plants and animals, and increased risks of diseases like skin cancer. Nationally, it could mean population shifts, and housing, energy, and economic adjustments. Regionally, it could mean the destruction of the farm economy as we now know it, and no region was more dependent on the healthy flow of agricultural money than Iowa. All those losses affected me, but I was waging my own, even more immediate, environmental battle. The drought meant the destruction of my garden, and without my garden I couldn't eat.

I cannot ingest the pesticides routinely sprayed on commercial fruits and vegetables. Yes, you can wash off some of the surface sprays with soap and water, but most Americans still take in an average of nine pounds of chemicals a year through their food. When apple growers, for example, regularly get exemptions to federal safety laws to saturate their crops up to eighteen times a season with pesticides, the chemicals remain in the very fibers of the fruits.

Here in the farm belt, eating organic vegetables sounds easy enough. Yet, here in the farm belt, very few vegetables are raised except in small, backyard plots. Instead, the government has encouraged farmers to narrow their crops to a few subsidized gems. In Iowa: corn and beans. In a state that has one of the highest number of tilled acres per person, we have a tough time buying a locally grown head of lettuce. We, like most of the rest of the country, depend upon corporate farmers in California and a handful of other sunbelt states to ship produce to us. We get in our cars and drive past acres of rich, dark soil or beautifully manicured lawns to a supermarket to buy a head of lettuce that comes to us days or weeks old, overpriced, often tasteless, wrapped in plastic, and full of contaminants.

In most of the Midwest, you can find organic produce only in a few select co-ops, health food stores, or farmers' markets. Without chemical preservatives to extend their shelf lives, or pesticides to protect them from blemishes, the California organics sometimes look less dazzling than their commercial counterparts. In turn, people buy less of them, the demand remains down, the cost up. Pretty is poison, I've come to realize as I watch consumers pass by the more nutritious piece of organic fruit and reach for the brightly colored and flawless commercials that have gained their luster through repeated sprayings, coatings of wax, or injections of dye. Most of us have become so used to dyed fruit that we don't recognize its natural color. We'll swallow eighteen applications of spray rather than cut away a single worm hole.

Then, the choice of organic produce is limited. Throughout the long winter, my co-op stocks only organic oranges and carrots. In the last decade, local organic truck farming has been on the rise in the heartland, but if you're lucky enough to find one near you, you'll soon realize that these farmers are at the whim of weather and have limited control over their supplies. During a drought in the early eighties, one truck farmer I knew sold freshly baked croissants, rather than spinach and kohlrabi, from the tailgate of his Ford truck.

Over the years, I've learned that if I want a reliable and affordable food supply, I have to grow my own. I've learned to garden organically, without a trace of chemicals, and have raised almost every bite of produce that goes into my mouth. I have experimented with new foods, with wide-row, square-foot, and vertical gardening. I've grown arugula in raised beds, bok choy in a cold frame, and buckwheat sprouts in trays on my dining-room table, the sunlight spilling through the picture window. I have learned to outwit bugs, choosing zone-specific species and variety-resistant seeds, building up my soil with manure and compost, and dusting and spraying plants, when need be, with wood ash, flour, or kelp and fish emulsion. In the past, my biggest problem was squash bugs. I interplanted marigolds and radishes to repel the beetles, then set out more plants to compensate for whatever loss occurred.

Mostly, I enjoyed the gain. No dessert at Chez Panisse could match the delicacy, the sugary delight of my open-pollinated sweet corn fresh from the garden, the steam rising off the cob. My peas, eaten raw and straight from the vine, were candy, and I grew to love the pop of the pod splitting open at the midrib under my thumb, the smooth break of the seeds rolling away from the funiculus into the bowl. Not even an Edward Weston photograph could capture the beautiful lines and sexy curves of my green peppers. My organic produce seemed like vintage French wine, while commercial vegetables were a cheaper Californian imitation.

During harvest, I learned the secrets and rhythms of preserving, the carrots root-cellaring in an outside pit, the canning lids pinging on the kitchen counter, the dehydrator whirling in the corner. I mastered the art of the pressure cooker, and everything I'd watched my grandmother do as a child suddenly took on a déjà vu–like quality. I remembered her selecting the best produce for canning, the blemishless tomatoes, the pristine green beans. I remembered her boiling water, sterilizing jars, inspecting the pressure cooker gasket, tightening the lid, watching the needle sweep toward the higher red numbers. The job became a ritual that connected me to generations of women. They stood in summer kitchens, aproned, their hands wet, their faces red, a stray strand of hair falling down into their eyes.

For my frozen goods, I sent away for cellophane bags, the plastic ones outgassing into my food, and rented freezer space at the local meat locker. After the plant burned one winter and destroyed months' worth of vegetables, I bought a small, used freezer of my own, only to have its motor die after several weeks' use. A day later, two strong men hauled its old carcass out of my basement and bounced a brand-new model down the steps. The new freezer lasted a year, then went out when I was away for a week one December. I managed to salvage a few soggy turnips, then purchased a dehydrator.

Whatever my method of preservation, for five winters in a

row I had subsisted on my larder of root-cellared, canned, frozen, or dried vegetables. I worked hard, sacrificing other pursuits. On Saturday nights when my friends went off to a smoky bar to listen to banjo and fiddle music, I turned on the radio and spent the evening tapping my feet to the rhythms of washed beets and diced squash. Again, I connected to a previous era, when work and play were one. I had no leisure time, devoting most of my energy to my job and my garden, watching my health improve as my horticultural skills grew.

Then came the insect plague.

"You need some birds to eat those grasshoppers," Mahlon told me. His chickens kept his infestation in check. "But guineas are the best, really. If a person has a few of them around, you won't see a grasshopper again. Course, you have to keep the guineas around too."

Fannie and Max had guineas, beautiful black and white speckled birds with bony casques on their heads. They darted out into the road, shrieked when you pulled into the drive, and rattled across the roof with a *click* and *tack*.

"Yeah, we had some guineas once too," Mahlon said. "They'd set up in our tree at night, then in the morning, be gone. A week later, we'd find them at a farm a couple of miles over."

Maybe, if I just wait, a guinea will appear, I thought. But I'd never been lucky, so I called the feed store to place my order.

"We don't get guineas in after the first of June," the dealer said.

I chastised myself for my tardiness, for not anticipating this grasshopper problem, for waiting too long. I should have acted that day in May when I found the first hatched nymph on a cabbage leaf.

"Ducks'll do real good too," Mahlon said the next night after I'd hailed him on the road on his tractor.

I *am* lucky, I thought. I knew a man north of town who raised ducks, hundreds of ducks, his farmyard overflowing with their webbed feet. Don's place was such a duck attraction that in the fall unsuccessful hunters stopped there and bought mallards. After crouching all morning in a blind in the bitter cold, the hunters didn't want to go home empty-handed.

I phoned Don. "I'd like to buy some adult ducks."

As fast as the birds mature, I knew I couldn't wait for hatchlings to grow up and begin their instinctual bug scavenging.

"I'm sorry to say, this year I don't have a duck on the place. Coons have been so bad—must be the drought—not enough for them to eat. They just walk into the yard in broad daylight, bold as you please, and a few minutes later sashay out with a duck in their mouth."

"Do you know of anyone who has ducks?"

"No, just about every guy I know who had 'em doesn't anymore. Same deal. Coons. I have geese, though. Plenty of those. Want some geese?"

"Will they eat grasshoppers?"

"Well, I don't know."

Who would? The county extension service agent was very interested in recording the exact location of my infestation, but confessed she didn't know if geese ate grasshoppers. I'd have to call the state poultry expert for the answer. "But why don't you just spray?" she asked. Several days and long distance phone calls later, I finally reached the poultry expert. He, too, wanted to make me a pin on someone's state map, but finally informed me that no, geese weren't especially good predators of grasshoppers. "Why don't you just spray?" he asked.

I tried to explain my plight. "Think of me as a pioneer," I said. "How did the pioneers cope with grasshoppers?"

He told me that the pioneers did have their disastrous locust plagues. (A locust is just a grasshopper gone rogue.) But a little more than a hundred years ago, when my great-grandparents settled in Iowa, before farmers tiled and drained their fields, the state was dotted with bogs and sloughs that supported dense populations of birds. Canada geese, canvas backs, and ring-necked ducks, mergansers, pelicans, and sand-hill and whooping cranes darkened the sky on their fall and spring migrations, and when they circled down to land, ate their share of grasshoppers. Year round, the native prairie chickens gobbled up thousands more of the insects, but the prairie chickens went the way of the buffalo, men hunting them for sport until near extinction. So here I was dealing with one human-made ecological imbalance on top of another.

I began reading the diaries and letters of prairie women, and found their tales of locusts ravaging their small settlements. 1874 came to be known as "The Grasshopper Year," when locusts swept across the plains like snowstorms, the insects dropping to the earth, covering every inch of ground, every bush or shrub like enormous-size flakes. Tree limbs snapped under their weight, and the grasshoppers ate right through sheets and quilts hastily thrown over precious tomato vines and celery plants. They devoured the leaves of fruit trees and ate through green peaches, leaving nothing but the pits hanging from the branches. They invaded homes and ate anything that wasn't encased in metal—even kitchen utensils, furniture, and wooden walls of the cabins. Window curtains were left in shreds, and young children screamed in horror as the grasshoppers wiggled through their hair and down their shirts. Men tied strings around their pant cuffs to keep the locusts from crawling up their legs. A Kansas woman even reported the grasshoppers eating a green stripe off the white dress she was wearing.

Pioneers learned that the grasshoppers would stop for nothing. The women's writings were filled with Biblical descriptions, accounts of locust plagues right out of Exodus that challenged the homesteaders' faith in themselves, their God, and the very idea of Manifest Destiny in the New World. The letters of Gro Svenson, a Norwegian immigrant, recorded her battle with locusts on the Iowa prairie near Estherville and explained that settlement's solution. Early in the spring, the pioneers doused their crude cabins and barns with water, then set fire to the surrounding fields and prairies in hopes of burning out the insects' eggs and young. Inevitably, the burning meant replanting and a late harvest, but the homesteaders were able to reap a crop from their one- and two-acre farms that year.

My garden isn't even a quarter acre, but the season was too dry, the plot too near the house to burn. Earlier that spring, brush fires had jumped across ditches, set fields smoldering, and threatened buildings all across the state. Day and night, the air smelled of smoke, and in April a county conservation commissioner told me, "Iowa's on fire." In early May, a friend in a small western Iowa town stayed up all night dragging buckets of water from her house to the edge of her yard to try to put out a wildfire that crept steadily closer, flames lapping toward her one-hundred-year-old family home, where her elderly and ailing mother slept inside.

Instead of the torch, I tried the phone and called an organic gardening magazine hotline. They told me to try some buckets of my own.

"Make grasshopper traps," the hotline woman instructed me, "by setting out buckets baited with molasses water. The grasshoppers will jump in and drown."

I combed the secondhand stores for small buckets, received donations from friends, and gathered up a stack on sale at the paint store, then covered their bottoms with goopy syrup. Sure enough, within minutes of placing traps out between my vegetable rows, grasshoppers leapt in, swam a few laps of breast stroke across the surface, then sank to their sugary graves. Dumbfounded, I stood out in my garden in the heat of the day among my tomato vines and watched hundreds of the insects plunge into the water. Hourly, the grasshopper carnage tallied up, yet more bugs kept coming.

I called the hotline again.

"Make a mixture of chili peppers and garlic and spray it all over your plants," the woman said.

The next day, spray tank slung over my shoulder, nozzle nosing the undersides of the leaves, I moved through the garden, coating all my vegetables with my homemade pesticide. At first, the concoction seemed to truly repel the grasshoppers, and I was jubilant. The insects still lurked near the garden, but had stopped eating it, their voracious hum quieted to a whisper. Occasionally, one would make a daring suicidal splash into a bucket, but most appeared slowed, almost listless, compared to their usual hyperactivity. I drove to the discount supermarket and bought a case of bottled chili peppers.

"Having some kind of party?" the clerk asked.

At home, the potion seemed to be wearing off, so I sprayed again, and this time the grasshoppers became excited, their wings vibrating, compound eyes sparkling with desire. The party had just begun.

"We got the salsa, you bring the chips." They buzzed, hopping and leaping from corn stalk to fence post, chomping and spitting more voraciously than ever.

I slumped down at the kitchen table. It was over. I spent the next few days foraging in the ditches and along the fences for lamb's-quarters and clover for my daily salads and tried not to even glance in the direction of my garden.

Then, a couple of mornings later, I woke early, remembering bug juice. Ah, yes! Bug juice, an old organic garden standby, a homemade pesticide that had never failed me. Bug juice, made from ground pest parts, was blended with water and sprayed back on the area of infestation. It worked, some-how, on the old holistic adage that like cures like. *Like* cer-tainly cures you from ever wanting to get up in the morning and fix yourself a nice quart of orange juice in the blender again. I'd read one source that speculated that the very smell of dead pests was enough to drive brethren away from the fold, and another source that claimed that dead pests spread viruses throughout the flock that killed fellow followers. Amen, I said to both theories and prayed the juice would work.

That afternoon, I sieved off the grasshoppers from the mo-lasses buckets and readied the juice. *Slish, slosh.* Masses of dead bugs swirled in the wire mesh, and just as I was about to whirl an Acrididae smoothie, Moses stopped by in his buggy.

He tied up his horse to the hitching post, bent over my buckets, and cocked his head. "Whatcha doing there?" he asked, and when I explained, he said, "Oh, you're cruel."

I may have been. When the blender gears began to grind mouths, claws, wings, ovipositors, and antennae together, I did have a moment of guilt, but as soon as I stood in the garden with the sprayer, I forgot my animal cruelty in hopes of saving the last shreds of my plants. The bug juice shot out over my cabbages, and once again I was optimistic, although guardedly so. I went to bed that night thinking I might have found a remedy to my problem, but at the same time was resigned to the possibility that I probably hadn't.

Days ticked by, and slowly I began to see some improve-ment. In Exodus, the Lord sent a series of plagues down on the resistant pharaoh who had enslaved Israel. The Egyptians suffered through infestations of ascending terror, from frogs, to maggots and flies, to grasshoppers. Then, finally, Moses parted the Red Sea, Pharaoh's army drowned, and all were delivered. My salvation was less dramatic—more like a re-routing of a small tributary—but little by little, the grasshoppers did begin to thin, and the cabbage, broccoli, and Swiss chard rallied to generate new leaves, fill in their flowerettes and heads, their fan-shaped leaves. After ten days, the garden had a different look and feel. No longer molested and limp, it stood up taller, stronger, more full-bodied.

When I reached the two-week point, I began to realize that I'd won, that the garden was definitely on the rebound, although it would never regain its original shape and hue. The grasshoppers still hovered thickly across the landscape, but I salvaged enough produce from my plot to make it through another winter. Yet, as I chopped okra (my only cultivated plant to make it through the plague unscathed), I began to wonder if my whole idea of gardening wasn't askew.

After years of organic gardening, I found it much easier to cultivate pest-resistant plants than to try to fight the pests themselves. So, to guard against future locust plagues, I thought I would delve into finding other species and varieties, like okra, which stood up well against the powerful jaws of the grasshoppers. Then I remembered that, in their journals, the pioneer women noted that the prairie grasses were the only thing that the grasshoppers left untouched. Plant a complete garden of okra and big and little bluestem grasses?

Was this *such* a crazy idea? Instead of prairie grasses, perhaps I could plant some of the prairie weeds that I had been reduced to foraging for my salads. Had I just said reduced to foraging? Foraging, like root-cellaring and dehydrating, which I ultimately found the cheapest and most satisfactory forms of food preservation, was our most ancient form of food production. Agricultural cultivation, as we know it, is a fairly recent historical development. What if I didn't plant at all? What if I just freed myself from all the hard work of gardening altogether—the plans, the seed saving and buying, the seed-lings and transplants, the cultivating and tools—and learned to forage for all my food?

I've come to rage at the way the prairie has been ravaged by the people who settled the Midwest, my ancestors and the pioneer women among them. In steamboats that crossed the Great Lakes, that made their way up the Mississippi, in cov-ered wagons that forded the Missouri, then creaked and moaned behind oxen along the narrow paths that wound west-ward, the early settlers brought their European values with them, and most of America today retains their idea of the ideal landscape. Trees, mountains, and large bodies of water, the familiar in the pioneers' past, were sought out and treasured. For the most part, the prairie was revered not for what it was, an ecosystem of magnificent intricacy and beauty in its own right, but for what it could become.

Naturally, it could become farms. It could be cultivated, and so destroyed, to produce plants that were familiar. Plants that could be raised and sold to others who found them fa-miliar. Never mind adapting to a new flora and fauna, of learning new ways of cooking and eating. Never mind the fact that this prairie had been sustaining populations of Native Americans for hundreds of years without much cultivation. The prairie was, and still is, devalued. With the introduction of the plow went the wildflowers and bluestems, the wetlands, the vast populations of birds, butterflies, and small mammals.

Sure, some understood. Gro Svenson marveled at the bloom-ing prairie flowers and the changing colors and nature of the landscape. Others were awed by the woolly calyxed pasque with its delicate yellow center, the first flower to appear in the spring. As spring moved into summer, a succession of surprises sprang up, from the buttercup and Johnny jump-up, to the puccoon, wild artichoke, wild indigo, spiderwort, wild garlic and onion, smartweed, butterfly weed, wood betony, and purple cone flower. The sunflowers dominated the midsummer with the opening of the black-eyed Susans and compass plants. Then the goldenrods and asters finished off the fall.

Today, we've nearly finished off the prairie. Now, you have to really search to find small patches of it in parks and preserves. Never again will we, like those pioneers, have the opportunity to experience the majesty of its vastness. When I walk through Doolittle Pairie, my favorite preserve in central Iowa, I try to imagine what this plot would be like if its waist-high grasses and wildflowers extended to the horizon, if it were unscarred by power lines and the constant din of passing traffic. In Doolittle Prairie, I began to wonder if gardening, this activity that I thought had been keeping me in touch with nature, was only, in a weird paradoxical way, destroying it. Perhaps I should give up gardening altogether, restore my plot to prairie, and just forage; then I truly would be in balance with my native environment. For wasn't my small garden a part of the larger farming problem that had so changed the landscape?

Agriculture does have its advantages, though, I reasoned. It has allowed us to be freed from hunter-gatherer society and stay in one place, build a stationary community. Yes, I could wander up and down the road, looking for a meal, but I might need to wander farther and farther, trespassing on others' "property," if this were my only source of sustenance. At last, I decided I would get out my field guide and make more of a study of natural food sources, do more foraging, but keep my garden, reducing my dependence upon it.

Then the two ideas—foraging and gardening—began to come together in my mind. I thought of Wes Jackson's work at the Land Institute in Kansas to find a perennial variety of wheat that, like prairie grass, would be regionally adapted and eliminate the time, cost, and contamination of planting seeds and applying pesticides and herbicides. Why couldn't I move more toward Jackson's idea in my garden?

I developed a plan for a native garden. I began to allow some of the common weeds—dandelions, lamb's-quarters, plantain, and purslane—to remain in my spring garden and combine with different varieties of lettuce in my salad bowl. I reserved a section of my garden to become a patch of perennial edibles—sunflowers, milkweed, and mullein. These hardy flowering weeds brought not only beauty but an array of butterflies to my plot. True, as staples, weeds took some getting used to in my diet, but over time they provided a delicious, free, and organic source of food that never needed to be shipped across country, sprayed, or watered.

I don't know if I will ever convert entirely to a native garden, but I'm willing to experiment. In the end, my own northern European roots may run deeper than those of prairie grass, and I may not be able to give up the grow lights, the seedlings, the straight rows and strings. I may cling as tightly to the familiar tomato, potato, peas, and beans as did the pioneers. "Let food be your medicine, and medicine be your food," Hippocrates, the medical pioneer, said. As tense as it was, my locust plague got me to thinking beyond my own rake and hoe to a new perception of food. In a small way, this new vision may begin to heal me and my landscape.

And what of the larger population and landscape? Big changes start with small decisions. What if, for starters, more of us returned to gardening, then each midwesterner nurtured his or her own prairie patch? Not just a "meadow in a can," but a real selection of indigenous plants that could be used for breakfast, lunch, or dinner. What if, deep down in our own tissues, we began to feel the changes these native foods brought? The return of a portion of control over our food sources, our physical and mental health, and balance of our natural environment. As long as the prairie is populated mostly by Euro-Americans, it will probably never return to its natural state, but a network of native gardens might be enough to keep its identity before us, reminding us how much we've lost and, with careful living, how much we might gain.

The big picture of a world of clean food, clean water, the return of local flora and fauna began to emerge in my mind, yet there were further leaps of thought I hadn't even entertained.

"Now, some people like grasshoppers," Mahlon told me later that summer when my infestation was in control.

"Like them? The birds like them, you mean."

"No, people like them."

"Why?"

"You may miss those grasshoppers yet."

"Why?"

"All this time you complained about not having enough to eat, you could've had *them*."

Of course! Didn't I have a crunchy organic protein source right in my own backyard? Didn't I have the guts to try them? Didn't Pharaoh's army get drowned? Hadn't I been delivered to the promised land?

E ARLY SUMMER is often a chaotic time of year for me, with job pressures and sudden storms in my health or personal life winding together and spiraling up the fence with enough force to make gardening not a pleasure but a chore. The spring of 1993 had already brought problems, with several heavy downpours that had washed out most of the first plantings in my garden. Every seed that slipped from my fingers one Monday morning when I knelt in my plot to replant was coated with worries, regrets, and nagging thoughts: deadlines to be met, a row of unpaid doctor bills.

Red-stemmed Swiss chard, deer tongue and Tom Thumb lettuce, radishes, tatsoi and arugula seeds became worry beads. I tried to console myself. This was the first time in days, I realized, that the sun was out and shining brightly and warmly enough to dry up the soil, soil wet and soggy from almost nine months of continual rain. But my pep talk and the meditational movements of planting did not quiet my racing mind. Instead, my emotions seemed way out ahead of my body and I wanted something to steady me, pull me back to the earth between my fingers.

Then suddenly, a horn honked and Moses appeared. Startled, I looked up and saw him leaning against my pickup truck, his arm through the open window. His buggy was stationed in my yard, the reins of his horse looped around an old hitching post.

"Thought that'd rouse you out," Moses said and laughed. We hadn't seen each other since Thanksgiving, he and Miriam having gone off to an Amish settlement in Florida for the winter and spring.

I hurried out the gate.

He opened his arms and kissed me.

Both of us a bit stunned at this very non-Amish, non-midwestern display of emotion, we stood there together for a moment, grinning, the early morning light slanting down across Picayune Creek and over Fairview School.

After Moses' greeting and our reunion, I returned to my garden feeling renewed. Yes, I thought, things do need to be accomplished, yes, things do change. But that's all part of a bigger scheme. People come in and out of your life, sometimes to be gone forever, sometimes to return. Plants struggle out of the soil, grow, die, break down. All living things have their cycles. That Monday morning, my garden became a symbol not of stability, nor of change, but of stability *within* change.

Little did I know how I would have to cling to that notion throughout the rest of the season.

For the next three months were rain, raining, rainy—intensifying and creating new fears each day. June was a dance of dark clouds and mighty mud puddles. The corn was only shin high by the Fourth of July, when gigantic lightning bolts crackled the sky and the Picayune rose so fast it sent my neighbor Bob's hogs swimming for higher ground. Two weeks later, storms hammered us again, and forty of the sows' newly delivered pigs washed away downstream.

The soil compacted, the weather consistently cool, the sun

having shone a total of only nineteen days all summer, every gardener in the region felt the effects of the Great Flood. Some noticed only a delay in maturation, their broccoli and cabbage late to head. Others lost their tomato crops, blights and fungi riddling the plump fruit. Those closer to major rivers and lakes saw their whole gardens go under for weeks at a time during the summer, the tips of their bean poles poking up out of the water. Gardeners in Des Moines watched in horror as a man just off Interstate 80 bulldozed his whole magnificent plot of young vegetables, scooping the dirt up into the air and dropping it down again in piles to build a dike around his house.

While news crews moved in and filmed houses cracking in two, floating down the Mississippi River, and interviewed flood victims living by the side of the road, not much thought was given to garden loss. But once the waters receded, cleanup efforts told a tale of agricultural and horticultural destruction. We lost much of that year's crop, and a portion of the previous year's in storage.

I drove past Hannibal, Missouri, on one of the first days the river road was open in early August, the water parting on each side like the Red Sea, and found a tangle of debris—cornstalks and bean plants from farm and garden—washed up on the shoulder. In Chelsea, Iowa, a small town on the Iowa River that was evacuated five times that year, a team of young teenage Mennonites cleaned out water-logged basements at the end of July, and dumped wheelbarrow after wheelbarrow of canned vegetables on the sidewalk for the trash.

"From now on, I'm certainly going to garden differently," Carl, my gardening pal in Iowa City, told me, explaining that with the recent swings between droughts and floods, he had searched out the most hardy and resilient varieties for his plot.

A friend near the Saylorville Reservoir in Ankeny, Iowa, where the lake waters had twice covered his garden by July and came within a hundred yards of his house, found himself becoming more resilient. "When I was flooded two years ago, I thought the world had come to an end. I dug all sorts of ditches, replanted everything, and looked upon the whole event as a huge man-versus-nature challenge. This time, I learned to accept and go with it."

As I struggled to bring in my own late harvest, the okra just reaching its normal height, the frost threatening to kill its pink blossoms, I realized that the summer had brought a lesson of resilience and acceptance to us all. Carl told me that when he dug his garlic that summer, he was delighted with the big, healthy-looking bulbs he placed on the kitchen counter, but when he cut into one, he discovered they were skinless, the pulp vulnerable and exposed. We flood gardeners appeared to be the opposite. The year's conditions toughened us on the outside and in. Cut us open and we stood up to the most intense stress.

Midwestern spiritual leaders from the far right to the New Age left called the flood a "cleansing," a time to wash out the old and welcome the new. Some conservative religious groups thought the flood a punishment for our sins. My Monday morning garden interactions with Moses opened the gate to a different perspective, one of personal calm. Pressures and losses seemed less crisis ridden and more a part of a natural whole.

But as the rains kept up, washing the soil downstream, the straightened rivers cutting faster and deeper at their banks, the fields turning into lakes around me, my vision enlarged even more. I still had a hard time buying the punitive-God approach, but did find a bit of truth in the biblical adage that the sins of the fathers would be paid for by the sons. The almost complete destruction of the prairie contributed to the severity of flooding in Iowa. Prairie plant roots grow deep and strong, holding in and filtering rainwater. Corn and soybean roots are not half as efficient.

As basic and satisfying as it is, gardening is an unnatural ethnocentric act. Our ancestors, who pioneered this land of promise, of milk and honey, wanted to eat, use, and sell the foods they were accustomed to in Europe, and so they displaced the prairie. If we alter one part of the ecosystem, we will eventually have to cope with other imbalances. The destruction of the prairie did not bring the summer's deluge, but it did exaggerate its effects. In 1993, as never before, we were forced to face the power of nature, its enormous ability to have its way—and both our significance and insignificance in that event.

I learned "my place" in my garden, and in my larger environment. Once I let go of my own worries, once I thought of my garden and the whole flood as a lesson in renewal, I began to see a majesty in the bigger event. While half my potato crops rotted in the ground, cattails—tall, spiky, and strong—shot up in my ditch. While my beets reached only half their normal size, huge great blue herons circled overhead.

One night, late in the summer, Moses appeared again, to eye the creek, assessing how far it had risen out of its banks.

"It's really been something this year, hasn't it?" I asked.

"It's been something, all right," Moses replied.

We fell silent, Moses and I, standing together again near my garden on the hill, watching as the summer of the Great Flood and some of our promised land flowed past in the valley below.

I WALKED OUT my door to pick some lettuce from my soggy garden and found a 1,500-pound black Angus bull loose in my yard, grazing on grass and clover, his tail swishing, his eyes gazing off down the hill toward the rising waters of the Picayune. Normally, the Picayune lives up to its name, a mere crack in the earth, a rivulet that drains this gentle, rolling valley with its corn, bean, oat and alfalfa fields, its fenced pastures of Holsteins and its large wooden frame houses that often hold three generations under one roof. Normally, the Picayune is just wide enough to dampen one shoe when you step across it to sit up on its bank with a fishing pole on a hot summer morning in hopes of catching a few small bluegills.

But this time the Picayune, and all the other creeks, rivers, and streams in the area that eventually wind their way into the Mississippi, was swollen. Its waters had overflowed and backed up in my neighbor Bob's fields, drowning out the young corn, flooding the barn, lapping water dangerously close to the foundation of his house, and creating a bog out of the pasture where he kept two prized bulls. And one of them was standing squarely in front of me. I slid back into the house and phoned my neighbor.

In a few minutes, Bob appeared in his pickup. His teenage son, who had already been sent off on a search, arrived soon after. Hands in the air and feet spaced a healthy distance from the bull, father and son tried to shoo the animal back down the hill toward home. With a stubborn sense of its own direction, the bull led the two on a chase through a cornfield toward the creek, its hooves sinking deeper and deeper into the mud. From my house, perched high and dry on top of the hill, I watched for nearly an hour as Bob and his son trailed the bull, matadors of the plains, never getting too close, yet close enough to finally herd the animal out of the mire and corral it safely behind its own barbed-wire fence.

While there was excitement and a kind of beauty in the moment, I couldn't help but feel for Bob. A lost afternoon, taking him away from pressing field work—beans that needed to be cultivated, hay that needed to be put up. And he'd already had so many losses that year. Once there had been two bulls in his pasture, but a week before, during a severe thunderstorm, one had been hit by lightning and killed. The other, lonely and agitated, snorted and cried for several days, then finally, with a surge of strength triggered by yet another storm, broke through the fence, eventually winding up at my house. Earlier in the spring, Bob had been counting on even a larger herd of cattle, but his cows gave birth in the muck by the creek and ten calves died. Earlier in the summer, Bob thought if his cattle didn't do so well, his hogs would.

Later in the summer, we could still hear the pounding, on through August into September, hammering and pounding, sloshing, drifting and floating. And when the waters began to recede, we found what had been carried down, down by the currents: tables and chairs, washing machines and dryers, books and bowling trophies, a whole freezer full of meat, the carcasses of Bob's dead pigs. Some things drifted out, others washed in. Later in the fall, the pounding stopped, the hammering and pounding. We drifted back up to resume our "normal" lives again. We waited, patiently waited for the waters to recede, then repaired the holes in our fences as we maneuvered our way back through the muddy fields toward home.

ONE HOT JUNE NIGHT, I stayed up with a sick kid goat, and by the next day had learned something about both animal and human disaster. I sat outside in the goat pen with Scalawag and the two of us worked to stroke and nudge, coo, coax, and pray her little five-day-old Mac back to life. With a crescent moon pinned in the sky above my acreage, the rows of young corn green and vibrant, parting in the fields on either side, the fireflies winking in and out of the ditch grass, the pastoral landscape did not reflect the desperateness of the situation. I fed Mac antibiotics, slipping a tiny rubber tube down his throat and shooting in the milky liquid with a syringe, while Scalawag wrapped her body around him as he sank into a gurgling, labored sleep. Then once an hour, the nanny roused him awake, nosing him until he staggered up on his feet to nurse. With the little strength he had, he butted her bag to stimulate the flow of milk, then stretched his neck to find the nipple.

"He's going to die," Karen, the vet, had told me. "We could perform heroics, but you're just going to dump a lot of money into that kid for nothing."

I wanted to try anyway. The first vet I had consulted, a well-intentioned but inexperienced large-animal doctor who had botched Mac's debudding and blinded him, had been wrong. Maybe Karen would be too, although over the course of a year of her treating my dog and cats, I'd grown to trust Karen as an extraordinarily skilled and compassionate veterinarian. Her diagnosis and treatment were always on target. As the first vet had packed us up to leave, he said that the debudding paste wouldn't drip into Mac's eye, and the kid would be fine when he came out of the anesthetic in a couple of hours. On the car ride home, the chemical seeped beyond Mac's lid. In his drugged stupor, Mac cried out in pain, his tiny mouth open, tongue out. Frantically, I tried to wipe the paste away, but the lye only advanced, slithering and sliding, toward the pupil.

"That paste is very caustic," the vet's assistant told me when I had rushed to phone. "Rinse it out right away, and really give it a good flushing."

I poured water over Mac's eye, and in my panic didn't think to cover his nostrils. He inhaled, suddenly ceased his crying, and lay limp in my arms. My God, my God, I've drowned my goat, I thought, and tipped his head forward to drain his nostrils. I blew down his nose the way I'd been trained in a CPR class, but nothing would revive him. Then the afternoon collapsed into a pool of adrenaline rushes: instant pneumonia, a dust-flying charge back down the gravel road to the first vet, only to find him away from the office, a call to Karen on her day off, finally a walkie-talkie connection, then static and a cutoff, another trip home to reconnect with her again, and at last, a ten-mile race to her office. She offered to see Mac, even though she specialized in small animals, and even though she held no hope.

Maybe it was the guilt I felt for my ineptitude, my inexperience with goats, maybe in the face of Karen's prediction

it was Donna's encouragement—that goat can pull through—
or maybe it was my sheer naiveté that compelled me to keep
hoping. But when Karen checked Mac's breathing with her
stethoscope, shook her head, and injected him with an anti-
inflammatory, I knew I had to hold on—to fight with whatever
energy I had—for both myself and the kid.

At the same time, having grown up in the rural Midwest,
I'd learned that disaster and letting go were part of the ev-
eryday. Small town Iowa life in the 1950s meant exposure to,
confrontation with, and acceptance of death and disability on
a daily basis. One of my earliest memories is the *clank, scrape*
of a girl walking past our house on her way to and from
school, her polio-afflicted leg bound in a brace. Many children
in town were stricken with polio, and it was all in the open.
I remember an eighth-grade boy falling over in the aisle in his
arithmetic class, to be placed in an iron lung, then on crutches
the rest of his life. Perhaps more sophisticated medical care
wasn't available at the time, or cost too much, or was inaccessible, but the town absorbed its mentally and physically
disabled without much thought of institutions, appliances, or
cosmetics. We lived with my grandmother and were surrounded by her elderly friends, almost all hearing impaired,
and none with the money or patience to acquire and adjust to
a hearing aid.

"Those dang things buzz all the time," I recall the complaints. "And amplify everything—even the rustle of my slip."

So the elderly shouted and we shouted back, and they
turned up the radio station that played polka music on Sunday
mornings, its *oomp-pa-pas* drifting down April Street toward
May. In a town of farmers and laborers, I'd guess nearly one
out of twenty-five men and several women I knew had missing
digits—hands caught in a thresher or wringer-washer. Bud
McMahon, the local feed and seed dealer, and our closest
neighbor, had been kicked in the face by a horse in his youth,

and had one sightless eye all his life. I'd named my kid goat after Bud, taking the "Mac" from the first syllable of my old neighbor's last name, and ironically enough, Mac's "christening" had taken place before his blinding. More amazing still, I chose Bud as a namesake because I'd always loved both his joie de vivre and his practical acceptance of fate.

Once, when I was in college, I dropped in on Bud for an unannounced visit to his acreage, where he and his wife, Elsie, had moved after retirement to be closer to their daughter and her family. I received the usual warm shout of greeting and a bear hug at the door, but as I sat down at the dining-room table, I knew something wasn't the same. The story came out. Earlier that afternoon, Bud had lost one of his prize Hereford heifers in a mud hole. The animal had mired herself into the muck, and while Bud pulled her free with his tractor, her spine was severed and her legs became paralyzed. That morning Bud had fed his tame heifer hay from his hand. That afternoon he held a knife up to her carcass, which hung after slaughter from a beam in the barn. I know it pained Bud to butcher his heifer, but he did it and went on.

As a child, every Saturday I cornered a hen in the coop, snagged her with a coat hanger, then slipped the bird under my grandmother's foot, where seconds later one whack of a corn knife sent the headless fryer flapping about the yard. I'd seen dogs shot for going after sheep, and whole litters of farm cats tied in a gunny sack and drowned. I'd held piglets up to the castration scalpel and chatted to the vet about the spring tornadoes as a barrow circled the corner of the barn and slowly bled to death. I understood that there was no room in the country for sentimentality. From my own family of farmers, I'd learned silent fortitude. By the time I was able to buy an acreage of my own and begin to raise goats, I could remember enough dining-room table scenes like Bud's to understand the rhythm of farm animals—the accidents, disease, birth defects that claim young lives before the slaughterhouse takes the older one.

Yet, I'd lived in cities most of my adult life, and as I rocked this five-day-old blue pygmy goat in my arms, his body quivering and gasping for breath, the rural emotional ethic fell away. Inside, I quivered too. I railed against his death. I couldn't let him go. Karen made a passing remark about "city slickers," and I began stroking Mac's peppered fur, his black hocks and hooves, the two stiff gray ears that stuck out from his head, already nearly as long as his mother's, his flat nose, the nostrils, two black peas pressed into this face. As he struggled to breathe, a rattle knocked through his air passages, from his sinuses down into his lungs, inflating, his white belly and chest expanding, then deflating with a sudden slump.

"Come on, Mac," I whispered. "You can do it. You can make it. Live, live, live."

In my early thirties, I'd used the same chant on myself as I lay in a hospital, unable to eat, unable to see little more than hazy figures at the bed railings, the oxygen mask and tube my cord to consciousness. My shallow breaths eased, became lighter and longer with each inhalation from the green tank beside my bed. During those dark days, I tried to rally all the strength I had to hold on, keep living. I fixated on getting back on my feet. I feared I'd have to remain in this hospital bubble forever, so I concentrated on going home and back to work. Every passing day was a financial and emotional drain.

My earphones on my head, I closed my eyes, floated out of the ward to the music. I saw myself secure, nestled in a little boat on a lake, the horizon clear and stretched in front of me, the morning sun warming my body, filling me with the energy to get well again. I rocked with each lap of the waves, *live, live, live.*

"Live, live, live. Come on, Mac. You can do it," I said as my kid's body gasped for air.

Just five days before, I'd whispered the same thing to Scalawag as she lay in the straw, bleating with each new contraction, Mac's head and right front hoof out, but his shoulders yet to appear. *Come on. You can do it.* Her eyes meeting mine, Scalawag stayed right with the pain, taking her time, breathing, crying in a steady rhythm, reaching down to clear her teats and assure a steady flow of milk. But throughout her pregnancy, Scalawag had taken her time. The blustery day I'd brought her home from the auction, I didn't know she was pregnant. In the ring at the Sale Barn, Scalawag stood alert in the midst of a herd of thirty-five to forty pygmies, her black legs and gray-blue fur setting her off as something more exotic than the more usual white and buff-colored goats.

Five, five, five, now ten, ten, ten. I waved my number in the air, and bid for choice of the herd, outlasting the fifteen or so other bidders who were squeezed in among the crowd that took up every seat in the arena. Pointed cowboy boots and round-toed work boots blurred the distinctions of the different rural cultures in this part of Iowa.

Thirty-five, five, five, forty. Do you want her? Yes, I did! Number 308 became mine, to hoist into the back of my pickup truck and drive home. There, Scalawag huddled inside the makeshift hut I'd made from hay bales, and was neither enthusiastic about coming out nor in making friends. Thirty-mile-an-hour winds pelted rain against the roof of the hut while Scalawag grew fatter, tame enough to come up and nibble a few blades of grass from my hand.

"That goat's pregnant," my neighbor said, and an inspection revealed an enlarged bag. Then the long wait began, tomatoes and squash planted, peas and lettuce up, Scalawag's sides bulging as she nipped off the weeds on the edge of the garden. By June first, Scalawag was so big she could barely waddle up the hill, her bag so full it almost scraped the ground, her teats squirting milk. Every morning I rushed out to the pen expecting to find twin or triplet kids born during the night. But nothing happened. She passed her mucus plug, and still nothing. I began to wonder if something was wrong, if the kids were positioned incorrectly, if the kids were even still alive.

"Pygmies take forever," Karen had advised me. "You just wonder, when, when, when?"

I tried to stay close to home as I waited, and soon my whole circle of friends became involved. Some wagered on the full moon to bring on the birth, and when it lost its bright glow, bets shifted to the northern lights. One evening, three of us sat on my front steps and waited to catch a glimpse of the predicted aurora borealis. We talked for hours as we sat in the dark and scanned the sky, studying the stars to locate the major constellations—the Big Dipper, the Little Dipper, the Milky Way. But we tired before we saw the sky deliver its show, and in the morning Scalawag remained in her own orbit.

Finally, it took a larger-scaled cosmic event to tease Mac into the world. On June 15, the first time since the mid-eighteenth century, Venus, Jupiter, and Saturn were in alignment. The three planets shone down with a light that carried me all the way back to the Revolutionary War. The next morning, as I tied up the tomatoes and harvested chard for a luncheon salad, I heard three short squawks from Scalawag inside the shed. The nanny lay on her side, hooves trembling with each contraction. Soon, I held a single beautiful, perfectly formed kid in my arms. The battle had been won.

But standing in Karen's office five days later, I knew the war had just begun. I may have been naive to enlist on the side of hope, but I now realize that that's the dilemma disability presents. You can either hold on or let go. Sometimes one or the other is the obvious choice. Other times, you're unsure. More often, you must strike a balance between the two—fighting to preserve what you can while finding the grace to accept the inevitable. Karen showed me how to tube feed Mac, then packed up a small box full of oral and optic antibiotics. Just as I was about to leave, she examined Mac's eye.

"Do you think he'll have any vision left in it at all?" I asked.

"Well," Karen said. "Let's put it this way. You can pass the Iowa driver's license test with only one eye."

"Just live, live, live," I repeated over and over that night as I sat outside in the straw, Scalawag nuzzling Mac the same way she had in the first moments of his life. In my attempt to hold on to Mac's life, I now find it astonishing how easily I accepted his vision loss. Today, it seems tragic that this animal's eye will be forever scarred, and callous that I worried so little about it at the time. But perhaps that callousness is just one more twist in the tug and pull between hope and acceptance. Once your hands are locked in a grip on the rope, everything else slips away.

Eight years before, when I'd lain in the hospital, my vision loss wasn't even entered into my chart. I could still make out large objects and type, but my roommate had to read me the fine print of the release forms that needed to be signed. In my attempt to hold on, I concentrated on finding foods I could eat without reacting, trying to get off the ward and home. I turned up the volume of my Walkman and tolerated my weakened eyes. Too dizzy to sit up, who wanted to pick up a book or magazine?

But weeks later, when I did go home, my immediate crisis past, my optical problems began to register. Kind friends sat beside my bed and read to me, but often I was too spacey to concentrate and lost track of the thread of the writing. Later, the Iowa Commission for the Blind sent a tape recorder and books on tape, and I wore out the gears. After a while, my eyes began to regain focus. Now, I can read again without too much difficulty, but for two or three days a month my vision relapses into a blur, a blur no glasses can correct.

But oddly, now that many of my other symptoms have disappeared, my eyes really bother me. Not that my vision problem is so difficult to handle for three days a month, but that it is a reminder of what has been and what could be. It's scary. It's something I don't want to accept. It's shameful. I'm angry or depressed every time I have to fish through my backpack for my magnifying lens, and humiliated when anyone walks into my office and finds me using it. During my crisis, I'd given myself over to others to care for my most basic needs, but now I don't want others to see the smallest hint of my disability.

The morning after Mac's blinding found him unashamed, lungs still rattling, yet up on his feet and using his one good eye to search out Scalawag's nipple. His other eye was swollen, nearly closed, burned tissue surrounding the socket, yet prominently there on his face, undisguised and already assimilated without a hint of embarrassment into this small animal's identity. Why, I wondered, couldn't I be more like this little goat? Why couldn't I be even more like Mac's namesake, Bud, who had the same bold attitude?

Bud's bad eye must have itched and hurt, because he stopped two or three times a day to take off his small wire-rimmed glasses and unabashedly wipe the eye with the white handkerchief he kept in the back pocket of his khaki pants. Day in and out, to his feed store or the Saint Patrick's Day party he threw every year at the American Legion Hall, Bud wore a khaki shirt and pants, the neck open at the collar, a clean white handkerchief peeking out of the pocket. Even into his eighties, Bud's hair was black, with only flecks of gray. His jaw jutted forward with stubbornness and determination, but his eyes—good and bad—held both the gentleness of a doe who might nibble on your pant leg and the mischievousness of a buck who might leap over the fence and dance across the pasture.

Despite the discomfort Bud's bad eye gave him, the pain wasn't enough to slow down his love of nature and enthusiasm for living. Bud first taught me the constellations, sitting outside on his porch with me on clear summer nights, my hand in his tracing the handle of the Big Dipper. Bud started most of the town's garden seedlings by the cycles of the moon, the flats of cabbage, kale, and tomatoes crammed into his tiny store off Main Street, where a pinochle game was usually in progress, the cards dealt out on a large wooden barrel. Bud led the whole neighborhood gang down to the railroad cut, where we received a caramel candy for every weed, wildflower, bird, or bug we could identify. For those we couldn't, Bud opened one of his Peterson's guidebooks, the spine cracked and broken, the pages worn smooth, bowed his head down near the print, nose almost touching the illustration, and read us both the Latin and common names. *Cannabis sativa* I learned at a much earlier age than most of my generation.

I saw Bud's disability stop him only once. Again, I was visiting Elsie and him at their acreage. Gregarious and friendly, Bud and Elsie had settled in quickly, and even though they lived in the country and were without a car (Elsie didn't drive and Bud's good eye had dimmed enough to restrict him from a license), made friends by attending the congregate meals in town. Twice a week, a county bus picked them up, took them to the meal site, and drove them back home again. Then, during a recession, a budget cut eliminated the bus. Still vigorous and strong, Bud could pitch a fifty-pound bale of hay into the loft with one arm, but his eyesight prevented him from getting to town.

"I'll get there yet," he told me. Staring straight ahead, he sat at the table with the letter in his hand and seethed. "If I have to get in a canoe and paddle down the Wapsipinnicon River, I'll get to town!"

If I stay in my house, safe and sequestered away from the larger world, I can "forget" I am disabled. Oh, you never truly forget. My daily routine completely revolves around my physical problems. I need more sleep, more exercise than the able-bodied person. I must eat different foods, wear different clothes, have different furnishings, and even breathe different air from the rest of the population. But in this world of difference, my routine now seems so normal that I can become lulled into complacency. Whole days go by when I'm not even thinking "disability." Yet one snag, one canceled bus ride is all it takes to confront myself again. And these confrontations always toss out that same question, that same frayed rope: Hold on? Let go?

During my last visit to Bud, just a few months before he died, I found him weakened from the surgery that had removed a cyst from his lung. But by hitching a ride with a neighbor friend, he was still attending congregate meals. When I arrived at his house that autumn evening, Bud had a lemon meringue pie waiting for me on the counter, made from one of Elsie's recipes he had learned after her death a couple of years before.

"If you see anything around here that you want," Bud told me, "just take it." Out of drawers and bureaus, he unfolded Elsie's handiwork—knitted pincushions and pot holders, embroidered pillow cases and quilts, the stitches small and even, the small squares in traditional patterns but juxtaposed in op art color sequences. A rag rug contained woven scraps from a red woolen coat I'd worn in second grade. Bud urged me to take home one of these beautiful pieces.

No, I thought to myself. That seemed so crass.

"Please," Bud insisted when the weekend was nearly over. "Just take whatever you want here."

Finally, I began to understand that Bud really did want me to take something from his house and make it my own, that while he moved ahead and fought with what he had—going to the congregate meals, baking pies—he recognized his limited time, accepted his impending death, and through this giveaway was letting go.

"Okay," I said at last. I picked up a pair of opera glasses and slipped them into my purse. Realizing her theater-going days were over, my mother had given Bud and Elsie this tiny pair of opera glasses during the early stages of her own illness, and the McMahons had used them to watch the cardinals that clustered around their feeder on January mornings.

The passing of the opera glasses was a moment of convergence, not only of one man's disability dilemma—holding on and letting go at once—but of two persons, two whole families' acknowledgment of that dilemma. There we were, a twenty-seven-year-old woman and a seventy-seven-year-old man confronting disability, confronting our own mortality, finding our place under the stars.

I keep those binoculars on the windowsill of Fairview School now, watching the birds glide over the fields. During Mac's recovery, I held them up to my eyes to peer out into the goat pen to check on his progress. A week after his tragedy, his breathing was still irregular and a lung infection lingered, but I crouched on the ground, head down, spine curved, while my little pygmy made a sport of leaping onto my back, sliding toward my neck, flopping off into the weeds, then hopping back up again for another romp. I laughed and encouraged Mac on, his inch-long tail wagging, Scalawag butting the cat out of the way and bleating a celebratory sound.

I took Mac back to Karen. "Could you take a good look

at his eye?" I asked and set him up on the examining table. Her pencil-thin white flashlight beamed in his face. I was constantly worried then about his eye, and wanted to make certain it didn't become infected, any more swollen than it already was, or in the end have to be removed. Every day, as I squeezed in antibiotic drops, I waved my hand and snapped my fingers in front of his face in hopes that he would blink. I was no longer holding on to his life. I was holding on to his vision. The rope shifted again.

"Look at that pupil respond." Karen smiled and predicted that Mac would have at least some vision in his left eye.

I pray that's true. When I look into his eyes, I feel a line of connection that reaches through both animal and human nature to the most basic tenet of all living things: we are mortal. Perhaps someday, as the French theologian Teilhard de Chardin surmised, in our mortality we will merge into one body, one consciousness, all our flaws lost to a higher perfection. But for now, we're stuck with what we have—just a variation of what our neighbor has. Disability connects us, creates a stronger spiritual glue for all earthly creatures.

Mac's depth perception is gone, but he is able to make out objects. I still can't quite believe the good news that he has sight at all. As Karen showed me how to dab the drops in under his lid, I whispered, *Thank you, God.* At that moment I felt that no matter what the imperfection, the planets were in alignment, the universe was in order. And I had my small part in it. When I carried Mac out of the office in my arms, I felt the power of the whole cosmos holding him up.

THE DAY I put to sleep my thirteen-year-old dog Bill, I took a deep breath, the drug already injected into his vein, and placed my arms around his broad chest to hold him through to the end. A matter of seconds. But instead of peacefully drifting away as I'd seen so many animals do when I'd worked for a veterinarian, Bill just looked up at me with this limpid brown eyes and wagged his tail. *Thump, thump.* I waited. One minute, two. He refused to die.

He lay on his beanbag bed on the floor at home, too weak to stand or eat, but alert and aware of his surroundings. Karen had given me the syringe full of pentobarbital the night before. Bill and I had been camped in her treatment room for three days, an IV dripping into his veins in hopes of reviving his failing kidneys and bringing him around enough to enjoy at least another couple years of life. But after seventy-two hours of pushing fluids without a sign of change, Karen didn't have to tell me what the next step was going to be. She simply pressed the syringe into my hand, hugged me, and held open the door, the dog's head flopping over my elbow as I carried him out to the truck.

"What kind of dog is that?" people used to ask when we waited in Karen's office for Bill's yearly vaccinations and checkups.

"A span-ter," I answered, and the curious seemed satisfied.

At exactly forty pounds, Bill was a medium-size dog, although his large head, protruding chest, and deep resonant bark gave the impression of something much larger. His love of water, instinctual ability to point, pink nose, and the brown spots that speckled his white body indicated some kind of spaniel—a loyal and lovable creature. Yet his high energy level and wiry fur cast a vote for a terrier, or terror, as I'd come to know the breed—an extremely intelligent, fun-loving, affectionate, but completely obstinate canine.

"Or he might have a little German wire-haired pointer in him," others used to speculate, petting his back.

"Or even some Saint Bernard. Or pit bull!" they guessed, trying to match his short, squat powerful legs with his barrel chest.

But it was his tongue—long, spoon-shaped, and slurpy— that finally won me over. I'd always loved dogs, grown up with them throughout my childhood, and found them comforting and companionable. When I left home to go off to college, I left my last dog and wasn't in a position to acquire another throughout my twenties as I moved about from state to state, city to city, and apartment to apartment with the not-so-fine-print of every lease reading: NO PETS ALLOWED. Finally, just when I turned thirty, I bought a tiny house, on a huge lot, with plenty of room for a dog.

A few weeks later, I searched the paper for a puppy but didn't find anything but yip dogs listed—miniature schnauzers, poodles, lhasa apsos—so I took a trip to the pound. There in a small kennel was a strange but friendly looking fuzzy dog with a loud bark. His voice rang and echoed through the concrete-block room, and when I approached his cage, he wiggled and wagged a wildly ecstatic greeting.

"I'd like to see that one." I pointed to his cage and the animal-control officer asked her assistant to bring the "spaniel" out to the waiting room.

"You mean the terrier?" the assistant asked.

"He's a spaniel," the officer insisted.

"Here comes the terrier," the assistant yelled as the mutt crashed through the kennel door.

"Here, boy," I beckoned and he leapt into my lap, licking my face over and over.

On the spot, I plunked down my forty dollars for neutering, the only payment required at the pound, and he was whisked off to surgery. "This is the kind of dog we like to do this to," the animal-control officer cracked, leading him away on the leash.

Once home, I named the dog Bill, after my childhood neighbor who was a bit of a stray dog too. An old bachelor farmer, the human Bill lived on beer and squirrels and wandered around the neighborhood, always whiskery, his cheeks full of chewing tobacco, doing odd jobs for a hot meal or a crisp one-dollar bill he stuffed into the pocket of his overalls.

I soon learned that my dog, like his namesake, was a good hunter, and would eat just about anything, including my moccasins, wristwatch—just as in the Timex commercial, still ticking when it was finally recovered—and two loaves of rising bread. And he had boundless energy, quickly getting to know each of my friends, springing up on them when they came to the door. He especially liked Kelly and Marie, the puppeteers. He knew the sound of their truck engine and would dance at the front door in anticipation of their arrival. In return, his likeness had appeared in several of their shows.

Heel. Sit. Stay. Off to obedience school we went, where we mastered only about a fourth of the commands, but bonded deeply. Bill and I practiced every day, walking together early in the morning, up and down the streets, stopping at garage sales, chatting with neighbors over their fences about their gardens, finding treasures like a perfectly good Schlitz cooler left out on the curb for the trash.

We filled the cooler with ice and drove off camping in Wisconsin and through the Upper Peninsula of Michigan, the two of us snuggled together in the tent, the sound of the tinkling of Bill's tags carrying out over the water, still and calm. After breakfast, we swam in the lake, Bill dog-paddling out to a sandbar to happily greet a flock of swans, who hissed and pecked, sending him scurrying back toward shore. In the winter, I lathered up his feet with Vaseline to prevent snow from becoming trapped between his pads, tied a red bandanna around his neck, his perfectly camouflaged body blending in with the landscape, and went cross-country skiing. He bounded through the woods, mouth open, tongue panting, his fur flying away from his face.

When we moved to Fairview School, he raced down the mud road through the snatches of native prairie in the ditch, his head bobbing above the black-eyed Susans and little bluestem grasses. He greeted every buggy that pulled into our drive with a bark and respectful bow toward the horses. Sometimes when we walked together down the gravel road, we'd meet Moses, who picked us up and drove us home, the three of us wedged into the seat, the reins snapping, Bill's head jutting out around the side of the buggy, his ears blown back by the wind.

During our thirteen years together, we saw each other through severe illness and near death. When he was only two, Bill got caught in a fence, and an infection spread through his body, huge hematomas swelling and bursting open all over the underside of his frame. Limp and dazed, he curled up on his bed and I sat for hours beside him, cleaning his wounds, massaging and rubbing his back. The vet thought then he should be put to sleep, but eventually he pulled through. I shot him up with massive doses of antibiotics twice a day, and when he saw me draw up the syringe and pull the cap off the needle, he raised up his leg to offer me the best large muscle injection site.

When Bill was six, despite the fact that he was on a preventative, he contracted heartworm. This time he breezed through the treatment, a dose of arsenic that kills many dogs. The regimen was a three-day course of medication, and the vet asked me to call every twelve hours. Morning and evening, expecting the worst, I dialed the phone. "Bill's fine," the vet kept reassuring me, and at the end of the third day, when I went to the clinic to pick him up, he leapt up on my lap with the same spunk he displayed at our very first meeting. The arsenic, though, did cause a permanent weakening of his kidneys, and I cooked him a special diet after that in hopes of further prolonging his life.

When I fell ill with Environmental Illness, Bill nervously paced the floor, back and forth between the bedroom and kitchen. He tuned in to my moods, wagging and panting in delight the first day I was able to get out of bed and walk downstairs, thrusting his head over my knee in sympathy on the days when I felt discouraged. Once, at two o'clock in the morning when I was having intense stomach pains, he sprang up on the bed, smearing his body against mine in a desperate attempt to comfort me. We pulled through calamity together, one human, one animal, each helping the other return to normalcy, each understanding and supporting the other's will to live.

So on the day Bill was assigned to die, is it any wonder that he wouldn't?

Duane had stopped over early that morning with a medicine that he gives his ailing cows. "You might try it. It's worth a shot," he said.

Then Moses peeked in on him. "Don't take it too hard," he'd said, placing his hand on my arm.

Friends had begun calling, offering their condolences. "You'll have to get another pup," they all said, then launched into their own dead dog stories, detailing fights, maiming by cars, and even a few accidents down wells.

But Bill just wasn't going to go. The stage was set. Inside, soothing music playing on the stereo, I'd surrounded him with his favorite chew bone and two of his favorite people, Kelly and Marie. Outside, a wild storm brewed, the sky suddenly turning purple and green, the wind picking up speed to nearly thirty miles an hour. Rain and hail pelted down, the puppeteers and I taking turns pulling on our slickers and digging a large hole under the cherry tree. We fought to open and close the door, the pull of the gust sucking a vacuum through the schoolhouse, the sky changing to black, the howl of the gale growing more and more shrill.

Wet, exhausted, and covered with mud, we sat there with Bill while he stared up at us, still alive, his lungs breathing normally, heart beating soundly, tail moving with a slow *thump-thud*. After ten minutes, Kelly and Marie sped off to Karen's for a larger, stronger dose of the euthanasia solution. I petted and cuddled Bill for the last time, the two of us alone together again in this limbo time between life and death, an eerie twilight hour that focused all our attention on the moment, the rest of the world falling away. I lifted him up on my lap, silently acknowledging our struggles and the passage his death was creating into a new era for us both.

"It's okay. You can go now. You can go," I whispered, the sound of hail pinging against Kelly and Marie's truck as it pulled into the drive, and at last, both of us—dog and owner—were ready.

4

To Breed
a Doe

TO BREED A DOE

The natural breeding season of sheep and goats is in September. It may be induced earlier by heavier feeding or by allowing the ram to run with the flock. Heat may occur 2 to 4 times at intervals of 13–18 days. Heat in sheep lasts about 2 days.

—Stringtown Grocery Calendar

A BIT NERVOUS and feeling as if we were trespassing, Donna and I pulled off the mud road into old man Sullivan's lane and tied Emily to a porch post, then with buckets and knives in hand, ventured into his garden to scavenge his Concord grapes. Sullivan, a bachelor farmer who had lived his whole life on the eighty-acre farm on top of the hill in this remote site, had died the previous winter; his place was scheduled to go up for auction in late autumn. For months, the farm stood empty, the screen door of his summer kitchen—a low-slung shed next to the house—flapping open in the spring winds, volunteer corn sprouting up in the garden through the tangle of lamb's-quarters and burdock.

The paint on the two-story house began to chip, the gingerbread trim wear loose, and the tin roof sag. Squirrels began digging their way through a hole in the attic wall until they found refuge inside, and raccoons soon followed. The neighboring Amish family milked Sullivan's Holsteins but didn't keep his fences up, so all that summer cows wandered out into the road and up onto the front porch of the house. Once, I came face to face with the bull in the middle of the road, his nose ring glistening in the sun.

"I feel like I should ask somebody's permission for these grapes," I said to Donna.

She agreed, but we didn't know whom to ask. Sullivan had been a recluse his whole life, alone, with only one sister rumored to live in a distant city.

"Those grapes are going to rot in a couple of days," Donna said.

"Right. Somebody should harvest them."

On top of the hill, the landscape billowed out and fell away from us the way the bunches of purple grapes did from the vines. On the east side of the house, the orchard of apple, pear, and cherry trees slanted up the slope, the branches laden with ripening fruit, and beyond on either side of the road Sullivan's pasture undulated over the tiny creek toward the bur oak grove savanna that had been an oasis for eons on the exposed prairie, the leaves already taking on a hint of orange. In the fall, the mud road says it all. A mile from Fairview School, the lane connects two well-traveled gravel roads, the dirt packed down from buggy wheels that rattle over the narrow path. An occasional car or tractor ventures this way, but the sound of an engine is a rarity in this place, where the high slurred *tee-err* of the red-winged blackbird dominates the air.

Back country mud roads, un-maintained by the county— without grading, gravel, snowplowing, or weed spraying—are sanctuaries, monuments to an earlier time. They still evoke an aura of wilderness. The fields of corn, browning and rustling, stretch to the horizon, and black-eyed Susans, compass plants, clumps of spiderwort, and cardinal flowers shooting up near the fence posts suggest a more primitive existence. Mulberries, red and ripe on their branches, and clusters of elderberries drooping down heavily on their stalks—juicy, fragrant, and free for the picking—recall a pre-agricultural age and the hunting and gathering societies of Native Americans.

In the fall, the senses are most in tune with this two-mile mud road. Here, there's no mistake. We're on a journey in the land of plenty, but it's chancy. Even the bright yellow county road sign announces the odds: ENTER AT YOUR OWN RISK. We might get stuck, mired down in the mud. As with anything else in life we really want, we gamble that our pleasure will be mixed with pain. As with anything else in life, we gamble because we know that the road is finite, then ultimately infinite. From Sullivan's, you can see both ends of the mud road meet the gravel, one mile in either direction. A beginning and an end. But if you drive around the square mile of roads—up past the tumble-down abandoned house with its yard full of waist-high weeds in the fall, past the pond where the children ice-skate in the winter, across the road where the small engine repair man tunes up my lawn mower each spring, then down again to the other entrance—the beginning becomes the end. Perhaps that's the beauty of our midwestern Jeffersonian road grid. The linear becomes the circular. The male model naturally gives way to the female.

In the fall, with its crisp air and the bur oak leaves about to launch their descent, we need to be reminded of the circular. "Márgarét, áre you gríeving / Over Goldengrove unleaving?" Hopkins wrote in his famous poem to a young child, explaining to her how her perceptions of spring and fall, or life and death, will change as she matures. I always come back to that line in this season that holds so many commemorations of loss—my mother's and grandmother's deaths, my father's departure from my life after my parents' divorce, the anniversary of the onset of my own illness, my own birthday and acknowledgment of mortality, and my secondary losses, like the early onset of menopause for a woman who loves and always wanted children. "Áh! ás the heart grows older / It will come to such sights colder."

In the fall on the mud road, I come to such sights with a more mature and integrated sorrow and sense of myself. My memories of loss in the distant past, and even the more recent past with old man Sullivan himself, put my life in an understandable framework. One loss helped prepare me for another, and the other helped explain the way I relate to the world today, finding reminders of pain at every turn but also such joy in the little pleasures that surround me in this environment. Almost every summer day for years, I took my dog, Bill, for a run down this mud road before breakfast. At seven A.M., we panted up the hill and loved the predictability of spotting the smoke rising from the chimney from the cookstove in Sullivan's little summer kitchen. I imagined him inside, fixing a breakfast of bacon and eggs, the same thing each morning, the grease swimming in the bottom of the cast iron frying pan, the smell of coffee wafting through the little shed.

Often, if we were just fifteen minutes late, we'd find him in his pasture driving around in his 1949 Chevy pickup, stopping to shoo his cattle through one rusty metal gate, across the road, and into another.

"Here, boss. Git-git-git," he'd chant, his arms in the air. He nodded toward me in greeting, and Scout, his brown mutt, nipped the cows' legs, then charged across the ditch, tail down, lips parted, teeth bared, staring at Bill, warning him not to cross over into his territory.

"Here, Scout," Sullivan would call, and the dog, obedient and attentive, snarled one more time at Bill, then turned and hopped into the bed of the pickup. Sullivan bounced forward, the wooden panels of his truck rattling on either side of his dog. Bill and I kept up our pace, my running shoes kicking up dust, his fur picking up cockleburs. We watched Sullivan move from spot to spot in his pasture, stopping his truck long enough to dig out a thistle, then another and another, with his spade.

We pushed on, pausing for me to reach up and grab a mulberry from a tree. I popped one in my mouth, so sweet and succulent, and tossed another into the air for Bill. He caught it and swallowed it down, licking his lips in happiness for the morsel. Then, near the oak grove, he disappeared, bounding through the brush. Sometimes he flushed out pheasants, his ill-proportioned body becoming rigid and still, right paw lifted comically into the air. Other times, he chased squirrels up the mighty bur oaks, driving them up the trees to take refuge in their aerial nests. Once, he hunted down a raccoon, a thirty-pound critter of nearly his own size. Bill sank his teeth into the coon's neck, and with two shakes, the animal fell limp. I couldn't get the carcass away from the dog, so for the rest of our walk, he dragged the kill along proudly in his mouth.

"You've got the wrong dog," I told Marvin, Moses' grandson, the next day. Marvin was an expert hunter, with three prize-winning coon dogs and several expensive rifles. During the season, he set off almost every evening around midnight in his buggy for the grove, a spotlight strapped around his head, a wide-beam flashlight tied to his waist. He stationed himself in the grove waiting for his dogs to tree a raccoon, often coming home at three or four empty-handed, just in time to sleep for an hour before getting up to do the chores.

"You didn't get a coon, did you? Not with that dog," Marvin said.

"Yup, and I didn't need no rifle nor flashlights neither."

DONNA AND I didn't need two buckets but four that day when we gathered the grapes, our harvest overflowing our containers. We piled up the fruit and cut some more. Finally, a buggy spun by. We lifted our heads and waved, but the occupants failed to acknowledge us. Good, maybe they didn't see us, I thought, still feeling as if we were on a clandestine mission, that if Sullivan couldn't catch us, at least we'd be punished by a charging bull.

"Those people are probably saying, 'Now, who's stealing old man Sullivan's grapes?' " Donna said, a plump purple cluster staining her hand. "We'll have to remember to give them some jelly on New Year's Day."

The buckets brimming over, we loaded up the cart, gave Emily a poke with the whip, and slowly, slowly, wound back down the road. New Year's, I thought, New Year's, the grove hovering on either side of me. By New Year's, Sullivan's farm would belong to someone else. Marvin would have moved to Indiana and Bill's grave would be almost a year old and iced over with snow. In the spring, I'd give up my early morning routine of walking the mud road. I'd get on my bike instead and take a wider swing, the circular route around the grid. It's what you have to live for. "It is Margaret you mourn for."

T HE COOL FALL day that we almost lost Ruby, the
barn fowl were out and about as usual, waddling into
my garden plot to feast on composting scraps and fertilize my
ground. Cochins, bantams, Blue Andalusians, Indian Runner
ducks, smaller, squatter blue, brown, and white ducks of
blurred genres—Groucho rounded them all up and herded
them inside the fence. He stretched his neck and hissed, pecked
at their tail feathers until they filed in at his command. It was
up and over the mulch, the roosters hopping to the highest
spot, where they screeched out their crows to the hens, who
would have just as soon been back in the coop warm in their
nests. Instead, they scratched at the hay covering my wide garden rows and pecked at the dried vines of a squash plant that
had escaped the end-of-the-season cleanup.

It's the geese who love the cool weather. Ruby burrows
down into the cold pond water, unfurls and flaps her mighty
wings, seemingly testing the air for takeoff. I worry every time
she appears ready to launch, for one time she did leave, her
long orange beak lifting into the sky. Friends, too softhearted
to slaughter their multiplying flock, had given me these geese,

warning me to keep them confined for several days when they first arrived.

"They need to adjust to your place and decide it's their new home," they'd told me.

Once unloaded from the dog kennel in which I'd transported them, Ruby and Groucho hunkered down for a four-day sentence in the coop. At first, they huddled in the corner, the two geese pressed together, their long necks straining to take in the new surroundings, but by the end of the second day, they'd begun to venture out into the middle of the coop to assess the situation. By day three, Groucho had become alpha fowl, ruler of the roost, hissing at the chickens and ducks, sending the bantams scurrying back behind the nesting boxes in terror. Even Speedy the rooster, the cock of the block, perched on top of a feed bag well out of the gander's way. Groucho, who received his name that day, honked and scolded every human or bird who came near, his wings arched, tail pointed upward, his bill widening just enough for his tongue, pink and pulsating, to jet out in warning to his comrades.

Released, Ruby and Groucho stepped out into the yard and hugged the fence, the chickens squawking in delight at their liberation from Groucho's domination, jumping into their incessant sex games, the ducks spilling toward the road in perfect step, a webfooted drill team, splashing in puddles left from tractor tracks. Scalawag wandered over to inspect the new residents, trotting toward the fence. She shook her head, quickly backing off when accosted by Groucho.

Suddenly, Ruby extended her wings and was in flight. She circled my house, her gray feathers cutting through the morning air, arching down toward Picayune Creek, buzzing my neighbor's machine shed and dipping and diving over his harvested fields, his Herefords gleaning the last kernels of corn. She wound back and tipped her wings over Moses and Miriam's farm. Above their corn crib and around their silo, past the old windmill that sits in the yard, rusted but still functioning, she flapped her way back to my place, where Groucho remained near the fence, staring up at the sky, his beak shut. Finally, she careened westward over the next ridge, and was gone—in the direction of her former owners, a hundred miles away.

Oh, Ruby, Groucho seemed to wail, his beak wide open now, head bobbing, his honking carrying out across the whole valley. And there he stayed the rest of the day, head back, eyes scanning the sky. And there he stayed the whole night when the other fowl dutifully climbed out of the pond, shook off their feathers and trudged up the hill, taking up their perches in the coop, locked away safely for the night from the jaws of the fox.

Oh, Ruuu-by, don't take your love to town, Groucho crooned.

Geese mate for life, their relationships surviving thousands of miles of travel, constant searches for good nesting sites, and the never-ending chore of raising new broods of goslings—a much more enduring bond than most human pairings. I could only guess at Groucho's sorrow, his neck rubbing against the pine boards, wings folded in, his macho display forgotten.

Yet, I held out some hope for Ruby's return. After all, I'd known a family in northeastern Iowa near Decorah that had owned a pair of geese named Salt and Pepper. Every morning Salt walked the family's two young boys down their farm lane to the school bus. While the boys waited near the mailbox, Salt pecked at a few weeds in the ditch, then lifted into the air with the arrival of the bus. The goose flew above, over the limestone cliffs and bluffs, down between the rolling hills, never losing sight of the bus bouncing and lurching the eighteen-mile trip to Decorah, halting and blinking its flashing red STOP signs through the school-year mornings of rain, fog, ice, snow, and sunshine.

When the boys hopped off the bus and scrambled across the playground, the first bell ringing, beckoning them into the building, Salt dove down close to their heads, circled the school, then glided a straight path homeward. She reunited with Pepper, then stationed herself again at the mailbox waiting for the boys' return in the afternoon. Salt earned her salt, and my image of the "mean" goose, the guard dog of the barnyard, softened while the idea of "Mother Goose" took on new meaning.

Sure enough, exactly twenty-four hours after Ruby's departure, I spotted a single gray goose circling my house. Clocked to almost the minute she'd disappeared the day before, Ruby reentered my slice of sky. In unison, Groucho and I raised and lowered our eyes in line with her flight pattern, my silence an attempt to allow her near, his noisy honking a signal of greeting. Finally, wings curling in, she landed, her feet—bright orange and wet with dew—coming to rest on the other side of the fence, just inches from her mate.

Groucho squawked and screeched, dashing back and forth, rubbing against the fence, furiously trying to find a way to reach Ruby. She poked her neck through the boards, nuzzling him. They bowed and beckoned, twitched and swayed, their beaks brushing against each other, then apart, exploring every knot in the wood, every ounce of air between the boards.

At last, Groucho unfurled his wings, launching himself from his matted spot in the grass, and dove westward through the sky. I feared he was now lost, returning to his original home, his body blocked from sight in the sun. This time, Ruby stood alone, her eyes riveted on the clouds, her honking a cry of distress. My distress was equally intense. The power of animal bonding to animal was there before me—unembarrassed and undisguised. Loneliness and loss personified. States we humans struggle so hard to deny or cover up.

Almost as quickly as he had headed west, Groucho circled

around to the north, looping down toward the creek, then south again and over the lightning rod on the top of my house. Ruby let out one last mournful honk, her eyes dark and penetrating. Groucho hovered above the garden, then carefully, ever so carefully, alighted on the other side of the fence, right next to Ruby—the two geese reunited and back home at Fairview School to stay.

MY LOST LOVED ONES in mind, I'm on my knees praying with the Beachy Amish congregation, facing the rear of the church, my lips moving, my folded hands resting on the pew seat. Beside me, Esther Chupp bows her head, her eyes closed. Throughout this service, I've taken my cue from Esther, squeezing into the seat beside her, with all the other women who take their position on the left side of the church, sharing her hymnal, my fingers supporting one side of the book, hers the other, my alto stabbing at the notes I sight-read, her soprano sliding up and down in familiarity. Though raised a Catholic, I've never quite gotten the hang of head bowing and eye lowering, so I stare straight ahead into the white prayer cap before me and take in the sleek, bare lines of this tiny church, its peaked roof and slanted ceiling, empty walls, its plain glass windows looking out onto the fall fields of corn and beans just waiting for the harvest.

Inside, the congregants' faces are as weathered as the church pews. The men, dressed in solid black trousers and lapel-less jackets that button high under their chins, showing just a flash of their white shirts near their faces, kneel on the right side of the church, shepherding their smaller sons close to their sides. Near the front of the church, the older children sit by themselves, boys on one side, girls on another. The girls, like their mothers, wear their hair long and swept up into buns at the back of their heads. The boys, like their fathers, wear theirs mid-ear in bowl cuts attended to at home by their mothers. The men's necks and faces are deeply tanned, their foreheads and ears a distinctly lighter shade from the protection of their summer straw hats. The women, with their younger daughters tucked close, are garbed in pastel dresses, white, pink, blue, and green, cut from the same pattern—puffed sleeves, pleated bodice, and full skirt. The minister stands at the front of the church on a raised platform. Nothing adorns this space but an oak podium where his Bible rests.

I have come to church with Esther as an act of friendship and solidarity, her gesture of welcoming me into the community, of declaring our bond in healing. I watch the stalks outside bend and sway in the morning breeze, thinking about my years of Catholicism, my knees imprinted with the lines of tongue-and-groove boards from hardwood floors, and realize what an odd thing I'm doing—kneeling in a Protestant church, this very strange deed probably a statement of dissent against my own religion.

I AM ON my knees praying with the Manning, Iowa, Sacred Heart Church congregation, facing forward toward the huge cross that hangs over the altar, lips just beginning to recognize a few words of Latin—*Dominus vobiscum*. It is 1956 and I am six years old and wedged between my mother and grandmother on the left side of the church. Closer to the front, older children sit by themselves, boys on the right under the statue of Saint Joseph with his blossoming staff, girls on the left under the serene pose of the Blessed Virgin Mary. My hands are folded, pressing against the pew, fingers pointed straight ahead toward the Lord, the way I was taught in Catechism class, my right thumb draped on top of my left.

Over my shoulder, I wear a strap dangling a tiny white patent leather purse that holds a tiny white rosary and pipe cleaners. The adults around me keep their gazes fixed on the altar and beat their fists to their breasts at the ringing of the bells, but I slump back against the pew seat and take in, on one extreme, the Stations of the Cross carved from oak depicting the bloody Crucifixion, and on the other, the life-size statue of the Christ Child the women of the Holy Rosary Society have dressed in a long, flowing lace gown and golden crown.

Sun pours through the stained-glass windows, the deep red and blue rays brightening the flicker and glow of the rack of votive candles, casting a tint across the faces of the women in their pastel dresses, the men in their dark sports slacks and short-sleeved white shirts, collars open. An usher, his neck and arms tanned a deep brown, his brow and face ghostly white in comparison, reaches up with a pole to unlock and open one of the windows. It tilts toward me. Cooler air and a fly rush in, and I make out the lettering on the pane: *In Loving Memory of Mr. and Mrs. Edward Signall* . . . my great-grandparents.

My great-grandparents, who homesteaded near this small town of just 1,500 people in Carroll County, donated the land on which this ornate red brick church was built, and helped hammer together the small plain wooden structure that came before it. They also donated the plot for the Catholic cemetery, a piece of pasture they fenced off where they had buried their nine-year-old daughter, the youngest of their ten children. My grandmother, who drops her envelope into the basket at the offertory, is donating money for the construction of yet a third church, a sleek, new modern one that will look like a gas station. Our Lady of the Pumps.

My grandmother was the sacristan for the original edifice, opening up its doors and building a fire in its woodstove when a missionary priest happened to come to town to say Mass, washing and ironing the vestments and altar cloths, polishing the brass candle holders and chalice, mopping down the floors, and even painting the building outside and in before her own wedding. Now, she often still takes a turn at laundering the priest's chasuble, the long, flowing white garment with its golden cross embroidered across the back, flapping in the breeze from our clothesline on clear fall days.

I have been taken to church by my family as a member of our nuclear unit, as a part of our larger rural community, as an initiate into the mores and customs of our Irish tradition. We are here because this ritual of Sunday Mass feeds our need for a spiritual center in our lives. We are here because this ritual affirms our place in the order of things. It links us to other townspeople with similar values, beliefs, and heritage. It links us to other congregations in the diocese, throughout the state, the country, and the world.

We believe in one Catholic and apostolic church, we pray at the Confiteor. We believe in the universality of our religion, but we know that, on a smaller scale, it provided a memory of home for my immigrant great-grandparents, a piece of the old country, a social context to their lives. Even at six, I know that we often spend more time outside the church visiting with relatives and friends after Mass than we do inside praying. During the early settlement days on the prairie, when there were no phones or cars, when families lived in relative isola-tion during the week, the trip to town to church on Sunday was a crucial rite.

Edward Signall, my Episcopalian great-grandfather who

converted the week before he died so he could be buried in the cemetery he donated, piled his wife and ten children into the buggy every Sunday morning, driving through mud, blizzards, and thunderstorms to make it to Mass on time. It was a sin *not* to go to Mass, but incentives also abounded. Gossip was exchanged there, business deals cinched, marriages arranged. My family had a deep respect for the church, but also cautioned not to take it too seriously.

"Those priests and nuns." My grandmother used to roll her eyes while she fed vestments through the wringer of her washing machine. "Don't get too thick with them."

My grandfather, an old country doctor, used to rise and genuflect, leaving the church to be "available to his patients," at the end of Mass before the priest launched into what could be an interminable sermon. When the homily was moved to the beginning of the Mass, he kept the same habits, exiting every Sunday after a mere ten minutes in the pew.

Agnus Dei.

Even at six, I recognize the bond that religion creates. I do not yet understand the terrible gulf and hatred it can also engender. Secure but bored with my scenario this Sunday morning, my mind wanders to Saturday cartoons and cowboy shows. I take out my rosary and wrap it around my neck like a lasso. I fashion a pipe cleaner into a horse and pretend that I am Mary, queen of the heavenly Wild West, riding out through the gates of my celestial ranch.

A HORSE GALLOPS into the yard outside my grandparents' house in Perry, Iowa, a man in a long, flowing white gown carrying a torch. Other men, in white hoods, their eyes peering out of holes as in Halloween ghost costumes, erect a huge cross wrapped in straw, quickly pounding its point into the ground. It is near midnight, the fall sky dark, the air clear, a breeze blowing the rag my grandmother uses to clean the line still clothespinned to the rope. The man with the torch bends down and sets fire to the cross, flames bursting into the night.

"Papists. Foreigners," he yells.

It is 1920 and my mother is six. She is the first one awake, her bedroom window facing the front of the house in the attic of their stucco bungalow. She stares through the glass, her body shaking in her flannel nightgown. She hops out of bed, watching the backs of the heads of the hooded men charging down Main Street toward her father's office. He has been in practice but a few months, after having left Clifden, Ireland, marrying my grandmother and completing a residency in Chicago.

"Papa," she calls and dashes downstairs through the dark to her parents' bedroom, her bare feet cold on the hardwood floors. "Papa, Mama!"

My grandparents light a lamp, toss on their robes, and rush out onto the porch just in time to see the wind pick up a spark and carry it to the clothesline, where the rag catches on fire.

"My God, they'll burn us out!" my grandfather bellows in his thick brogue, my grandmother already filling a bucket of water at the pump.

But soon the flames in the yard are doused, the rag stomped into the ground, the wooden cross nothing but a skeleton of ashes, and my grandmother scurries down the street to the office to check on its security, bucket in hand, as she does every morning at dawn to clean and mop down the examining rooms. Inside the house, my grandfather puts my mother on his knee, trying to ease her sobbing.

"Why did those men come and start a fire?" she cries, and he wraps his arms around her.

"They are hateful people."

"But why do they hate us?"

"We're Irish Catholics," he tries to explain.

"And they want to burn us up?"

"For hundreds of years certain groups of people have hated us."

"Why?"

"People learn to hate one another. But you must be strong—strong in your faith and yourself."

My grandparents stay in Perry only another year, just long enough for a Catholic medical practice in Atlantic, Iowa, to open up. Then they move farther west and live within the shadow of Saint Peter and Paul's Church.

BLACK-AND-WHITE snapshot number 1: I am nine, and we have moved to Davenport, all the way across Iowa to the easternmost border of the state, on the Mississippi River. I am dressed in white, my crinoline slip fluffing out the skirt of my Swiss polka dot dress, a garland of daisies in my hair, my patent leather purse slung over my shoulder, the pipe cleaners inside replaced by a small daily missal. I stand just outside Saint Paul's parish church, where minutes before I've made my First Communion. My hands are folded, my face peaceful but for the wrinkle of lines above my brows when I squint into the bright sun.

Snapshot number 2: Minutes later, tongue out, thumbs in my ears, hands waving fiercely at my tormentor, my face is scrunched into a grotesque scowl. One of my Protestant schoolmates from the public school has ridden by on his bicycle, jeering at me. He stops and pitches a rock in my direction. I pick it up and throw it back at him.

"Why are they throwing rocks at me?" I had sobbed in my mother's lap one day after school earlier that year.

I had gone to my new second grade, earned all A's on my

report card, learned new jump rope chants, *Down the Missis-sippi, down the muddy Mississippi, where the boats go push,* become playmates with Bobbie, the Jewish neighbor girl down the street with the Stop and Go earmuffs, but never become integrated into the class. Head down, I worked hard in school, then walked home alone, for many of my classmates' mothers forbid them to play with me because of my religion. Then, throughout the spring of the year, I was dismissed three days a week, for two hours of special training in preparation for my First Communion. I rather enjoyed the sessions of instruc-tion with the young priest, who laughed a lot and drew pic-tures of the Holy Trinity on the blackboard, but I dreaded leaving public school at ten in the morning, fishing my coat out of my locker and walking across the playground with taunts of "mackerel snapper" and the sting of small pebbles grazing my back.

"People learn to hate," my mother tries to explain.

"Why?"

"It's been going on for hundreds and hundreds of years. You must be strong in your faith and yourself."

The next day I walk home from school with Bobbie, tell her about the rock throwing, the talk with my mother. She tells me what her mother has told her about pogroms in Rus-sia, about Nazi Germany and the Holocaust. My eyes widen and I stop still in the middle of the sidewalk.

TWENTY YOUNG GIRLS and boys dressed in white, their families following closely behind, parade down the side-walk in Clifden, Ireland. They trail after a priest who leads the procession through the narrow, winding streets, a crucifix held high on a pole. Acolytes carry banners and a censer bob-bing back and forth on a long golden chain, smoke rising into the air. The sun illuminates the faces of the townspeople, who pour out of their houses and cheer the young parishioners with a radiance that warms the entire scene.

" 'Tis a lovely day," they say, craning their necks up at the heavens in wonderment that the rain held off long enough for the young people to show off their white outfits before donning slickers and galoshes. A man with a horse-drawn cart clops up the street, the mare whinnying in delight.

"Oh, they must be making their First Communion," I say to my companions, a family from Belfast. I am twenty-six and hitchhiking through Ireland for the summer.

"Aye," the husband says from the front seat of the station wagon. We are on a day's outing, eventually going to the Cliffs of Moher, where we will stand in awe at the power and majesty of the sea crashing against the rocks, the wind blowing so fiercely that we hang on to one another for fear we, too, will be swept away.

"Aye." The wife smiles and admonishes Dermit, her smallest son, who is sitting in the far back of the car, to keep his voice down.

In Dublin's fair city, where the girls are so pretty, he belts out.

The husband stops to let the procession cross the street, lifting his right foot off the pedal and braking. The young boys and girls begin to sing, their voices intertwining in a sweet-sounding purity with Dermit's raspy notes.

Holy God, we praise Thy name . . .

There lived a young maiden named Molly Malone . . .

"Dermit, please," his mother says.

The husband's left leg lies limply against the seat, his foot a prosthesis. Several months before he had bummed a ride home from a pub in Belfast with a friend, and as soon as the ignition turned over, the vehicle exploded, the husband's left foot blowing off and landing fifty feet away. Since then, the

husband has had a "nervous condition," and now the family
is on holiday in an attempt to get away from their strife-torn
city for a few weeks.

Infinite Thy vast domain . . .

*She wheels her wheelbarrow through streets wide and nar-
row . . .*

"You always remember days like that," the husband says,
staring out at the children streaming by. "Your First Communion. Such innocence."

The horse pulls up right beside our car, its nostrils flared.

"Aye," the wife answers. "To be that age again."

Everlasting is Thy reign . . .

And that was the end of sweet Molly Malone.

I AM SITTING on Moses and Miriam's porch swing,
both feet dangling, my toes brushing the floorboards, back and
forth, the seat squeaking *eeek, eeek,* creating its own rhythm
and breeze. It is late September, the corn across the road crisp,
drying to a golden light brown. I am thirty-nine years old and
the temperature is sixty-nine degrees. Earlier, I had walked
around the corner and knocked on Moses and Miriam's door
for a visit. We decided to congregate outside, as the evening
was so pleasant.

Now the leaves of the Norway maple tree in the yard rustle
faintly with an almost inaudible stir, the sun setting, a purplish
light spreading across the flat western horizon that stretches
taut and secure as the twine wrapped across the bales of hay
stacked in the barn. There, the stray cat has nestled in and
delivered a litter of scrawny kittens in all colors—calico, fluffy
white, solid gray, tiger stripes. A litter of cats can have several
fathers, and this one looks like it's been fertilized by several
denominations. In the morning, Miriam will cook oatmeal for
these varied creatures, half of whom will die in a few weeks

of distemper; Moses will carry the dish out to the barn, where the mother will slink up close, always alert, always suspicious, as any wild animal instinctively is, her nipples almost dragging on the ground, and lap at the cereal with her rough tongue.

One stray monarch butterfly drifts toward the windbreak of pines, and the gauzy outline of the full moon rises into the sky. A horse drawing a buggy ambles by, gravel clicking against wooden wheels, the battery-powered reflector blinking in the dark.

"Who's that going there?" Miriam asks, perched on the swing next to me in her nightgown and robe, her cheeks sunken into her face, a light chiffon scarf loosely draped over her gray hair, which falls down around her shoulders.

"Fannie," Moses says, flapping open the screen door with a huge bowl of popcorn he's fixed in the kitchen. "Sure, that's Fannie Yoder."

Fannie waves from the buggy, the horse slowing slightly.

"Fannie? That's not Fannie," Miriam says.

"Well, sure it is."

"Where's she going then so late at night?"

"I don't know. She didn't tell me," Moses jokes, scooping out popcorn from the larger bowl into smaller ones, handing one to his wife.

"I won't have any. Don't have my teeth in. But did you bring napkins?"

"Yes, I brought the napkins."

"Fannie? She's got church at her house tomorrow. You'd think she'd be at home getting ready."

"You go to church?" Moses turns to me.

I nod, not wanting to expound on my "recovering Catholic" status, the troubles I've had all my adult life reconciling many of the tenets of the church with my own convictions, the pull and tug I've felt between staying with and leaving an organization I've found at once stabilizing and repressive.

"Where do you go?"

"In Lakeland."

"Lakeland?" Moses swings around and stares me in the eye, knowing that there's only one church in that nearby town. "You're not a Catholic, are you?"

I nod again. "I was raised a Catholic."

Moses drops his hand into the popcorn bowl and Miriam stops still in the swing.

"Well," Moses says after several seconds' silence. "That's all right. That's all right too."

THE HORSES ON the cover of our history books in the convent school are decked out in flashing armor, metal covering their whole bodies, their tails poking out on one end, their eyes on the other. Knights in matching armor perch atop the mounts, swords in scabbards slung across their waists. A knight in the foreground dressed in blue carries a crucifix held high on a long pole, the knight next to him in red hoisting a banner into the air. They are galloping off across the continent of Europe to attack the Muslims and attempt to secure the Holy Land.

"The Crusaders were searching for the Holy Grail," Sister Mary Aquinas says, standing in front of my fourth-grade class. "The Turks had stolen it and the pope sent his army to fight to bring it back."

My parents have given up the fight and sent me to a Catholic school, not the overcrowded parish school near our home but a more exclusive one, in Rock Island, Illinois. They can ill afford the instruction I receive in the Villa de Chantal, this gothic structure modeled on a French castle, and philosophically object to its elitism but hope that it will not only provide refuge from the stone throwers but an excellent education that includes French and piano lessons. So every day, I climb into a green bus and ride forty-five minutes each way, through the bustling Quad Cities and up over the drawbridge that spans the muddy Mississippi.

"Pope Urban II promised that the journey would count as full penance for each knight's sins," Sister says, and even at that young age I wonder how killing someone else can absolve you from all the other bad things you've done, and raise my hand to question this logic.

"In the church, we have what's called the Just War Theory," she tries to explain, launching into a winded explication of the doctrine. Confused, I stop listening and realize that there are some contradictions I will never understand. Take Sister Aquinas herself, for example. She has no thumbs. And while she teaches us history she also teaches us penmanship. *Oval, oval, oval. . . .* She writes beautifully, though, and we all emulate her, holding our pens between our index and third fingers. *Push-pull, push-pull, push-pull and off.*

After history we have French and curtsey our *Bonjour, ma soeur* to Sister Mary Ignatius, who lays out the streets of Paris on the blackboard to a bunch of second-generation Irish and German girls whose midwestern accents will give them away even when, in their early twenties, they navigate through the city as if they've lived there their whole lives. For now, my life is centered here, where a crucifix hangs above every door, the nuns' long black habits swish across the marble floors, and the strains of "Frère Jacques" float out the window, down the bluff toward the water that winds southward through the United States, flows into the Gulf of Mexico, and mingles with all the great oceans of the world.

Inside the blessed womb of the Villa, the world is safe, although during the years that I am there, the outside world begins to stir. The civil rights movement is born, Kennedy is shot, and Vietnam becomes news. Sister Aquinas has us write term papers on world affairs, and everyone, it seems, "justly" or not, is fighting everyone else over race or religion. It isn't cool to be different, neither inside school nor in the world at large. In eighth grade I finally shift my pen to rest next to my thumb.

OUTSIDE MY BOYFRIEND'S eighth-floor dormitory window at Georgetown University, a National Guard helicopter hovers, dropping tear gas on Pete Seeger and other protesters below. Cambodia has been invaded, students at Kent State University gunned down, and Washington, D.C., is filled with striking students who are demonstrating against President Nixon and a government that has once again escalated the Vietnam War.

I'm in Washington, D.C., because all my life I've longed to get a bigger picture of the world than Iowa has to offer, and at this moment this city is a vortex for the currents of a troubling but exciting historical time. I attend Georgetown, founded by John Carroll, brother of Charles Carroll, signer of the Declaration of Independence, and after whom Carroll County, Iowa, has been named.

My boyfriend and I are just back from a protest at the Washington Monument, and from seeing my childhood friend Bobbie off at the train. She had come down for the weekend from her college in Massachusetts for the demonstration. It is 1970. I am twenty and still wearing a black armband, still feeling the press of people surrounding me as we linked arms and sang *All we are saying is give peace a chance,* the scent of dope smoke in the air, the warm sun pouring down, some people out of their clothes and standing naked in the throng. National Guardsmen were stationed atop all the surrounding buildings, their rifles aimed down at the crowd.

Eugene McCarthy spoke, then George McGovern. Then a white-haired bespectacled man took the platform, opened his arms, as if he were embracing us all, and boomed into the microphone, "My children." We roared with laughter and applauded Dr. Spock. Next, Jane Fonda took the stage, a movie star I'd known only for her sex-kitten roles, and I was astounded to hear her talk about Vietnam and the women's movement in the same sentence.

"The oppression of people everywhere is linked together," Fonda said. "The killing of a people of a different race, religion, and political philosophy in Southeast Asia is linked to the killing of civil rights workers at home. The oppression of blacks in America is linked to the oppression of women throughout the world."

My boyfriend and I slam the window against the tear gas, and lie back on the bed, our feet dangling on the floor. We are exhausted from the walking, the chanting, the emotional charge of the day. A life-size poster of Ronald Reagan hangs from my boyfriend's closet, the governor of California riding a horse, dressed in cowboy boots and hat, his pistol drawn. "REA-GUNS," the caption reads.

My boyfriend and I wrap our arms around each other and vow we will study this evening. We do not know yet that exams will soon be canceled, the entire university as well as universities across the country shut down. I worry about writing a long paper for my theology class on the Just War Theory, the doctrine my Jesuit professor had so aptly debunked in class a few weeks before.

"There is no such thing as justified killing," he said, standing before us in his collar and black shirt and slacks, his hair covering his ears, a large crucifix dangling around his neck, his feet in sandals. "Violence stems from aggression and aggression is all around us. People are aggressive all the time and it grows in increments. Pick up the newspaper and all you read about is aggression. People jostled me in line at the supermarket last night. That's aggression on a smaller scale. People honked and darted in front of me in traffic this morning. And that's aggression too."

In place of aggression, Father McSorley lectures on nonviolent resistance, Martin Luther King, Jr., Gandhi, and conscientious objectors. He takes us off to a retreat in a meetinghouse in Maryland to plan a protest to lay our bodies down in front of buses that will transport draftees off to boot camp. There, we join hands with Quakers and Mennonites in a prayer for peace.

THE LARGE WHITE TRUCK, "MENNONITE DISASTER SERVICE" stenciled on its side, is parked in the lot of Saint Joseph's Church. Life jacket, slicker, and knee-high rubber boots thrown into the back of my truck, I drive through a foot of water to find Mahlon and some of my other neighbors, Amish and Mennonite volunteers, who have come to Chelsea, Iowa, to help pump out basements in this flood-ravaged town. It is 1993, I'm forty-three, and this is the fifth time this year that the waters of the Iowa River have rushed through the streets and forced the evacuation of all 376 of Chelsea's residents.

Now, the waters have receded enough so that you can drive to the fire station and pick up cleaning supplies, but the town still has boats tied to front porch railings, carp swimming in large puddles in yards, and the smell of rotten sewage in the air. Here on a journalistic assignment, I slip my tape recorder into my pocket, sling my camera around my neck, and find my way into the Catholic school, which has been converted into a Red Cross center.

It is dinnertime, and three gray-haired women in hairnets scoop hot dogs and beans onto plastic trays in the gymnasium, Mahlon and his crew in their plain clothes sitting at one long table under the statue of Saint Jude, patron of lost and hopeless causes. Chelsea townspeople rummage through the free-clothing boxes set up in the corner of the room, plop down at tables with food, stare at the television set on one wall, tuned to the local news station showing shots of their own homes, and stare into space. Children sit docilely beside their parents, too confused to move. Parents try to attend to their children but their energy has been drained out of them like the air from a flat tire.

I interview a young couple who carried their four children high over their heads out of their flooding home, the water up to their necks.

"We can't break down," the husband and wife say in hushed voices. "We can't cry in front of our children. Instead, we fall back on our Catholic faith, our faith in God."

I interview the town mayor.

"This is an old Czech town. Catholic. I know I might catch heck for calling in the Mennonites, but they know the job and have the equipment, see?" Suddenly, the mayor looks up at me nervously, realizing I'd come to town with the disaster service and might also be a Mennonite.

"They're my neighbors. I'm an old Catholic."

"Oh." The mayor relaxes back into his chair.

I interview one of the disaster service volunteers, a woman in her thirties.

"Are you getting a sense of the town?" she asks. "Catholic." Her voice and eyes take on a hint of tension that she quickly fights off. "You might want to talk to the priest. He knows everyone and everything that goes on here."

I thank her and head down the long school corridor to find the pastor. The cornfields, which come right up to the edge of town, are decaying and stunted, having stood in water a good three months of the summer. Sofas and canning jars, piles of magazines and newspapers, photo albums and books—all the things that people keep in basements—are dumped in wet slimy clumps on their lawns in front of their houses. Clothes that have been washed three and four times but never come clean hang from the lines like dirty rags.

I am at once amazed and encouraged, amazed that this town still exists at all, having been flooded over and over for as long as its oldest residents can remember. I am amazed to think that after a hundred years, the town's religion is still its center and that that center still holds. I am also amazed that in the midst of such a disaster, religious prejudice could still crop up, could still be considered an issue. Still, I am encouraged that here today, two groups, Catholics and Protestants, whose antipathy runs deep, are working side by side.

Now I have come full circle, facing backward and forward, from one part of the state to the other, from one part of the country to another, one continent to another. I am facing backward and forward, understanding how my small experience with prejudice in my small state opened up my consciousness toward a larger world. I am facing backward and forward, wishing that we could retain our sense of community without built-in bias toward others. Now I am leaving Saint Joseph's School, the doors flung wide. I am thinking of my place at Fairview School, an outsider surrounded by a "peculiar people," people who are true outsiders to the rest of the world, people who have taken me in. Now I am wading through water toward a church, a cross on top that I see bursting into flames.

BOB RACED ALL day and night to harvest his soy-beans, the headlights of his combine flashing out over the field well past midnight in hopes of bringing in the crop before another storm drenched us. Then, early the next morning his manure tank truck wound its way back and forth, up and around Picayune Creek and over the stubble. By eleven, a thick acrid odor was burning my nostrils, pervading my house, a stench so pungent you didn't want to open your mouth for fear of tasting it. Ah, the sweet scent of autumn. Just as I was about to flee and head into town, another odor wafted through the screen door, this time a sugary smell that immediately con-jured up pancakes and popcorn balls. *O season of mists and mellow fruitfulness.* The Amish were pressing sorghum!

Sorghum, a member of the grass family, looks a lot like corn, although the seed is clumped in a panicle rather than an ear. Probably indigenous to Africa, it is one of the longest cultivated plants of that continent, and because its deep branching roots make it drought resistant, it has done well in the warmer Great Plains regions of the United States. Innu-merable varieties abound. The fibers of broomcorn sorghums are used for brooms, grass sorghums for pasture and hay, and pulverized grain sorghums for livestock and poultry feed. Only a small amount of sweet sorghum, the cane juice boiled into molasses, is grown at all, and most of that is locally consumed.

So instead of driving into town, I meandered a mile down the gravel road, following my nose past the General Store into Max and Fannie's long, sweeping lane, rows of white fence boards leading me up a gentle hill. There, the molasses mill stood on top of the rise, the building a series of pole sheds nailed together and open on three sides to the elements, the roof a piece of tin tacked to the beams, a gaping hole deliberately left near the peak to allow the steam rising from the copper coil-lined cauldrons to escape. A stovepipe poked through another hole in the tin, smoke from the rusty, wood-fed boiler billowing out over the valley—the still unpicked cornfields, golden and rustling in the Turneresque light, the stand of timber, its trees' leaves muted soft red and orange by a September of drizzling rain.

The mill was homemade and run by a family of three: Max, Fannie, and their youngest daughter, nineteen-year-old Lydia. The family worked together harmoniously, Fannie feeding the cane into the mouth of the press, Max hand-pumping the green juice out of an old sink and up into a rain spout, where it trickled down into a horse trough filled with clay, Lydia stirring the mixture with a long paddle until it turned a rich mocha color. Yet this division of labor wasn't rigid. When Lydia grabbed more scrap lumber to pitch into the boiler, her mother took up the paddle. Or when Max ran after his four-year-old grandson, who announced in Deitsch that the sow had just delivered a litter of pigs in the barn, so please come quick, Lydia filled in at the pump.

"We all do everything, know every job," Lydia explained, skimming the foam off the top of the cauldron with a wire spatula. "See, I've been working here as long as I can remember, and Dad as far back as he knows. His father built the mill in 1928."

Steam clouded the shed and Lydia, small and lithe, seemed to float from task to task in the vapors with the fluidity of a supernatural spirit. Tied tightly under her chin, a yellow babushka framed her face, her complexion strikingly pretty and clear, a sprinkling of freckles dotting her nose and cheeks. On that cool afternoon, she wore a purple sweater pulled down over her long denim skirt and white ankle-length apron. She adjusted the steam jet, suctioning more juice out of the trough, up through piping above our heads and down again in the cauldron.

"From start to finish, the whole business takes about six hours," Max told me, spooning a bowlful of molasses from the cooling pan. On a large blackboard above him, he had scrawled the names of seven families, mostly relatives living within a radius of two miles, who had already had their molasses prepared. "Most have it made up just for themselves, although we sell some at the General Store. Now, taste a dab of that." He motioned for me to stick my finger into the syrup.

"It's finger-licking good! Best on fried mush," Lydia said, waving to a group of Amish schoolboys walking up the road on their way home from the one-room school, their tin lunch buckets in hand, their books slung over their shoulders in a strap. She pulled a cord near the boiler. *Toot-toot,* the steam whistle blew. The boys giggled, waving back.

Sticky and sweet, the molasses pooled on my tongue. Then I, too, felt part of the process, as if I'd boarded a train, its cars separate, carrying their individual loads, capable of going their own ways, but much more functional when linked together in one consorted action. Here was a nuclear family working together as members of a larger extended unit, neighbors bonding with neighbors, a community solidifying.

Soon, two horse-drawn wagons piled high with sorghum

made their way up the lane. On one, the canes were neatly stacked five feet high, the shafts green and reedy like bamboo, cinched with a cable and held in place with tree branch braces stuck into the wagon sides. On the other, the canes were pitched helter-skelter onto the wagon bed, four or five young boys splayed prostrate on top to keep the sorghum from spilling out onto the road.

But whether metal or human, the bindings got the job done, and reminded me of how most of us in the outside culture have never known this concept of family and community attachment. Instead, alone in our cabs, we chug along, each with our own engine in separate directions, our headlights shooting out over the prairie in the dark. Even in rural life, in modern agriculture, family self-sufficiency is almost gone, and it takes a sect living in the past to reconnect us to our sense of people and place.

A friend in the extension service at Iowa State University said he was involved in an innovative project that would encourage farmers to work together, sharing equipment and jobs. "Instead of each farmer buying a big expensive combine, neighbors might go together and buy one, then work as a team at harvest, helping one another."

"Imagine that!" I said.

Then suddenly, Lydia and I were left alone, her father again in the barn with the sow, her mother driven off in the buggy to round up some chickens on her son's farm for butchering in the morning.

"We won't work in the mill tomorrow," Lydia said. "It's going to rain and thunder makes the molasses bitter."

So, while Lydia knocked the clinkers out of the fire, I swept the foam from the cauldron, the sun setting over the hill, the sweet smell of molasses enveloping us together in the mist.

SCALAWAG WAS NOT cooperating the day I tried to round her up in the fog to transport for breeding. Annually in the fall, I load her into Bill's old dog kennel in the back of my truck and drive a hundred miles to the farm of a friend who has a champion blue pygmy billy. Jet black, Dominic is a strikingly handsome goat, his build stocky and wide, his coat sleek. When I bring Scalawag down the long hill to his barn, Dominic dashes into the outside pen, head high, eyes flashing, beard sweeping his chest. The alpha goat of his herd, he hops on top of a barrel and stands firm, protecting his territory. Butting one of the wethers away, their horns clashing, he charges the fence, Scalawag bolting away toward the trees. With corn and pieces of apple, I lure her back toward the barn and into Dominic's stall. Within seconds he understands his role and drops his territorial aggression long enough to mount her and get on with the action. Down, down, down, hammering and pounding. Stunned, she stands motionless, surrendered to him, her elongated pupils never wavering.

"Dominic?" one of my old Georgetown friends who now lives in New York said when I told him about the breeding process. "Dominic? Oh, an Italian. . . . They met in church?"

Scalawag boards with Dominic for a few weeks—just to make sure that things are "taking." Slowly, they become friends, she adjusting to the new barnyard, learning to nibble at the weeds that shoot up around the barrel, learning to drink from the creek and mince around the Muscovy ducks who splash in and out of the water. When I load her up to return home, a silence, cold as the creek waters, registers from the back of the truck. No friendly nudges or affectionate tugs on my pant legs does she give me. Neither does she emit cries, grunts, or bleats of protest. Stoically, she stares straight ahead, the tailgate closing, the lines of the interstate disappearing under the wheels of the truck. For the first few miles, I talk to her and call words of encouragement. "That's it, Mama, soon we'll be home." Then after twenty minutes, together we fall into the rhythm of the road, the rhythm of the classical station on the radio, she, standing perfectly still the whole way, me, hoping her bladder will hold, the notes of Handel's Water Music lulling us toward Fairview School.

"How lucky you are, how pampered to have a goat's life rather than a sheep's." I try to explain things to Scalawag. Donna, Stu, and I keep sheep in the pasture from March until October. These animals have short existences in comparison to the goats, whose life spans are around twelve to fourteen years. The sheep mow the grass, then provide a freezer full of organic meat for the winter. We approach the sheep with reverence, providing them with the best life we know how, realizing that they will become part of our own bodies soon enough, that our contract with them is one of mutual dependence and nurturance. The day we take them to the slaughtering house is grim, for try as we may not to get attached, we are still mindful of the weight of our deed.

To cheer up ourselves and the sheep, we make their last day as festive as we can, giving them extra corn and a little bit of hay before their trip to the butcher's. Since we usually raise only two sheep, Donna thinks it a waste of money to call Duane to transport them in his trailer, so offers the backseat of her hatchback. Besides, Donna recalls the last time Duane hauled Bob's cattle to the Sale Barn. She had been sleeping and was awakened to the sound of May Chadek's voice.

"That gate don't look like it's shut," May Chadek yelled to me from the grove, where she'd gone early one morning for morel hunting. She pointed toward the back of Duane's trailer as he drove away toward town, faces of black Angus cattle visible behind the bars.

"Uh-oh! Uh-oh. Yup. There they go. There they go!"

One by one, the cattle slipped out the trailer gate and spilled onto the road, wandering off through Donna and Stu's yard. Donna looked out her bedroom window to find one grazing on her flower bed.

"But, Donna, are you sure you want those sheep in your car?" I ask.

"Nothing could hurt that clunker," she says.

In they go, propped up on their haunches, mesmerized and playing statue the way they do when they're sheared. We strap seat belts around their middles, plop straw hats on their heads, and offer them one last cigarette before we speed down the gravel road, their long ears and black faces bobbing in the rearview mirror.

"It could be worse," I tell Scalawag when we arrive at Fairview School, home at last from our breeding expedition. Released from bondage, she hops out of the truck and rushes past me, running around the fence, climbing up on top of the wood pile and, chest out, legs splayed, leaping the five feet to the ground into the pen. There her silence ends as she bleats and calls Mac to her side, licking and stroking him with her tongue.

"Goats are the only animals besides humans that I know

that recognize their own offspring after a separation," Karen had told me once, and these reunions always confirm all the studies I've ever read about parental bonding—even on the so-called lower level. Round and round they go, Madonna and child, rubbing up against one another, cooing and snorting their greetings and endearments.

Once she's reestablished her connection to Mac, Scalawag wiggles her way through the fence gate to seek out Emily, her other attachment. Goats and horses form a special kind of bond and the cliché "get your goat" comes from the fact that once a goat is removed from a horse's sphere, the horse can become irritable and agitated. Who would've guessed that Scalawag would have had a calming influence on anything? But when she wasn't trying to eat Emily's food, the horse mellowed in her presence, seeming to even enjoy having the goat dance around her, running in and out between her legs.

So close did the two become that once they executed the great escape together. Working open the latch on the pasture gate with her teeth, Scalawag released the entire barnyard to the outside world. While I was in town and Donna and Stu slept, Emily took a field trip down the gravel road, trotting along at a good clip, her mane flying, Scalawag jogging beside her.

"Why, Emily's in the yard!" Moses said, peering out the window.

"And some little dog's running behind her," Miriam said.

"That's no dog."

"Well, what is it then?"

"A goat."

"A goat?"

Folklore has it that goats are much dumber than dogs, but Scalawag ranks right up there with Lassie and Rin-Tin-Tin. Whenever I can catch Scalawag to tether her out in the yard, I pull her to me with the rope to clip her hooves and brush her fur. She hates these captive activities, and digs her legs into the sod, bracing herself against my advances. She darts away from me, and unless I stomp my foot down on the rope, circles my legs, binding up my ankles until I topple helplessly on the ground.

Once, when I'd introduced Shenanigan, another goat, into the menagerie, Scalawag's behavior took on all the vengeance of an older sibling. I tethered both Scalawag and Shenanigan out in the yard, just close enough for company, but far enough apart so that they wouldn't tangle each other's ropes. Scalawag tolerated Shenanigan's presence for an hour, the two goats grazing on the high grass, then she could control herself no longer. As Shenanigan began to feel at home and venture out farther and farther away from the fence and closer to Scalawag's territory, she reached over and placed her hoof firmly on his rope—just the way I'd done with her. Shenanigan's head jerked back, eyes bulging in surprise. After that, he stayed within the confines of his own designated radius.

I had Scalawag confined to the pen, the gate tied securely shut, the day I tried to catch her in the fog. It was October and we were already behind schedule for breeding; then, the morning we were to head west, a thick damp mist rolled into the valley, forcing cars to slow down to a buggy's pace, creating a gigantic mud puddle out of the pen. Perhaps it was the dog kennel that I dragged out of the basement and lifted into the truck that gave me away, but that day Scalawag wanted less to do with this planned parenthood idea than ever.

"That's it, Scal," I said, holding out a piece of apple. "You like Dominic."

Scalawag leapt up onto the roof of the goat shed, defiant, hooves spread wide apart.

I held out my hand, inching closer. "He's a handsome boy."

She bolted off the roof, and over a tree stump.

"A very handsome boy."

Cautiously, I made my way around the stump and offered the apple with the very tips of my fingers. Scalawag stood still, contemplating. I came closer, hoping to back her into a corner of the pen.

"Such a stud!"

She glanced at my hand, then the apple, my hand, then the apple.

"Look at your nice boy, Mac."

She nibbled the apple, then pulled back against the fence.

"It's fun to make babies."

She pulled the rest of the apple slice into her mouth; then, with one quick swipe of my hand, I grabbed her collar. She butted my leg and yanked away, my fingers still pressed tightly against her fur. She bounded over the tree stump, my legs collapsing underneath me, my forehead clashing into the wood with a smack. I lost hold of her collar, then fell into the slick mud, a lump above my eye beginning to swell, a trickle of blood oozing down my face.

Angry now myself, I left the pen like a tag team mud wrestler and went into the house to hold a piece of ice to my head. There, I filled my pockets with corn, and after I'd regrouped, went back for another round. If only I could trap her inside the shed, I thought, dumping the corn into a bucket and placing it inside the hut. There had to be an easier way.

"Scal-a-wag," I called. "Sweet Scalawag . . ."

She stood motionless near the gate.

"Remember what happens to sheep."

Then Mac and Shenanigan charged into the shed and began gobbling the corn. Darn, I thought, this isn't working either. But maybe it was! Suddenly, Scalawag rammed Shenanigan, then Mac, sending the two of them scurrying outside, dipping her own head down into the bucket to fill herself with corn. I blocked the entrance to the shed with my body and knelt down into the straw, reaching around behind Scalawag to clutch her collar. My fingers wrapped around the strap, I caught her in a half nelson, nearly pinning her to the ground. I thought I had her at last, when with one powerful surge, she broke away, flying over my shoulder, out of the shed and back into the fog.

"The descent of the Holy Spirit might be an easier way to conceive," Donna called, appearing near the fence. "I'll help."

Within minutes, the two of us had Scalawag trapped inside the shed, a rope snapped to her collar. Then with perfect grace, up and over the tailgate she bounded and into the dog kennel. At last she gave in and waited in the truck in silence. Muddy, bruised, and battered, I backed out of the drive and headed down the road westward into the haze. Once again, our journey was about to begin.

OUR BLACK VAN sped through the black night, an evening just before Thanksgiving that Moses, Miriam, their family, and I had agreed upon to go out to dinner and celebrate my birthday. We twisted and turned over the back road, a smooth blacktop, "The Orval Yoder Turnpike," named in honor of a long-term resident and lobbyist for its upgrading from gravel. Outside, a fierce wind blew, and a cloud cover obscured what little light shone from the slivered moon hanging above, but inside we generated our own warmth as we squeezed together—Moses and Miriam, their Mennonite son at the wheel, and his wife, eight children, and a few assorted cousins all crunched in around me.

Our stomachs growled and we debated our orders. Would we get chicken and Swiss steak for all? Or pork chops and steak? Each one of us imagined the bowls of mashed potatoes, the cole slaw, sauerkraut, and mounds of brown bread, the sweet corn and green beans that would fill our table. Rosie, the red-haired waitress, would burst through the swinging door from the kitchen, a huge tray balanced on her shoulder and, plopping our food down on the blue checked tablecloth, joke in German about the size of small families these days.

"Now, let me count, thirteen of you tonight? But the Kinder don't eat, isn't that right?" she'd tease the children. "Oh, you might take a bite of an old chicken wing, but you won't touch that chocolate cake."

We'd bow our heads in prayer, hungry after working all day and into the early evening on this year's late harvest, but happy to be having this celebratory meal together, neighbor to neighbor, kith and kin. Moses would pass each dish to his right, his long gray beard bobbing into the gravy bowl, his rough, eighty-year-old hands meeting the tiny tender ones of Truman, his youngest grandson. And then we would eat, and eat, and eat, and when we finished the last morsel of that chocolate cake, we'd drive home, groggy and sleepy, the smaller girls, babushkas tied down over their ears, resting their heads in their mother's lap.

It was a small wonder we'd even set out on our trip at all, for arranging such a journey was not easy with my eating restrictions and without the convenience of car or telephone. One morning in late October I'd heard a horse whinny and had looked out my window to find Moses, slow and stiff-legged, climbing out of his buggy in my front yard.

"Would next Tuesday suit?" he had asked, standing in my doorway.

We agreed, then hands on the rail, he descended my front steps backward, an idiosyncratic technique he'd developed to put less stress on his arthritic knee. He whipped Willy's rump, then drove off down the road and up the hill toward his son's place, the wooden buggy wheels churning up dust.

"Tuesday don't suit the other folks," Moses told me several days later when he reappeared in my drive. So, we picked another date, and the whole process began again, Moses and Willy making the rounds from homestead to homestead, back and forth, with different dates clear of church meetings, ball-

games, and quilting bees. After about the third try, we settled
on that late November night, my birthday long gone, but the
black van washed, gassed, and willing to make the fifteen-mile
trip past fields now dark and barren, with only a skim of snow
covering the corn stubble.

We chattered as we drove, discussing everything from the
price of beans to the price of world peace, the road winding
before us in its serpentine fashion, up and around one bend,
one curve, and into another. Suddenly, plastic and glass flew
up in front of our eyes, the van's radiator bursting into steam.
We coasted several hundred feet before any of us realized we'd
been in an accident, and when we'd awakened to the realiza-
tion, we pulled over near the edge of the road and sat there
motionless in silence. At last, Moses swung open the heavy
door, scanned the scene, and said, "We hit a calf."

There the calf lay when we all spilled out of the van—a
black Angus steer, the color of the night, on the shoulder of
the road, still alive but breathing hard and bellowing, too hurt
to get up. I heard something swish behind me and turned to
make out a small herd of calves prancing down the road, dim
inky shadows. Then Moses hobbled across the blacktop and
pointed toward the ditch. A bull—massive, powerful, and
dark—pawed at the brome grass, his breath steaming his brass
nose ring. The adults shooed the children back into the van
and one of the older cousins set off in search of the farmer
and owner of the runaways.

Magically, a butcher knife appeared and Moses took it up
into his hand like a baton. With a steady, sure grip, he leaned
down and cut a firm slit across the calf's throat. The animal's
eyes rolled back, the tongue relaxed, lolling out of the corner
of the mouth, and with one last long moan, a whole note held
for several measures, the steer mercifully finished its final tune.
We all stared straight ahead into the horror, acknowledging
and confronting the death. Within minutes, the farmer had the

bull and herd corralled back in the pasture, the dead calf lifted up into the bed of his pickup, its head hanging over the end of the open tailgate. Truman, who had escaped our notice and still stood there with us on the road, stepped forward, his eyes wide, and Miriam pulled him back into the folds of her skirt.

"Don't look," she said, fixing her gaze on the truck bumping and bouncing down the lane toward the barn, where within an hour the calf would be hoisted up on block and tackle, butchered, wrapped in white paper, and deposited in a freezer. Then, shivering and hungry, as we waited in the night for the sheriff, we orchestrated our own score, and it wasn't the accident and slaughter as much as this chorus of midwestern voices singing a familiar refrain that was finally memorable.

"It could have been worse."

"Oh, ja. Just think. Twenty below."

"The snow drifting against the fence."

"My, we could've been bruised and cut."

"The children pitched head first through the windshield."

"Moses and Miriam right behind."

"We could've been charged by the bull in the ditch!"

"What matters, we're all safe, no one hurt."

"Ja, that's the main thing."

What matters at Thanksgiving for every good midwesterner is not so much what happened this year, but what did not. Here, we count our blessings according to the magnitude of our near misses. We give thanks to the tornado that blew the roof off the barn but left the house intact. We're grateful to the illness that almost killed us but didn't, to the drought that ruined the corn crop but spared the beans. We bow our heads to the flood, that horrible deluge, that washed away forty pigs but left the bridge still standing. We are not a culture of straightforward praise, of boastful-sounding strong melodies, but rather, we recognize our riches in our rests. What is not there but could have been. That silence, that gap in our existence that consoles us, and celebrates the beauty of our grim compositions. Oh, yes, we say, slicing our knives across the turkey necks on our tables, it could have been just awful. We might never had gotten back home that night at all. So much worse.

"BY THE POWER invested in me as your emperor, I do decree that everyone in the Roman world must find his way back to his home town to register." Caesar Augustus stood in the middle of Fairview School, fifty shepherds, sheep, kings, and angels gathered around him. He read from a long scroll, enunciating perfectly and booming the words out with clear authority.

"A census will be taken of my entire kingdom."

A few days before Christmas, I assembled friends from all over the area and we reenacted the Nativity scene. The living crèche. A traditional place for Christmas pageants, Fairview School provided the perfect setting, with the ground frozen but not yet impossible, the Iowa flag flying from the pole in a steady breeze but not yet a howling wind, and a few snowflakes just beginning to fall but not yet turning into a blizzard. There was no script, and parts were not assigned, although cross gender roles were encouraged. And first, we had a good old-fashioned midwestern potluck dinner.

Beginning in the late afternoon, just before the sun set, the guests arrived, toting casserole dishes and bread boards, halos and staffs.

"Peace be with you." A local realtor was the first to appear, with barbecued chicken wings under his arm and a scraggly beard pasted to his face. He stood before me in a long flowing robe studded with rhinestones, a pair of pointed slippers on his feet and a crown on his head. "I come bearing gifts," he said and turned my oven on low to keep the chicken warm.

Next, Donna showed up at the door dressed as another king, and a friend's twelve-year-old daughter as the third. Yet a fourth, a Jewish journalist, came with his press tag dangling from his shirt: Mr. Weissman III. An artist, originally from Alabama, stuffed a pillow under her dress and became the pregnant Saint Elizabeth, cousin of Mary.

"Who are we?" she said, standing next to her husband. "Baptists. Southern Baptists."

Another friend bobby-pinned furry children's mittens in her hair and transformed herself into one of the sheep. Several women musicians, the heavenly hostesses, arrived with tiaras in their hair and numbers designating Table #38, 39, and 40. Caesar Augustus' commanding nature was authentic. He was played by a real English lord, who spends half of his time in Iowa with his law professor spouse and the other half in Parliament. The lord brought along his Lebanese brother-in-law, a Broadway composer home for the holidays, who took up the role of Saint Joseph. I, of course, wrapped in a blue bedsheet, played the Virgin Mary.

The schoolhouse lit up the countryside. In each of the eight tall windows, a candle glowed brightly, reminiscent of the older, traditional Yuletide ceremonies celebrated in this space. In the more modern, "English" fashion, blinking Christmas tree lights, secured by big red bows, looped across the loft and up and over the bookshelves. A tiny papier-mâché Nativity scene, a gift from some vacationing friends in Mexico, took up a quiet but important place on the bureau, its presence seemingly becoming more muted while the pile of coats next to it grew up higher and higher.

Invitations to thirty people somehow produced sixty guests. In they poured, grandmothers in hair nets and grandchildren playing kazoos, couples and singles, friends of friends, visitors from California and Hong Kong who just happened to be passing through on their way to Michigan or North Carolina. The table filled with goodies, the offerings as diverse as the crowd. Plates of plump Christmas sausages and hot German potato salad were wedged up against sushi and braised duck in Creole sauce. Children stuffed their mouths with angel food cake and chocolate pie before their parents could encourage them to try some baked beans or a few bites of turkey.

So Joseph went up to Judaea from the town of Nazareth in Galilee, to register in the city of David, called Bethlehem, because he was of the house of David by descent; and with him went Mary, who was betrothed to him. She was expecting a child, and while they were there, the time came for her baby to be born.

We listened to the Bible reading, then another from a book of myths, tracing all our customs—the wreaths on the door, the trees decorated with ornaments in the corner, and even the Yule log—back to the celebration of the winter solstice. Pagans, Catholics, Protestants, and Jews, we tucked our heavy winter coats under our bedsheets and stepped out into the dark.

"It came upon a midnight clear," we sang at last, assembling on the front stoop. Saint Elizabeth threw me the pillow and I crammed it up under my costume.

Eeeee, aaaaaa, Katie brayed, her mouth open wide, ears pointing straight up into the crisp air. I hopped up on her back, and Joseph, lantern in hand, took the lead. Then we were off, Katie trotting at a faster rate than we'd ever seen her go before. I was Mary, the Virgin Mary, Goddess, queen of the Wild West. A French horn carrying the melody, our voices rising up in harmony, a life-size cardboard star guiding our way, we rounded the garage, heading for Donna and Stu's mudroom door—the Inn.

"That glorious time of old." We ambled along and sang, buggies rolling by on the road, those inside, I'm sure, wondering about the event. For a moment, I felt a tinge of fear that my neighbors would think my party was sacrilegious. Throughout the Midwest, living crèches are a common occurrence around Christmas time, church groups gathering each year for these reenactments. Usually, they have to search for a donkey, though. Of course, I approached this occasion with a sense of irony, but not with the intention of making fun of the significance of the day. On the other side of my world, some of my friends asked how I could celebrate such a patriarchal occasion.

"First of all," I told them, "I'm playing the Virgin Mary, who had a leading role in this chapter of the story."

Second, this is the myth I grew up with. It's as simple as that. I've examined it now from every angle. I've found its cracks. I've figured out its evolutionary roots, and acknowledged my anger over its faults. Yet I've also discovered that I like the celebratory nature of the holiday, as well as the sense of sacredness that it forces me to contemplate. And there is something very dangerous in completely rejecting your heritage. It's good to step back, even move away for a while from one's childhood assumptions and indoctrinations. Even the

Amish allow their youth a period of experimentation when they are free to rebel against the mores and strictures of their religion. Fuzzy dice hanging down in front of the windshield of a buggy tell me that the teenage driver is moving through his dissidence period. But if not a return or reconciliation, then at least a reconnoitering of one's original mythical structure seems a key to the health of the human—for both body and soul.

Saint Joseph knocked at the mudroom door, and Stu appeared.

"See if they'll take Mastercard, will you, honey?" I called.

"Could we stay here for the night? My wife's about to have a baby."

"Do you have a reservation?"

"We didn't think to call ahead."

"I'm sorry."

"Ohh-ohhhhhh," I moaned from the donkey.

"My wife's going into labor."

"There's the barn . . ."

We made our way across the yard, up into the pasture toward the barn, the new red building with its sturdy manger where two sheep, Emily, and Scalawag—her own belly beginning to bulge—waited in the freshly strewn straw that Donna and I had laid down that morning. Joseph and I arrived first. I pulled out my stuffing, and from the manger picked up and held in my arms a rag doll that Donna keeps on hand for her grandchildren. We'd planted the prop in the hay that morning when, donned in rubber boots and work gloves, the two of us shoveled and raked the manure out of the barn, then ceremoniously spread it on our gardens.

"Joy to the world!" we sang, flinging the brown crusted clumps with our pitchforks. "Let earth receive her King . . ."

The earth itself seemed to be both king and queen that night in the stable. The star led the shepherds into the stall, and angels suddenly appeared in the barn's "miscellaneous" area. All sixty of us crowded in, Katie looking down on the scene with the nonchalance that only a donkey can provide, the children looking up with awe and amazement. Real sheep and costumed sheep pressed in to create a warmth of body and spirit that suddenly became more hallowed than anyone expected. We stood there in silence for a moment, the laughter, singing, and merriment stopped.

All the Christmases of my past flashed before me, from those of great joy and festivity of my youth, to those rather barren ones of the past few years. Trees and stockings, wrapping paper and bows, even the great beauty of the choirs during Midnight Mass, all fell away at this moment. Another beauty took over. One of simplicity and starkness. Of living your life on the animal level, of going through the miracle of birth on the basest plane, finding your god, finding your place, your connection to all life in a wooden shelter with the smell of droppings around you. In that instant, the Christmas myth became wilder, more feral, more full of energy and raw female power, closer to the primitive spirit world, closer to me.

Silent night! Holy night! All is calm, all is bright.

"Thank you all for coming to my home and sharing this celebration with me," I said to my friends after we'd finished the last carol and were about to wind back along the path to the school, the stars in the sky shining brightly down upon us. Inside, I had a box of oranges that Moses had sent me from Florida. I planned to give one to every guest. "Have a wonderful Christmas and New Year." I couldn't find the words to say more.

HOW DO THEY find their way? By the stars? Wherever I've gone, wherever I've lived, I've looked for them —the monarchs, those majestic gold and black butterflies that dip and dive over milkweed plants and alight on garden stakes, their wings spreading in the sun. In their transience, they are one of the most anchoring images of my present life in Fairview School. Through the stages of their metamorphosis, they are one of my most vivid memories from my first childhood home.

In Manning, a tiny town in western Iowa, thousands of monarchs gathered every year in the fall. For one night they landed in the silver maple tree right outside my bedroom window in our old white house. Their legs clinging to the sappy branches, their wings extended, they became a huge ball of orange fire descending upon the maple. With their wings folded in at sunset, they mimicked the tree's leaves, their bodies swinging and swaying in the cool autumn breeze that blew in from the north over the rustling and browning cornfields. In the morning, their wings opening again, expanding, they launched back into the air and drifted south.

In the 1950s, we knew where the butterflies summered, but where they wintered was still a mystery. The western monarch's overwintering site had long been known—a grove of pine trees, oddly enough, near a motel in Monterey, California. But the eastern monarch's route had never been quite determined, and their overwintering site in the mountains about one hundred miles north of Mexico City wouldn't be discovered until 1974. When butterflies took off on those fall mornings, I watched them float away toward some unknown destination. Where were they going? How did they know when to leave? How did their offspring, several generations later, know how to retrace the same route, landing in the very same tree year after year?

As the monarchs came and went throughout my childhood, so have they followed me through my adult life. Like most from my generation of baby boomers, I've moved around a lot—probably twenty times in the same number of years. One year I moved six times, and since then, still have things— photograph books and mementos—that have never been taken out of boxes. They've sat in attics, packed and ready to go at the slightest warning. I learned to pride myself in how easily I could make moves, keeping a wad of money stashed away just for damage deposits and first-month's rent checks. I thinned out my wardrobe and weaned down my furniture to light items I could lift myself and preferably fold up and put in the trunk of my car. I got to know two movers, swarthy, muscular men who looked like pirates in their sleeveless T-shirts with tattoos engraved on their bulging biceps. They became experts at piling up four or five boxes of my books at once on their backs and carrying them down three flights of stairs.

"See you again next year," the pirates said when I paid them at the end of the day.

Moving became an avocation. Routinely, I read the rental

ads and kept my eyes trained for signs posted on lawns and in windows. I listened for friends who were leaving town and asked about their apartments. I helped other people find places to live, matching landowner with lessee, renter with sub-letter. I moved unnecessarily. I moved just to be three blocks closer to the commuter train or to have a bank of windows with a southern exposure.

Throughout my teenage years, I'd lain awake at night and dreamed of moving. This wasn't the usual adolescent desire to mature and leave the nest, but a deeper, more shame-ridden kind of longing. This was a longing intrinsic to the small towns and moderate-size cities of the Midwest. This was Willa Cather leaving Red Cloud, Nebraska, on the hot, dusty train for Pittsburgh. This was F. Scott Fitzgerald bidding good-bye to Saint Paul, Minnesota, Hemingway to Oak Park, Illinois.

"I've got to get out of this dump," I told myself when I left Iowa for college in Washington, D.C., and rejoiced in my good fortune to be moving away from a place where the world perceived its people to be as flat and boring as its landscape. I was never coming back. No, I would never return. The thought made me giddy. The thought made me panic. Nothing would ever be familiar again, but oh well, there was nothing for me back *there*.

"There's no there there," Gertrude Stein said of her home in Oakland, California, as she glanced back across the ocean from her domicile-in-exile outside Paris. Her remark became emblematic for me as I slid through my early twenties, my nuclear family dispersed or dead. There was no there there. There was no one home there. There was no home to go home to.

There was still a house. That huge, rambling childhood house. It stood in the center of town, on the corner of April and First streets. Once, it had been the banker's home, and ever since had been known as the old Dutton place. At the turn of the century, the Dutton place was the kind of house the Midwest is made of, a house in a town with twenty trains a day whizzing in and out and a burgeoning farm economy, a house that dripped of immigrant optimism and faith in life in the New World. Its widow's walk, its gingerbread porch railings, its stained-glass windows, its gazebo with the circular drive where the Dutton daughter rode her pony round and round, all spoke of an affluence that the rest of the townspeople at once grumbled about and aspired to.

By the 1930s, the Dutton place stood empty, the wind blowing through the broken windows, the Virginia creeper vines pushing in through the holes in the glass. The Depression had a leveling effect on small town life, and most of these fine old houses had been either chopped up into rooming houses or converted to funeral homes. My grandparents bought the ailing old Dutton place for $1,000, having moved back to my grandmother's hometown to live out their final years. They went about their business in the downstairs while a succession of schoolteachers and laborers took up residence above, the smell of a boarder's soup warming on a hot plate wafting through the air in the early evening, the sounds of snoring echoing down the stairway at night.

In 1950, my mother made the migration home to Iowa from Chicago, pregnant and with two small boys and a husband whose Illinois naval reserve unit was about to be called up for the Korean War. The change of residence was to be a temporary thing, until I was born and the war was over. The schoolteachers were moved out and our little family in, the hot plates replaced by a full-size stove and refrigerator. But then the years stretched out, and even when we did move across the state ten years later to Davenport, I returned to the old Dutton place every summer to live with my grandmother. It was there, and only there that ever seemed like home.

In my mid-twenties I inherited the old Dutton place and

went back for a summer to clean it out of four generations' worth of accumulations. I worked alone, fixing the house up for sale, the heat one hundred degrees in the attic, where piles of boxes held piles of other boxes: my great-grandmother's tea tin she brought from Ireland, my grandmother's crate of crucifixes she'd saved from the coffins of twenty-five family members she'd buried, my mother's jewelry box with the locket she'd worn and nervously put in her mouth, the teeth marks still indented in the gold-plated metal.

Downstairs, one generation's stuff bled into another, the result of a Depression mentality that stuck with us for decades. In our household, money was saved by saving things, recycling and putting even the smallest scrap of scratch paper to good use. Take my grandfather's equipment, for example. Just before I was born, my grandfather died and left his office full of old books, glass vials, and torturous-looking stainless steel instruments. My family quickly utilized these belongings in its own mundane way, and I arrived into a world of medical metaphor. I grew up watching my mother pluck her eyebrows by staring into my grandfather's magnifying mirror, which he wore clamped around his head for eye, ear, nose, and throat exams. My brother clipped the dog's fur with a pair of old surgical scissors, and I used surgical tweezers to spread the wings of the mounted butterflies in my collection. My grandmother threw a tablecloth over my grandfather's examining table and shoved it into her breakfast nook. Every morning I drank my juice and ate my toast bumping into stirrups.

Flashlight in hand, that hot summer I sifted, sorted, and stacked things in piles in the dark reaches of that attic and thought about home. What was it? A geographical location? A physical structure? A house? A tepee, igloo, or boat? A bunch of junk handed down from one generation to the next? No, no, I told myself, it's the people who inhabit that structure. But as I moved downstairs to scrub out the kitchen sink, I realized even more than ever before that those people were gone and still I felt that this house—now almost empty of furniture and artifacts, the rooms ghostly with echoes—still felt like home.

Memories, then, I told myself, taking down the heavy draperies in the living room that Olga had made, her gray hair bent over her sewing machine. A home is not so much the people as the memories of the people who inhabited it. I remembered Olga on a step ladder, slipping the draperies over their three-pronged hooks, my mother feeding the material up to her, and when they were finished, the two of them sitting at the kitchen table for coffee and doughnuts, Olga's full lips parting in laughter when our little wire-hair fox terrier sat up on her haunches, begging for a bit of the pastry.

"Ach," Olga said, slipping the dog a few crumbs, "who can resist that?"

Recollections, who can resist those? I asked myself. Recollections are what's important, I said, dragging furniture, books, and kitchen wares out on the street for an auction, these last items too big, heavy, or insignificant for me to carry around for the rest of my life. Watching buyers load up a box of old canning jars on their pickup truck, I realized I was sending on memories, that another family would incorporate these items into their lives, and like a quilt made of scraps of clothes, these objects would have another life, another layer of reminiscence. I have my memories, I told myself repeatedly when the For Sale sign went up in front of the old Dutton place. I can't hold on to the house anymore, but my internal picture of it is still intact.

The house was sold right after Labor Day. I sat down on the front steps and wept, but then felt a strange presence surrounding me. I raised my head out of my lap to see one monarch butterfly, then another glide in over the lawn and alight on the silver maple. They were back, the monarchs on the same tree, making their migration. Scientists have speculated that the butterflies may find their way to the same roosting trees through the use of pheromones, or hormonal scent markings, not sensed by the human nose but strong enough to attract insects over a hundred miles away. Human behavior is influenced by pheromones too. On a subtle yet powerful level, our own smells attract the opposite sex in a much more dramatic way than any perfume. Pheromones keep us hormonally attuned, even in same-gender situations. Women living in close proximity, as in college dorms, tend to synchronize their menstrual periods through pheromones.

Perhaps my attraction for the Dutton place went beyond the reach of happy childhood memories, of family solidarity, to a deeper, intangible bond. Twenty years and twenty living spaces later, that's the home of my dreams, the bedroom that brings me safety and refuge in my happy reveries, the driveway I'm trying to reach over and over again in my nightmares. My peers, fellow graduates of the baby-boom-moving-school, suggest that a sense of home has nothing to do with actual geography or physical space, that home is something internal, spiritual, what you carry around inside you.

This is certainly a mobile concept, and much more uplifting than Frost's home-is-the-place-where-when-you-have-to-go-there-they-have-to-take-you-in mode of thinking. But most of my friends, especially those in academia or the corporate business world, plunk themselves down in a locale or a house for which they have no affinity. Many of them live for five to fifteen years in a spot that does not tug at their psyche or soul. They aren't interested in the history of the place, nor the evolution of its landscape and environment. Instead, they hope nearby are good restaurants and schools, and a cheap fitness club. No, as much as I like the ephemeral notion of home, I like exploring the opposite idea, that home may be an almost physiological tug toward a concrete physical place.

AFTER I SOLD the old Dutton place, I went back to Chicago, lived there for three years, and thought of the Zen story of the two men who were moving to the same new town and feeling a lot of anxiety about the transition. They both went to the Zen master and asked him if their new town would be a good place in which to live.

"How did you like your last home?" the master asked the first man.

"Oh, I loved it. It was wonderful," the man said.

"You'll like your new town very much," the master said, then turned to the second man, asking him the same question.

"I hated that place," the second man said. "It was a horrible town."

"Then you'll be very unhappy in your new home," the master said.

Perhaps it was my karma, then, not to fall in love with Chicago. I didn't dislike it. I loved riding the el downtown on Friday nights to attend the Chicago Symphony or a poetry reading at the Museum of Contemporary Art, grabbing a quick meal first at Berghoff's, the waiters whisking the plates and silverware on and off the white tablecloths with enormous speed and efficiency. I loved walking along the lake at dusk, the water a deep turquoise, rolling out toward the horizon. I loved clicking on my radio to the Studs Terkel show every morning, his gravelly voice interviewing everyone from Itzhak Perlman to the national champion Irish fiddle player. But when my Chicago job began to implode, I knew the city was not the kind of place I was tuned into enough to stay and settle for good. Quite surprisingly, I found myself thinking about moving back to Iowa, not to Manning—that would be just too isolated and cut off—but to Iowa City, a larger, university town that had made cameo appearances in my life since I was very small.

The money from the sale of the old Dutton place was enough for a downpayment on Ida's place, an old five-room house in Iowa City built about the turn of the century. The house stood in a humble neighborhood of very old and very young home owners—widows and retired laborers, singles and newlyweds in their early thirties buying "fixer-uppers." Just on the other side of the tracks, a block outside the official inner ring of student ghetto housing and the roundhouse of the Northwestern railroad, the neighborhood withstood the head-splitting midnight bangings of the coupling cars, tolerable only to the poor who could find no escape, the deaf, and those still too engrossed in the newness of their own couplings to care.

Ida's place was a story and a half, the two tandem bedrooms upstairs squatting squarely above the living and dining room below. A great old brick chimney ran up through the center of the home, the plates over the opening for the wood-stove pipes still there, unpainted, plastered, or papered over, their pastoral winter scenes complete with sleighs and red-cheeked children. The dwelling had once been on the outskirts of the city, a small farmhouse on the edge, surrounded by open prairie. Until the 1950s, this was still mostly the case, until lots were subdivided and most of the other houses in the neighborhood moved in. Outside, its large yard, almost a quarter acre, with its fruit trees and garden space, its grapevines, lilac hedges, and raspberry canes, was more alluring than the home itself, the tin roof rusting, the old fishscale shingles covered by asbestos ones.

Ida's had been standing empty for three years when I bought it, the windows cracked and vandalized, the Virginia creeper vines winding their way inside. Like my grandparents, I saw a bargain, and the price tag for this house included everything that was in it, the complete belongings of the ninety-year-old woman who had lived there for twenty years. The day I got the keys, the contents of the place were exactly the same as the day Ida left, carried out on a stretcher by paramedics and rushed to the hospital after a stroke. Her coffee cup was still in the sink, her apron slung over the kitchen chair, a load of laundry strung on a rope in the basement to dry.

Her son and daughter, in their seventies with health problems of their own, did not have the energy or sentiment to go through the mother's belongings. Even with a housing shortage in the city, the place did not sell.

"I'd show the house," the real estate agent said, nudging me to sign my name on the final papers, "and unlike you, people just couldn't see beyond the mess."

Yes, I knew mess, and had to mess with the mess before I could move in my collapsible furniture and boxes of books. First, I let the family come and take whatever they wanted. They carted off the photographs, the silver, china, and an old Victrola, then on my first day of ownership, I hired a dump truck and literally scooped and carried out eight loads of junk. Anything that wasn't worth anything went: newspapers and magazines, old industrial-size cans full of lard, mattresses, canning jars full of homemade grape juice, a thin layer of botulism and mold swimming along the top. I pulled up the tattered rugs and down the heavy draperies. I washed the windows and scrubbed the floors, disinfected the bathtub.

Underneath the refuse were some nice antiques—a caned rocking chair, a library table, and a bureau—and underneath the *Organic Gardening* magazines stuffed in the drawers of the bureau unfolded Ida's life. From her scrapbooks and artifacts, I pieced together her history, how she'd grown up on a farm near Iowa City, and been courted from Kalona, fifteen miles away, mostly through penny postcards in the mail.

March 20, 1908
Dear Ida,
Just to let you know that I made it home from the dance okay. Didn't get back until 2 a.m., though, with the horse pulling as hard as she could through the snow. I hope to be back in town near Easter.

Until then,
Ed

I found Ed's gun and spurs from the Spanish-American War, Ida's wedding dress, and their son's baptismal gown. I followed her children through their schooling and report cards. I found Ida and Ed's fiftieth anniversary card. Different plates and mugs with insignia from various dorms across campus traced her career as a cook for the university. Everything was marked and labeled in a wobbly scrawl. *This is the shirt Ed wore when he took his last breath. This is the pillow where Ed laid his head when he took his last breath. This is the rag I used to wipe Ed's brow when he laid his head on the pillow to take his last breath.*

This plain country woman who lived a simple life in a simple house was very emotional and sentimental. Perhaps most moving of all were the numerals she had saved from the other houses she'd lived in during her adult life. Wrapped in a silk handkerchief, they fell out into my hand, the numbers and little pieces of paper providing the street addresses: *2308 Muscatine Ave.* and *109 Governor.* In her scrapbooks and letters, she constantly navigated by her sense of place. *He gave me this in the Muscatine house,* she scrawled under an old valentine from Ed, and *That was in the Governor house,* she added under their daughter's birth announcement.

Ida's identity with place pervaded the house. As I sorted through her belongings, I felt like an intruder. And I was. Ida, you see, was still alive! A massive stroke was not enough to fell this strong woman, just enough to land her in a nursing home for the rest of her days.

"Whatever you do, don't sell my house!" she'd told her son as soon as she moved to the long-term county care facility. "I'm going home."

"Don't worry, Mother. Your house'll be there for you," her son said, and a week later the For Sale sign went up in the yard.

For five more years, after I bought her home, Ida hung on, pushing a hundred before she finally died in the nursing home, her son having passed away three years before her. During that time, not a day went by when I didn't think of her, didn't make some psyshic space for her, didn't run into some little reminder of the life that had inhabited that home before me. Her home was still there for her, and she was there for me— both with curses and blessings. Through the quirks of her house, I began to slip inside the workings of her mind.

One day, with the robins whistling in the mulberry tree, I dragged the stepladder outside to remove the storm windows, only to find them nailed onto the house. Lily, the eighty-year-old neighbor woman who pushed her lawn mower ten blocks to the shop every spring to have the blades sharpened, told me that in Ida's last years in the house, she had gotten fearful that someone was going to break in. Winter and summer, she kept the storms on, long two-penny nails securing them to the window frames. I swore at her that day when I had to climb onto the roof with a crowbar, a rope tied around my waist for safety, to pry loose the windows from the second story.

I praised her, though, when I glanced down at the flower

bed below: there were her plantings, which heralded the beginning of spring—crocuses, tulips, and the beautiful white
pasqueflower. Inside, Ida's whole household attested to the
fact that her real focus was outside. Her gardening gloves, her
trowel, and muddy black rubbers that fit snugly over her ox-
fords rested on the basement steps right next to the back door.
In the cellar, she'd set up a summer kitchen, complete with an
old cookstove, a huge pressure cooker on the burner, and dozens of blue mason jars, some with dates stretching back before
the Civil War.

Without a window that would open, the hot, steaming water of August canning season would have made the upstairs
kitchen unbearable, but there was something hidden, and sacred, about this catacomb operation that appealed to the primitive, private side of myself. Here was energy at the very core,
the very bottom of things—fuel and food. Here was a place
of hibernation, of preservation, the long winter wait before
renewal. Eleven short steps up, the yard opened into the rough
terrain of Ida's former vegetable plot, the grass grown over
the rows. I reopened her plot and began the first garden of my
adult life there.

Following the chronology of her scrapbooks, I watched
Ida's adult life yield back to childhood. Her early books contained themes she had written in a one-room school, describ-
ing the May baskets she'd filled with wildflowers from the
fields and groves around her house. The margins of the yel-
lowed paper were covered with drawings of bluebells, spring
beauties, and pasqueflowers, large bold butterflies resting on
the petals. Then, in her last years, her books again returned
to the simplicity of a mind delighted by nature. Drawings and
photographs of birds, chipmunks, and deer clipped from newspapers and church bulletins were pasted on her black pages.
A large color shot of a monarch butterfly drifting above a
milkweed plant graced the last page of the last book.

One evening that first fall, the canning jars full of beans and tomatoes neatly arranged on the cellar shelves, I stepped out onto the front porch to rest in a lawn chair, and spotted monarchs gliding over the garden, their wings folding and unfolding like the pages of Ida's scrapbooks. First there were twenty butterflies, then thirty. They circled and landed on flowers, shrubs, and trees until they settled at last on the low-hanging limbs of Lily's sugar maple, its leaves just beginning to turn a bright orange, one shade lighter than the monarch's wings. The butterflies' numbers weren't enough to transform the sugar maple into the roosting tree of my youth, but they did make me feel that I had something right. I'd found a spot along my route where all the conditions were perfect for me to land and thrive—for at least another year.

I never met Ida, never went to visit her in the nursing home, as many friends and acquaintances had urged me to do. I never knew if she'd ever been told that her house had been sold and I preferred to leave her memories intact. I preferred not to interfere with that pull she felt toward home, and the hope that she would eventually migrate back there again.

"Don't you dare sell my house." I heard her voice in the attic, in the cellar, in the pear tree outside. It was as if her words were pheromone molecules, markings she'd left on the place. She'd lived in that house twenty years. Why couldn't that be her roost for five more years in her mind?

The couple that had lived in the house before Ida had occupied the place for some fifty years, but never felt the same bond. Instead, they were pulled back to their ancestral home.

"You've never heard the story of Mr. and Mrs. Story?" Lily said to me one day over coffee and doughnuts. "They were from Ireland, but lived here all these years, planted these fruit trees, tilled the first garden spot. Then he decided he wanted to go back home to die. They left. Just like that. Sold the house to Ida. He wasn't even sick, but when they got to Ireland, he died. Happy, I guess."

MIRIAM ROTHCHILD, a renowned self-taught naturalist and researcher on butterflies and moths, was never happy unless she was living in a home outside the city. "All the big dramas happen in the country," she contended. Her work showed how the monarch butterfly uses plant toxins as a defense mechanism. By storing within itself poisons drawn from the milkweed plant—poisons to which the monarch has evolved an immunity—the butterfly makes itself quite unpalatable to birds and spiders.

The circumstances surrounding my illness pushed me out of Ida's house and along another migratory route. By sheer fluke, several years later, I found Fairview School, and the minute I peeked in the door and saw the view of the rolling hills open up outside the bank of the six-foot-tall windows, I was certain that I could be happy to make my home there. By coming to a spot in the middle of the Amish community, isolated and as far away as one can get in this society from the reaches of the world, I knew I'd find sanctuary, if not immunity, from the birds and spiders of my life that sought to consume me.

Fairview School was still serving the area until 1985. The student population was about ninety percent Amish, although some neighborhood English did attend, blending right into the fabric of the whole. A certified teacher taught classes with twenty-five to thirty students, or "scholars," squeezed into the 25-by-25 space at any given time. Then, in the mid-eighties, the students were moved into town and the doors of Fairview School were closed, the desks, books, blackboards, and even the bell tower put up for sale at auction.

When I bought the place, the school had—what else?—

been standing empty for three years, the farmer owner thinking he would use the structure for haying his cattle. "I thought
I might build a loft and manger in here, open the doors, and
let the critters roam through," he told me. "Then I said, no,
I'd try to put it up for sale first."

When I roamed through, instead of holding a herd of Herefords, the place was filled with dust, cobwebs, and mice. The
walls were painted hospital green, and what plumbing there
was creaked, spit, and leaked, the well filling up with water
after every snow melt. I swept and scrubbed and lived there
for six weeks before renovation began, camping out on the
floor in my sleeping bag, mouse traps clicking their way into
the night like castanets. I had no phone, no oven, no refrigerator. I kept my food cold by placing it in a box outside. I
cooked soups and stews and heated water on top of the
woodstove.

I had a table, a chair, and a stool, my clothes hanging on
a hook on the back of the door. I used the phone next door
in the Amish phone booth, and drove into town and took a
shower at the gym. Life was pared down about as far as I'd
ever known, and once or twice, when a couple of friends
stopped in to visit, their eyes widened in disbelief. But I simply
pulled a couple of mugs out of the "library" cabinet and we
slumped down on the floor to tea.

Even without the maps and globe that the library once
held, in the isolation of those weeks I began to figure out
where and who I was. I knew none of the neighbors, and the
cold winter weather kept our contacts down to a minimum. I
knew what it was to live in a house alone, but this time the
extreme emptiness of the situation, in contrast to the clutter
of the Dutton place and Ida's house, opened me up at that
moment and in the years to come to big and small dramas of
the country. Here, I've watched turkey vultures circle over the
road, their wing spans cutting the air, landing, their talons

clutching a squirrel, stiff in the ditch. I rounded up a whole herd of stray Holsteins on Christmas Eve, securing them in my pasture, the gate shut tight, only to rise the next morning to find them vanished, gone without a trace like Santa's reindeer.

I watched a khaki duck build a nest and lay six eggs under the lilac bush, then for over a week attempt to fight off the chickens, who pecked and finally destroyed five would-be ducklings. I watched the khaki sit on her remaining egg another day, then in a weird reversal and surrender to forces of nature, turn on her own young and peck that last egg to oblivion herself. I watched a rooster sit on a nest. I watched tadpoles hatch from eggs. I watched a turkey ride on Emily's back, then dismount and chase Magic into the pond and away from his hens. I watched the chrysalis of a monarch attach itself to the dorsal side of a milkweed leaf, then push out of its confinement, one glistening black leg, then another. I watched the legs of horses lifting proudly into the air or pulling buggies down the road, the weather turning hot again, a whole family jammed into the carriage, seven or eight people at once, a little boy's bare foot sticking out, the strains of harmonica music washing back over my schoolhouse.

Miriam taught me to predict rain from the wash of red light on the horizon of sunset, and I learned how that horizon was formed, from which glacial plain. I learned the soil type and the names of the prairie grasses, quickly becoming adept at spotting little and big bluestem grasses in the ditches, remnants of the prairie that had covered this region for hundreds of thousands of cycling seasons, remnants of a prairie that was almost completely destroyed in just sixty years. I read about how a Native American woman who had lost her knitting needles improvised from a set of big bluestem grasses, how the Chippewa used the grass as medicine for indigestion and stomach pains, how the Omaha made a concoction of the lower leaf blades to treat general debility from an unknown cause. I sensed what these vast fields had been like before they were planted and cultivated, how the roots of the prairie grasses sank down into the soil eight to ten feet deep, and how they made the perfect harbingers for another grass—King Corn.

I perfected my own corn crops, my own cultivations, my garden changing and developing each year. Instead of moving "forward" as most gardeners do, searching through catalogues for more and more specialized hybrid seeds, I moved "backward," thumbing through the Seed Saver's yearbook, cracking the code to make contact with gardeners just a few counties away, receiving heirloom, non-hybrid seed from them in little smudged, recycled envelopes. Their successful crop, their seed became mine, and mine went back into the envelopes again. What once grew and did well in conditions very similar to mine, reproduced itself. The science of the narrow niche became supreme. In order to understand the larger world, to satisfy that adolescent longing to commune with the bigger scene, I learned that I had to understand the smaller realm, the anatomy and physiology of "my own backyard."

"Home is where you know what's going on," Greg Brown, a friend, fellow Iowan, and folk singer said to me once when he moved from Minneapolis back to Iowa. "And I'm heading home."

Inside my current home, the curtains went up on the day-to-day life of Fairview School. From Max, Mahlon, and Duane, I heard about the regimens of reading, writing, and arithmetic. The switch from speaking Deitsch to English, the figuring of sums. From Fannie, Lydia, and Esther, I heard about pounding chalk board erasers, and hauling in water, keeping the woodbox filled. The exploits of their youth flooded their faces with memories, returning them to the glow of their childhood. Their childhood became mine and mine theirs. Fairview School—with its pages of mental scrapbooks opening and closing like wings, gliding in the wind—became a place to land. Joshua became Rudy, Duane became Ott, Mac became Bud, Bill became Bill. Esther became Ida, who became Olga. At once, Moses and Miriam became my parents and grandparents. Donna and Stu became the aunt and uncle I never had. Frogs became princes. The wind became water became earth became flame.

"Having any trouble with that well?" Max asked.

"Yes, it's been filling up with water."

"I was one of the eighth-grade boys assigned to climb down into the pit to bail it out."

"Want me to paint that flagpole, too?" Duane asked.

"That would be great."

"I used to have to shimmy up that thing with the flag at dawn. Whew, that metal could be cold on a winter morning."

"I spent most of my time down here," Mahlon said on the cellar steps.

"Here?"

"Yup, this is where the bad boys had to go and sit."

Up and down those men and women went. And up and down the road the buggies drove, pulling into my lane, my neighbors knocking to ask if they could stick their heads in the door and see "what you done with the schoolhouse." One fall night, I sat around the dining-room table at Moses and Miriam's, their whole family home for an auction, and listened to their reminiscences about their schoolhouse. Most of all, they recalled holidays. They remembered descending those cellar steps, the lights out on Halloween night, their hearts thumping, the older boys hiding under the landing, grabbing the younger children's legs as they entered the basement "spook house." They remembered boiling a gooey mixture in a huge kettle, then pulling it out, watching it harden into round, sugary candies for Christmas. They remembered shoving the desks to the side and building a tiny platform for the pageant, their parts memorized and running through their heads.

"I walked out on the stage," one of Moses and Miriam's daughters said, "pulled back the tiny curtain we strung across the room, and said my line: 'We'll have pork chops and sauerkraut on Christmas Day.' I'll never forget that. Somehow they couldn't get a turkey, so they had pork chops and sauerkraut on Christmas Day. All the parents were there at night, little presents left for the teacher on her desk, the lights shining brightly through the windows. Every time I go by at night now and see the lights lit up, I know it's you in there, but it always reminds me of Christmas."

In a sense, every night has been Christmas in Fairview School, with many gifts bestowed upon me. What have I been given? A home. A place to experience the dramas of my own internal growth. A place to find a sense of place, to feel grounded both physically and spiritually. A place to feel confidence in myself develop with my confidence to nurture plants and animals. A place to nurture myself and build up my bodily and psychological defenses. A place, as a single woman, to find a community, a group of people that made me feel part of a family again. A place where even as an outsider with strange ways and a strange illness, I found acceptance. A place to find strength in solitude, connection in being alone. Here, I've discovered that only alone could I heal, could I feel both intense physical and psychic pain and then relief. Here, as I've entered middle age, I've felt all the grief, all the exuberance of my youth descend in a single evening, only to float out again the next morning, the cool fall breezes reminding me that we all migrate up and down, and down and up again.

Last Christmas, my friend the English lord gave me a large red and green candle. Every night I light it and stare into its flames, letting the glow carry me into a trance, the wax never seeming to melt, the candle never burning out. Instead, I watch the yellow flame turn to a deep orange; then wings open and all the past spirits of this house enter again, all the little boys and girls with their books in straps, all their sleds leaning against the side of the building, all the teachers with apples on their desks, all the parents here once a year for the pageant, standing in the back of the room, their necks straining to get a glimpse of their children. I feel a convergence of people, a synchronization of lessons learned, of daily exercises and chores, of hopes and aspirations soaring in and out of this room, heavenward, toward the one bright star.